Intimate Violence

INTIMATE VIOLENCE

Reading Rape and Torture
in Twentieth-Century Fiction

LAURA E. TANNER

INDIANA UNIVERSITY PRESS

Bloomington and Indianapolis

The paper used in this publication meets the minimum requirements of American
National Standard for Information Sciences—Permanence of Paper for Printed
Library Materials, ANSI Z39.48-1984.

Manufactured in the United States of America

Library of Congress Cataloging-in-Publication Data
Tanner, Laura E., date
Intimate violence : reading rape and torture in twentieth-century fiction /
Laura E. Tanner.
p. cm.
Includes bibliographical references and index.
ISBN 0-253-35648-2 (cloth : alk. paper)
1. American fiction—20th century—History and criticism. 2. English fiction—20th
century—History and criticism. 3. Victims of crimes in literature. 4. Body, Human,
in literature. 5. Reader-response criticism. 6. Violence in literature. 7. Torture in
literature. 8. Women in literature. 9. Rape in literature.
I. Title.
PS374.V53T35   1994
813'.509355—dc20   93-47318
1 2 3 4 5 99 98 97 96 95 94

177825

For my father, Donald Tanner (1931–1990)
In loving celebration of his life

CONTENTS

PREFACE

This book grew out of my own fears and frustrations as a woman who felt—in the hills of upstate New York, on the streets of Brooklyn, in the neighborhoods of West Philadelphia—vulnerable to the threat of a violence that I could neither understand nor control. My study of reading represents a move toward empowering myself and other readers with the ability to resist the pull of violation, if only in representational terms. In the pages that follow, I attempt to chart my resistance not only to the acts of victimization these novels describe but to the acts of imaginative violation they sometimes perpetuate.

Much of the power of violence as I address it here stems from its "intimacy," the force with which it violates the personal boundaries that define the autonomy of both victim and reader. My interest lies in forms of violence that originate primarily out of the desire of one human being to inflict pain upon another, and in the dynamics of reading that allow the reader to become surprisingly intimate with the power or the vulnerability that results from such violation. The intimacy of the reading experience often allows us to come close to characters and experiences that we might otherwise never encounter; by the same token, however, it can force our intimacy by subtly pushing us into imaginative landscapes of violation from which it is difficult to extricate ourselves.

In the pages that follow, I approach representations of rape and torture using various aspects of diverse theoretical models. As reader-response theory helps to locate the reader in the text of violation, feminist film theory unveils the gendered implications of the reader's placement in that text. Poststructuralist theories of subjectivity check an easy bid for coherence by revealing the constructed nature of the readerly subject and textual meaning, while Marx's materialist framework offers a means of denaturalizing representations of violation that obscure the material specificity of the victim's body. In developing what might be described as a materialist semiotics of violence, then, I appropriate elements of different analytical models to sketch a theory of reading violation that emphasizes the reader's status as negotiator between the conventions of representation and the material dynamics of violence.

The issues that I raise almost all emerge out of close analysis of specific representations of physical violation; underlying my use of different critical frameworks, then, is the assumption that theoretical exploration need not—and indeed should not—be divorced from a close study of the way that individual texts operate. Although I concentrate on twentieth-century works of fiction, the texts that follow are chosen not because they display a pattern that speaks to the definition of genre or historical period[1] but because their representations of violation are controversial, offensive, critically unsettling. As a result of their shocking content, representations of violation may be said to exist at the margins of literary discourse; the texts that I explore here exist at the margins of those margins, and as such raise forceful and sometimes disturbing theoretical questions.

Intimate Violence focuses largely on representations of violence written by white male authors; it begins and ends, however, with works written by women of color. When placed alongside texts by Faulkner, Orwell, Thomas, Selby, and Ellis, depictions of violence by Naylor and Erdrich uncover dynamics of race and gender that operate with equal power but less visibility in all of the study's representations. As it creates critical dialogues that unsettle the authority of individual representations and denaturalize hegemonic assumptions about violence, this study points to the need for further exploration of the complicated ways in which issues of gender and race surface in representations of violation.[2]

Chapter 1, "Reading Rape: *Sanctuary* and *The Women of Brewster Place*," uses reader-response theory and categories developed by Laura Mulvey in her film theory work to focus on representations of rape in two very different twentieth-century novels. In Faulkner's *Sanctuary*, the "empirical objectivity" of rape disappears altogether and is replaced by an imaginative construct created by the reader and endorsed by the text; within the frame of that construct, the reader identifies with (imaginatively becomes) the violator while the victim remains an object of imaginative manipulation, his or her body merely the text on which the crime is written. The reader who responds uncritically to the novel's structured blanks thus silently embraces the possibility of rape without pain, of violation without its attendant dehumanization. Whereas *Sanctuary* exploits the reader's bodiless status to invite a voyeuristic participation in the scene of violence, *The Women of Brewster Place* attaches the reader to the victim's tortured body, subverting the scopophilic gaze of the reader by turning it inward to focus on the victim's pain. By denying the reader the freedom to observe the victim of violence from behind the wall of aesthetic convention, Naylor disrupts the connection between violator and viewer that Laura Mulvey emphasizes in her discussion of cinematic convention. The power of the reader's imagination is not unleashed in a tumult of speculative violences but is channeled within the confines of the victim's body. Confronted with the task of representing an experience that refuses to be translated into words, Naylor forces the reader past a limited system of linguistic referentiality into the immediacy of an emotional and experiential idiom that *the reader* must create.

Chapter 2, "Reading Torture: *1984* and Amnesty International," uses George Orwell's *1984* to explore the way in which reading torture complicates the dynamics of reading fiction and to assess the way in which literary conventions function to manipulate the reader's role in the novel of violence. Reading involves a purely imaginary participation in the novel's fictional universe; the reader's presence in the text, therefore, is defined by the absence of a body. Because violence depends upon the vulnerability of the victim's body, such an absence becomes particularly problematic in a text about violence. In the process of torture, the body's pain constitutes such a monolithic reality that it overwhelms all distinctions of the nature of truth; to assent to a torturer's demands within what Elaine Scarry describes in *The Body in Pain* as "the thick agony of the body" is to testify to the absence of reality as it is known, to the total irrelevance of distinctions of intellect and mind. The representations of torture in *1984* both expose and problematize the gap between intellectual relativity and physical absoluteness. By blurring the lines that separate character and critic, perpetrator and reader, victim and observer, Orwell violates the conventions of reading; in the process of reading *1984*, the reader is thrust out of disembodiment and subjected not only to the representation but to the experience of torture.

The literary strategies used in *1984* to manipulate the reader's imaginative response to violence are revised and extended in visual portrayals of torture offered by Amnesty International. Chapter 2 concludes by exploring two different representational strategies utilized in Amnesty International's television campaign against torture. While one commercial manipulates its visual text to restore the power of imaging to the viewer, another strips the viewer of imaginative freedom to situate him or her in the position of image receiver rather than image creator. As the conventions of reading that define response to novelistic representations of torture give way to the conventions of commercial viewing, the uneasy balance between the representation and the reality of torture, between imaginary participation and embodied experience in a scene of violence, is rendered visible.

Chapter 3, "Sweet Pain and Charred Bodies: Figuring Violence in *The White Hotel*," unveils the consequences of the unself-conscious reader's imaginative endorsement of a symbolic perception of violence. D. M. Thomas's novel cultivates the reader's intimacy to elicit his or her participation in Freudian interpretations of violence that the novel endorses only long enough to undercut. Because the symbolic framework of the novel is accessed only through an immediate perception of the work's violence, the process of reading involves an act of redirecting the gaze, not away from violence entirely, but *through* violence to its symbolic meaning. By "grasping" Freud's symbolic interpretation of the pain of the novel's protagonist, the unself-conscious reader participates in an act of imaginative violence paralleling that of the soldiers who grasp her body and the Nazis who occupy her country. Once the reader is firmly located within the text's symbolic framework, the novel draws back from its self-created universe to reveal the extent to which the reader has been entrapped by the subtle persuasions of literary form. In exposing the implications of the reader's imaginative assent to the force of its representations, *The White Hotel* forces the reader to question not only the particular definitions of violence that the text appears to endorse but also the very process through which fiction simultaneously creates and disguises its own ideologies.

Chapter 4, "Envisioning Violence: Seeing/Selling the Body in *Last Exit to Brooklyn*," uses the writings of Marx and the work of feminist theorists to explore representations of the victim's body in Hubert Selby's novel. Issues of narrative veiling and reader complicity articulated in *The White Hotel* are rendered visible in the "Tralala" section of Selby's text; as the victim's body disappears beneath the force of narrative abstraction, the act of reading becomes itself a form of consuming. The reader's response to Tralala, the prostitute who is gang raped in Selby's novel, is manipulated by a text that only gradually lends the victim's body narrative visibility. In rendering her body visible to the reader, Selby reveals not only Tralala's embodied presence in the narrative but the cost and consequences of the reader's interpretation of her absence; the reader is forced to acknowledge the way in which Tralala is forcibly coopted both by the men who rape her and the text that lays her bare. The reader's way of looking becomes connected not with pleasure but with pain as the object of narrative vision, Tralala's body, becomes not a creative absence waiting to be filled with a story but a destroyed presence speaking the story of its own loss.

Although the body that is absent in Selby's work becomes visible in Bret Easton Ellis's *American Psycho*, the relationship between body and subject is still obscured through narrative means. Chapter 5, "*American Psycho* and the American Psyche: Reading the Forbidden Text," traces the way in which Ellis's narrator unveils bodies only to deny their subjectivity and represents pain only to redefine it as a sign of the psycho's power rather than the victim's resistance. In using the victim as a vehicle through which to articulate a voice of resistance created and controlled by itself, the narrative appropriates without seeming to appropriate; even the victim's pain ceases to belong to the victim and becomes part of the violator's text. Ellis's narrator wields his power unchecked so that he seems to act on the reader in much the same way that the psycho acts on his victims. We as readers are produced by the very text that alienates us, seemingly denied the right not only to define but to resist the subject position that the novel offers us.

The final chapter of the study, "'Known in the Brain and Known in the Flesh': Gender, Race, and the Vulnerable Body in *Tracks*," uses Erdrich's novel to explore the ways in which issues of race and gender complicate the dynamics of bodily violation; Pauline's response to rape in the novel cannot be separated from her essentialist understanding of a body that marks her vulnerability in racial as well as gender terms. Erdrich's narrative points to a definition of intimate violence that acknowledges its material and immaterial consequences; "known in the brain and known in the flesh," the victim of violence is assaulted not only as body but as subject. Pauline's attempt to preserve her subjectivity by manipulating the materiality of her body represents one response to these dynamics. Because she fails to acknowledge the way in which that body's significance is constructed through the interpretation of a hegemonic culture, however, Pauline's material manipulations of her form fail to lend her the inviolability that she seeks. The reader, on the other hand, ignores the materiality of the vulnerable body to focus on the way in which it is constructed in the act of representation; the reader's concentration on Fleur's rape as a literary or symbolic phenomenon may blind him or her to the dynamics of violation that the text naturalizes. Even as Pauline ignores the textuality of the body, then, Erdrich's reader may fail to recognize the materiality of the text.

This study attempts to articulate the reader's ability to participate in, conspire with, and resist scenes of intimate violence contained within a series of twentieth-century American and British novels. Reader responses to these texts, like any others, are shaped not only by the content of the representation and the conventions of reading but by the individual assumptions that each reader brings to the text; in attempting to focus on the *act* of reading, therefore, my intention is not to generalize my own responses or to reduce the complexity of possible reactions but to provide a map of one reader's excursions into the intimate domain of violation represented and imagined. In addressing the force of representation, the act of reading, and the consequences of their intersection, I aim not to designate one form of response to representations of violence but to open up avenues of imaginative opposition that allow the reader to resist the forceful imposition of any narrative, including my own.

ACKNOWLEDGMENTS

Chapter 1 of this study appeared in different form in *American Literature* 62.4 (December 1990): 559–82. A version of chapter 3 appeared in *boundary 2: an international journal of literature and culture* 18.2 (Summer 1991): 130–49, and is reprinted with the permission of Duke University Press. My thanks to Helen Garrett and the staff of Amnesty International for access to the materials on torture that appear in chapter 2.

I am grateful to Boston College for the Research Incentive Grant that allowed me to complete this project, and to my colleagues in the Boston College Department of English for their willingness to raise more questions about violence than I could answer. Andrew Von Hendy, Robin Lydenberg, Paul Lewis, and Christopher Wilson all read portions of the manuscript with care and insight; Mary Crane and Judith Wilt provided advice and administrative support throughout the writing and editing process. I am particularly grateful to Anne Fleche not only for reading lengthy drafts but for initiating dialogue, questioning theoretical assumptions, and offering her personal support.

I owe a permanent debt to Houston Baker, Wendy Steiner, and Peter Balakian, for shaping not only the way I read literature but the very ways in which I think. Paul D. Travers lent me access to his many valuable resources, the greatest of which were his own thoughts. Susan Greenfield read portions of this book with the careful perception that characterizes her own critical thought; Allyson Booth shared her uneasy responses to *American Psycho* in a late-night conversation that shaped my thoughts on that work. My thanks to Alan Nadel for his astute observations about the introduction, and to William Cain for his generous correspondence about this work.

The always challenging process of writing a book has been complicated in this case by the overwhelming subject matter that I attempt to address here. For hours of provocative conversation and the occasional early morning phone conversation after a nightmare, I want to thank Wendy Wall, Jennifer Green, Lindon Barrett, Martin Danahay, and Cristine Levenduski. Thanks also to Jessamine and Beth Tanner for their joyful exuberance, which always offered a welcome contrast to the sobering aspects of this work.

Some debts are impossible to acknowledge properly. My mother, Nancy Clark Tanner, taught me what it means to love words; my father, Donald Tanner, taught me the importance of making things that last. Gray Tanner arrived in time to celebrate the completion of this project and to lend it new meaning. Most of all, I want to thank my husband, James Krasner, for the endless hours of passionate dialogue that we shared in pursuit of the occasional moment of revelation. His thoughts echo behind every word written here.

Intimate Violence

INTRODUCTION

In the chapters that follow, I attempt to explore the issues at stake in the process of reading fictional representations of rape and torture. Suspended between material and semiotic worlds, the reader in the scene of violence must negotiate a position relative not only to victim and violator but to the attitudes about violation encoded in representation and experienced through reading. The force of the narrative impulsion that aligns the reader with victim, violator, or observer and the reader's reaction to that force create an interactive power dynamic, an intimate and sometimes unsettling play of readerly response and resistance in which the reader's own sense of embodied subjectivity comes to be at risk.

The victim of violation is the object rather than the subject of violence, a human being stripped of agency and mercilessly attached to a physical form that cannot be dissolved at will. In acts of intimate violence such as rape and torture, the paradox of the phrase "human body" becomes visible: the victim is at once consciousness, emotion, subject, and at the same time physicality, material, object. As material, the human body consists of a physical form that exists in space, is limited by gravity, is vulnerable to injury. That material is connected to but never fully owned by a human subject who may use the body but who is also used by it, for whom the body is both an extension of the self and an exposed receptacle for pain. Although it is the materiality of the body that defines its susceptibility to violence, it is the vulnerability of the subject accessible through that body that renders the victim susceptible to violation. In referring to the material dynamics of violence in the pages that follow, then, I mean to invoke not only *the body* but *the suffering body* as I trace the victim's subjective experience of embodiment in the scene of rape or torture.

The dynamics of violence often involve a violator who appropriates the victim's subjectivity as an extension of his own power, turning the force of consciousness against a victim for whom sentience becomes pain, consciousness no more than an agonizing awareness of the inability to escape embodiment. Acts of intimate violence, then, transform human interaction into a struggle for power in which the victim is stripped of the ability to define and control his or her participation. The violator usurps the victim's body, forcing it to assume the configurations of the violator's decree; intimate violence thus results in what Bard and Sangrey describe as a physical and psychological "disorganization of the [victim's] self" (35). As the literal points of reference by which the victim confirms his or her presence are transformed by the violator's force, conventions of self-definition are often unsettled. The

3

fragmentation of the victim's physical form is accompanied by an assault on subjectivity that leads to a radical alteration of worldview:

> If the world doesn't make sense, people can't do anything with confidence. . . . Victims . . . need to find some way of pulling themselves together. They go through a mental process to reorganize and reunderstand the world that has become chaotic. This process helps to reintegrate the violated self, reducing the dissonance caused by its fragmentation. . . . (Bard and Sangrey, 65)

Violence, then, has the capacity to destroy not only the form of the victim's body but the familiar forms of understanding through which that victim constructs him- or herself as subject.

In acts of intimate violence, the assault on a victim's physical form thus comes to assume psychological implications for both violator and victim. In his study of gang violence, Bruno Bettelheim describes the apparently random violence of youthful gang members as a means of empowerment through which gang members confirm and extend their own fragile subjectivity: "In a single act of unpremeditated intensity, they at once establish a sense of their own existence and forcefully impress this now valid existence on others" (41–42). Whether the incident of violence is an act of rape or torture, the forceful imposition of the assaulter's form on the victim may serve as a means of empowerment for the violator; the victim's body acts as a blank text on which an insecure individual's worldview may be written. "A disembodied idea that has no basis in the material world . . . can," as Elaine Scarry observes in *The Body in Pain*, "borrow the appearance of reality from the realm that from the very start has compelling reality to the human mind, the physical body itself" (125). The wound that is the physical manifestation of victimization by violence is also the mark of a much more subtle confrontation, a confrontation of forms and of worlds. For the violator, violence may come to serve as a temporary affirmation of an unstable self, a material manifestation of a disembodied ideology, an expansion of one's own insubstantial form out into an alien world. For the victim, however, violence is defined by a literal and psychological destruction of form, a threat to personal coherence, a sacrifice of self-control.

In defining the way in which the body is culturally constructed, recent criticism has called into question the conceptual splitting of mind and body, while current technology has unsettled distinctions as fundamental as the notion of the "inside" and "outside" of a body.[1] These categories remain useful, however, in articulating the ways in which the victim understands the experience of violation. Victims of intimate violence often appropriate the categories of mind and body, subject and object, only to describe the way in which the experience of violation seems to dissolve many of the boundaries between them. What Scarry defines as the "compelling reality" of the physical body constantly asserts itself in the act of violence; it is that material domain on which both the victim's struggle to escape pain and the violator's attempt to appropriate power are first waged. The body's susceptibility to pain lends the violator power over a victim whom he attacks not just as body but as subject; the victim's body becomes the material extension of vulnerability, its susceptibility to pain rendering it the locus of attention for a victim for whom subjectivity and materiality become hopelessly entangled.

Testimonies of victims of rape and torture frequently describe their attempt to avoid violation by asserting their identities as "human" beings as well as bodies. One victim of gang rape traces her desperate attempt to reclaim an autonomy wrested from her physically by manipulating her attackers verbally:

> *Ms. Davis*: I talked constantly, trying to show them that I wasn't freaked out, that I was a human being and not something that they could just pick up and do this to without any feedback. I tried to reach them, to make human contact with them. I felt that if they were aware I was a human being, they would not be able to do it. But it didn't work. . . .
>
> I didn't feel I could get through without talking. I felt I would go crazy if I didn't talk. I also wanted to prove that they couldn't destroy me by doing this. So I would talk to them as if I were perfectly at ease. Of course I wasn't, I wasn't fooling myself. I was only showing them I wasn't totally destroyed.
> *Interviewer*: You thought that's what they wanted you to be?
> *Ms. Davis*: Yes, I definitely think so. (Russell, 165–66)

As the rapists appropriate the victim's body through violence, she attempts to reclaim her autonomy as subject by positing a distinction between body and mind. The rapists' ability to violate her is predicated upon her material vulnerability, her connection to a body that exists in space as "something that they could just pick up and do this to." By forcing the violators' recognition of her as a "human being," Ms. Davis hopes to forestall that assault on her physical form. In the context of rape, however, she becomes an appropriated body attempting to reclaim herself verbally rather than a self speaking to other selves.

The violators' silencing of their victim—she is allowed to respond only to their questions, and then only by answering yes or no—demonstrates that their physical violence functions as a means of claiming the victim not only as body but as speaking subject. The penetration of Ms. Davis's body results in an experience of physical and emotional instability that effects the "total destruction" the rapists seek:

> After it was finally over . . . I grabbed the guy in the back and held onto his arm, because I needed somebody to hold on to. I was shaking. I think that it bothered them that I was seeking some kind of human comfort from one of them. It was all so crazy. (Russell, 167)

The effect of rape is to pin Davis's subjectivity to her body; she can no longer posit a human subject separate from the trembling, violated body in the back seat of the car. She no longer "reaches" for "human comfort" figuratively, but does so through a literal, physical act; as she grasps the arm of her violator, his body emerges as the stable entity against which she measures her own tenuous existence. The victim's sense of powerlessness reduces her to a violable body that is not only the literal site of physical violence but the figurative doorway to a subject that the body renders vulnerable to assault.

While semiotic systems are based on the function of signs as vehicles of intellectual mediation, violence thrusts its victims into the status of uncontestable embodiment; instead of manipulating language to construct a representation, the violator offers a hermeneutics of destruction in which the basic unit is physical rather than semiotic, a piece of the human body rather than a word. Representations of violation, then, emerge at the intersection of linguistic and material worlds, between which the readerly subject negotiates. Because the process of making meaning involves a motion between words and bodies, the reduction of representations of violation to linguistic practice obscures the tensions that result from the interplay between both.

In their introduction to *The Violence of Representation*, Nancy Armstrong and Leonard Tennenhouse attempt to return violence to a critical plane on which the linguistic and the material exist side by side. Their volume consists of analyses which often assert the continuity between historical and representational violence:

> Others of us are less careful of the line between data and analysis, between forms of violence that are represented in writing and the violence committed through representation. They consider writing but one more symbolic practice among the others that make up cultural history. From their point of view, writing is not so much about violence as a form of violence in its own right. . . .
> We have offered a distinction between two modalities of violence: that which is "out there" in the world, as opposed to that which is exercised through words upon things in the world, often by attributing violence to them. But our ultimate goal is to demonstrate that the two cannot in fact be distinguished. . . . (2, 9)

As Armstrong and Tennenhouse rightfully assert, representations of violence are intimately connected to violence in the world; "politics and poetics," as they claim, "are inseparable concerns." In defining writing as but one symbolic practice among others, however, Armstrong and Tennenhouse risk obliterating any distinction between semiotic violence and its empirical counterpart. Although literary language is never simply referential, the act of reading a representation of violence is defined by the reader's suspension between the semiotic and the real, between a representation and the material dynamics of violence which it evokes, reflects, or transforms.

The mimetic qualities of fiction function through a series of complex mediations involving not only the gap between sign and referent but that between the text and an empirical subtext drawn from the reader's assumptions about violence—an understanding of its impact, dynamics, and consequences drawn from experience in the empirical world as well as from fictional and nonfictional representations. As "extratextual" realities surface in the fictional text, they are, as Wolfgang Iser observes,

> always in some way reduced or modified, as they have been removed from their original context and function. In the literary text they thus become capable of new connections, but at the same time old connections are still present, at least to a certain degree (and may themselves appear in a new light); indeed, their original context must remain sufficiently implicit to act as a background to offset their new significance. (69)

Iser's depiction of the relationship between textual and extratextual reality points to the way in which empirical violence hovers in the background of its representational counterpart to qualify the reader's response to a literary text. At the same time, literary representations of violence perpetuate, revise, or transform the reader's attitude toward empirical violence, often in ways of which the reader is not fully aware. As the dynamics of violation emerge within the conventions of representation and reading, fiction's ability to generate "new connections" allows it to introduce the reader to assumptions about violence that the text itself naturalizes. The victim's body may be reduced to literary convention or unveiled with agonizing specificity; the text may recreate the rhythms of the violator's force or mark the jarring disruptions of the victim's pain. The reader's experience of a representation of violation thus involves accepting or rejecting assumptions about the dynamics of violation that the text itself seldom makes explicit; those assumptions qualify and are qualified by the reader's experience of violence as an empirical as well as a representational phenomenon.

Because the experience of reading implicates the reader in specific attitudes toward empirical violence, criticism of representations of violation must establish a means of reintroducing the suffering material body into literary analysis. Marx's introduction of the laborer's body into his discussion of capitalism offers a materialist model that serves as a basis of discussion in several of the chapters that follow. Marx unveils the apparently "magical" economy of capitalism by tracing the way in which its success depends upon the capitalist's ability to cover over or deny the cost borne by the laborer's body. As he traces the origin and consequences of capitalism, Marx uncovers the laborer's suffering body in all its material specificity and attempts to reestablish the connection between the body that labors and the subject that suffers. Although Marx concentrates on the operation of capitalism rather than its representation, his theories point to the way in which the capitalist's power derives not only from ownership of the laborer's body but from ownership of the sign. Elaine Scarry's reading of Marx in *The Body in Pain* is especially useful here: "Marx's own labor is the work of restoring the original referent, not just pointing to the human authors again and again, but carrying their portraits forward into the analysis, so that the sentient origins of the made world stay visible and accompany the progressively spiritualized or sublimated reappearances of that object world" (272). By tracing the material impact of capitalism on the human body, Marx reintroduces empirical reality into an otherwise magical economic system; as the terms of Scarry's analysis demonstrate, that system thrives on the capitalist's command not only of the making and selling of objects but of their interpretive significance. Marx, in a sense, rewrites the capitalist's representation of the commodity such that it becomes impossible for the reader to disentangle the materiality of the laboring body from the material which its labor produces.

Marx's unveiling of the way in which the laborer's suffering body is rendered invisible by the machinery of capitalism thus provides a critical model for understanding representations which obscure the materiality of bodily violation. Positing a parallel between the capitalist's acts of oppression and the violator's acts of victimization, my study reveals the issues at stake in acts of representation that reinscribe violation within a magical system devoid of human suffering and pain. As the victim's body disappears beneath the force of narrative abstraction or is rendered purely material through a focus on its mechanistic functions, narrative may implicitly endorse a vision of violence that divorces an act of violation from its human consequences. The "original referent" of violence which my analysis attempts to restore is not a single incident or historical event but an empirical dynamic that demands, at its most basic level, the acknowledgment of the painful materiality of the victim's body.

An accurate theory of reading violence must account for the reader's experience of the text as a negotiation between that empirical dynamic of violence and its representational counterpart.[2] In "The Violence of Rhetoric," Teresa de Lauretis makes a motion toward such a theory as she introduces the semiotic theories of Charles Peirce to redefine the relationship between empirical reality and the activity of semiosis. Citing the importance of Foucault's symbolic order, de Lauretis emphasizes the distinction between violence itself—which exists outside that symbolic order—and its conceptualization and expression, which exist inside it:

> It seems to me that of the three—the concept, the expression, and the violence—only the first two belong to Foucault's discursive order. The third is somewhere else. . . . Now, for those of us whose bodies and whose pleasures are out there, where the violence is . . . if we want to attempt to know them, we have to leave Foucault and turn, for the time being, to Peirce.
>
> For Peirce, the object has more weight, as it were. The real, the physical world and empirical reality, are of greater consequence to the human activity of semiosis . . . than they are to the symbolic activity of signification, as defined in Saussure's theory of language and re-elaborated in contemporary French thought. (38–39)

Peirce's focus on the significance of "the real" in the activity of semiosis lends itself to a theory of reading violation that emphasizes the reader's status as negotiator between representational and empirical violence. The path from semiosis to reality that Peirce maps involves a chain of meaning made possible only because it "comes to a halt, however temporarily, by anchoring itself to somebody, to some body, an individual subject" (41). De Lauretis's emphasis on the subject who mediates between semiosis and reality leads, in her essay, to a discussion of how that subject is engendered by a rhetoric of violence.

Her announcement of that subject as not only "somebody" but "some body," however, points to additional concerns about the way in which the intrusion or absence of the reader's body complicates the dynamics of representational violence that she describes. Because the materiality of the body and its susceptibility to pain constitute one of the principal dynamics of violence, an analysis of the representation of violence demands not only a recognition of the reader who serves as the semiotic subject but an exploration of the way in which that reader experiences him- or herself as a body. To what degree can the reading subject be said to be a reading body? The analyses that follow explore the necessity of rendering visible the way in which representations of violence may exaggerate the disembodied status of the reader or, conversely, lend him or her a textual body which delimits the reader's experience of the text. My study, then, will focus on the process of reading as it conceals or discloses the violated and violating body through a reading act to which the reader brings a varying awareness of his or her own empirical body.

The reader accesses the fictional world of violence by abandoning the body that anchors him or her to a material universe and entering imaginatively into a fictional scene. The reader's admittance into the scene of violence is thus achieved only at the expense of disembodiment; the victim's experience, on the other hand, is defined by the overwhelming presence of a vulnerable body. The distance and detachment of a reader who must leave his or her body behind in order to enter imaginatively into the scene of violence make it possible for representations of violence to obscure the material dynamics of bodily violation, erasing not only the victim's body but his or her pain.

The disparity between the disembodied reader and the embodied victim may lead to a sense of detachment that is perpetuated by the distanced dynamics of the reading process. Even as representations of violation invoke and revise the reader's understanding of the way in which actual violence works, they do so through the manipulation of words, images, and literary forms that often function to efface rather than unveil the materiality of the victimized body. If the conventions of reading that emphasize the distance between a reader and the intra-textual acts of violence about which he or she reads are exaggerated, the immediacy of violence may be obscured and the victim may emerge as an object of imaginative manipulation, his or her body simply another text on which the reader inscribes meaning. In such a case, the reader's freedom parallels the autonomy of the violator, who creates a narrative of violence in which the bodies of others are molded to fit the configurations of the violator's desire. Insofar as the reader's imagination manipulates the victim's body as a purely textual entity, the reality of pain and the vulnerability of that body may be obscured by the participation of a reading subject who perpetuates the dynamics of violation.

The social consequences of such readerly disembodiment may be profound. The reader brings the conclusions generated about violence through representation back to the empirical world, even as he or she brings the empirical experience of violence to the representation. Reading, as Robert Scholes suggests in *Protocols of Reading*, "has two faces, looks in two directions. One direction is back, toward the source and original context of the signs we are deciphering. The other direction is forward, based on the textual situation of the person doing the reading. . . . [R]eading is almost always an affair of at least two times, two places, and two consciousnesses . . ." (7). Eliding the distinction between the representational and the "real" can be just as dangerous as failing to acknowledge their connection. The seductive power of representation lies, at least in part, in its ability to naturalize its own conclusions, to obscure its manipulation of the experiential dynamics of violence by veiling the ideological assumptions inherent in its linguistic maneuvers. In the representation of violence, such a phenomenon may result in a text that seems to represent the dynamics of violation even as it obscures the reader's perception of the victim's body and relegates to background the reality of the victim's pain.

In order to reveal rather than obscure the suffering body, literary representations of violence must often work against themselves to subvert their own distancing conventions. Because representation is defined by mediation, the subversion of reading conventions lends the text one means of unsettling its own dynamics and pushing the reader into a position of discomforting proximity to the victim's vulnerable body. Frequently, the body emerges in the text of violence at the moment when representation works against its immaterial biases to unveil the suffering body and the conventions of reading break down to collapse the distance between a disembodied reader and a victim defined by embodiment. At such moments, the reader's sense of discomfort or entrapment by the text enforces an experience of intellectual limitation that parallels the physical limitation of the victim, pushing the reader to acknowledge both the parameters of representation and the restrictions of material embodiment. A similar process of unsettling the reader's expectation may occur when the reader finds him- or herself located in discomforting proximity to the violator, pressured toward a subject position that he or she finds repugnant and frightening. In such circumstances, the experience of reading may become an opportunity for interrogating the mechanisms of representation and the conventions of reading through which the material dynamics of violence are depicted.

Teresa de Lauretis identifies a similar potential for self-critique in cinema's representation of female subjectivity:

> [B]y foregrounding the work of its codes, cinema could be made to re-present the play of contradictory percepts and meanings usually elided in representation, and so to enact the contradictions of women as social subjects, to perform the terms of the specific division of the female subject in language, in imaging, in the social. (*Alice Doesn't*, 69)

Literary texts can explore the ramifications of that which is normally elided in representations of violation in much the same way that de Lauretis's cinematic texts expose the "contradictions of women as social subjects." Feminist film criticism offers powerful models for the analysis of readers who are, like the viewers de Lauretis describes, located in an "impossible" place (69). The reader's position as negotiator between empirical and representational violence in the act of reading is echoed in cinema by the position of spectators who "are not, as it were, either in the film text *or* simply outside the film text; rather, we might say, they intersect the film as they are intersected by cinema" (de Lauretis, *Alice Doesn't*, 44). The means through which the spectator constitutes him- or herself as subject in relation to the representational reality of the screen has, as both Laura Mulvey and Teresa de Lauretis explore, important ideological implications for the viewer and his or her attitudes toward gender. In exposing the conventions associated with the representation and viewing of woman as body or spectacle, film renders visible many of the dynamics that also underlie acts of representing and reading violence, especially violence against women. Feminist film theory extends film theory's focus on reception and the act of viewing to explore the way in which ideology infiltrates the act of spectatorship; in so doing, it points to complexities of response that underlie reading as well as cinematic viewing.

In this study, film theory functions both to establish parallels between literary and cinematic representation and to mark significant differences in the conventions associated with these forms. My focus on the materiality of violation and the way in which it is revealed or erased in the act of literary representation makes the issue of narrative visibility crucial for the literary analysis that follows; at the same time, literary conventions ensure that bodies are "visible" or "invisible" to the reader only in a metaphorical sense. The terms of film theory make it possible to translate textual conventions into visually perceptible form; references to the reader's "gaze," his or her way of looking at a literary scene of violence, render the metaphor of narrative vision critically immediate in much the same way that references to the reader's textual body render his or her presence in the scene of violence visible.

Such a translation functions as a vehicle for unveiling textual dynamics that are often hidden in literary representations because they are played out not on a screen located spatially in relationship to the viewer's vision but in the reader's imagination. My appropriation of the language of film theory to explore the act of reading representations of violation is thus an attempt to explore rather than to deny the tensions that arise when filmic and literary conventions are compared; the moments at which such a metaphorical equivalence breaks down are as important to the study as the moments at which it is seemingly naturalized by the literary text. Frequently, in an attempt to reveal the body in all its material specificity, literary representations of violence appropriate the conventions of film, either relying upon a highly visual mode of narration or undermining the distancing conventions of reading to direct the reader's gaze upon a scene in a manner similar to the enforced perspective of the camera's frame. Representations of violence can thus impose themselves upon the reader's imagination in the same way film imposes itself upon the viewer's vision. Film metaphors are least applicable to literary texts that emphasize the disembodied conventions of reading; the ease with which such representations efface the materiality of the victimized body is in direct contrast to a cinematic genre the conventions of which dictate the viewer's focus on the material location of violence (this is not necessarily the same, of course, as a focus on the implications of the subject's materiality). In appropriating filmic technique, therefore, literature must work against itself; as it does so, it unveils the very conventions that it manipulates.

Literary appropriations of cinematic convention lead, in representations of violation, both to new forms of narrative vision and to enforced blinders that obscure the material and human dynamics of victimization. The language of feminist film theory can be used to describe not only literary works that subvert their own conventions in order to introduce the reader into the scene of violation with forceful immediacy, but those that adopt a cinematic focus on the material location of violence without exploring the way in which subjectivity and materiality are linked in the human body. Several contemporary works of violence, for example, reflect the assumptions of a contemporary film culture without exploring their implications for the representation of violence. In a literary representation, the absence of visible form may render a subject immaterial and his or her body merely conventional—and therefore absent from the scene of violence. Conversely, the emphasis on pure physicality in a cinematic novel like *American Psycho* may have the opposite effect; in rendering the violation of the human body in mechanistic terms, such a representation once again severs subject and object, reducing the human body to pure material. In such cases the reader is offered an embodied gaze, but it is the gaze of the physically powerful violator, perceiving the victim's body as a subjectless mass of matter. The conventions of neither reading nor viewing are in and of themselves more appropriate to the representation of violence; both can be manipulated and appropriated to reveal or obscure the implications of bodily violation.

Representations of violence must subvert the disembodying tendencies of the reading process in order to offer the reader the fullest experience of reading violence. They must, in effect, remind the reader of his or her own violability. This does not suggest, however, that the reader becomes passive. Negotiating the representation of violence, the reader finds him- or herself more vigorously placed and more intensively manipulated than in most texts. The reader's response to such narrative harrying, his or her attempt to break free from imprisoning or emotionally painful narrative structures, must be an element in the reading process just, as de Lauretis notes, it is in the process of viewing cinema: "[N]arrative and visual pleasure need and should not be thought of as the exclusive property of dominant codes, serving solely the purposes of 'oppression'. . . . [I]t must be possible to imagine how perceptual and semantic contradictions may be engaged, worked through, or redirected toward unsettling and subverting the dominant formations" (*Alice Doesn't*, 69). Joel Black's recent critical study of literary representations of violence,[3] *The Aesthetics of Murder* (1991), perpetuates the vision of a disempowered reader overwhelmed by the representation of violence. According to Black, the passive reader or viewer[4] of the scene of violence is gendered female:

> [T]he conventional masculine gaze . . . is voyeuristically directed at an arousing spectacle or desirable object. In contrast, the object of the feminine gaze is typically a scene of violence. "Abject terror," maintains Clover, "is gendered feminine"; this accounts for "the femaleness of the victim" in the modern horror film, and even for the "incorporat[ion]" of the "feminine" in the spectators who are collectively violated "in ways otherwise imaginable, for males, only in nightmare." But the female victim's look of terror is not the only expression of the feminine gaze; there is also the female witness's look of anguish as she reacts to a tragic scene of suffering and violence with the classical responses of pity and fear. In the passive role of spectator, the reader of a text or the viewer of a film hardly becomes a victim, but rather assumes the role of (feminine) witness. . . . (66–67)

In the scenario that Black describes, the woman is offered the "power" of the gaze only to be overpowered by the horror of what she sees; suddenly, agency is overwhelmed as pleasure turns to pain and looking provides not vicarious enjoyment but a form of self-inflicted torture. The look in this case is tied to powerlessness; the witness or reader-viewer, in her terror, becomes "abject" like the victim. Her pity and fear are "classical responses" destined not to disrupt a scenario of violation in which the witness does not—and the reader-viewer literally cannot—intervene.

Black's reluctance to characterize such passive spectatorship as a form of victimization may be traced to his recognition that with the status of reader-viewer comes a special aesthetic dispensation from assault:

> Identification with the murder witness . . . allows the reader or spectator to experience terror-at-a-distance, so to speak. . . . [I]f the relative safety of the reader-viewer and murder witness allows them to pass beyond the victim's terror, it initiates them into the mysterious experience of the murderer himself and invites them to participate in his otherworldly "suspension of earthly passion." (67)

14 Intimate Violence

Black's formulation converts the frozen gaze of a reader-viewer gendered female into the narrative liberation of a spectator free to distance him- or herself from the victim and even to indulge imaginatively in the murderer's suspended passion. No longer locked into the gaze, this observer roams the text to try on the various subject positions it offers, donning and discarding the attire of victim, violator, and observer without recognition of conflict or attention to consequence. Black's reader-viewer is released from the position of "abject terror" that results when her powerless eyes are forced open only to be liberated into a form of blindness that announces itself as sight; instead of wresting away the violator's power to confront and resist the violation that she is forced to observe, the reader-viewer is lulled into "seeing" violence without its attendant consequences, experiencing the "rapture" without recognizing its connection to the very pain she seeks to avoid. Such aestheticization not only fails to empower the reader-viewer but often blinds her to her own complicity in the violence enacted by the text.

Black's positioning of the reader in the text of violence, then, affords that reader little strength to engage fully with the power of its representations. Once pushed outside the "ethical world of human reality" into the domain of the text, it would seem, the reader must give up the right to resist not only the violence it represents but the narrative force it exerts. Recent work in reader-response and narrative theory, however, questions the reader's relegation to the status of textual thrall. In *Discerning the Subject*, Paul Smith observes that

> there is a distinction to be made between the subject-position prescribed by a text and the actual human agent who engages with that text and thus with the subject-position it offers. Clearly, any given text is not empowered to *force* the reader to adhere to the discursive position it offers. . . . [W]hat always stands between the text's potential or preferred effect and an actualized effect is a reader who has a history of his/her own. (34)

Only through an understanding of the way in which narrative force is constituted can a reader hope to resist a narrative that both represents and enacts violence. Recognition of the way in which meaning is generated—both through the process of representation and in the experience of reading—empowers the reader with the ability to refuse not only a problematic subject-position that reinforces the dynamics of violence but the very notion that the reader is *subjected* to the text that he or she reads. In *Room for Maneuver*, Ross Chambers describes a type of literature that actively encourages the reader to resist its "force":

> [L]iterature can designate itself, in its "textual function," as a site of discursive oppositionality; that is, that it produces, as the context that makes it meaningful, a context of oppositional relations to power. But such oppositionality, I further suggest, takes the form, precisely, of a split between the "narrative"

and the "textual" functions of discourse such that the "narrative function," as the site of an address to the narratee in the position of power, comes to be relativized—or, more technically, *ironized*—by a "textual function" that distances the reader from the narratee position and requires the "narrative function" to become part of the text *as an object of interpretation.* (43)

Several of the texts that I will address here fit Chambers's category of oppositionality in that they offer a subject-position to the reader only to expose the problematics of donning it. In doing so, they invoke the power of the reader's imagination to unveil and resist the very dynamics of violation that they reveal. In these representations, the reader's ability to identify imaginatively with a fictional universe is used to communicate the victim's experience of violation, to expose the reader to the power dynamics of intimate violence not by enlisting the reader's imagination as part of the magical force of the violator but by subjecting the reader to the consequences of a violation that his or her imagination helps to create.

In Chambers's terms, it is *the text* that "designate[s] itself" oppositional; it does so through "a 'textual function' that distances the reader from the narratee position." Although Chambers's reader thus appears to be utterly constricted by the text which he or she approaches, Chambers's conclusions point to the possibility of an oppositional *reader* as well. "Everything thus depends," Chambers observes, "on the intervention of a reader capable of manifesting the discourse as a mediated phenomenon by producing the crucial split between 'narrative' and 'textual' functions. Discourse that is not, in this sense, read cannot be oppositional" (43). In the pages that follow, I will argue that representations of violation even in texts that do not explicitly foreground the gap between their narrative and textual functions may be read oppositionally if the *reader* is self-conscious about his or her own role in the construction of textual meaning. The gendered model of viewing violence with which Black begins posits the reader's passive vision of rather than active participation in the representation of violence. The reader's response to such a dynamic of disempowerment, however, should not be to offer up such vision in exchange for the aesthetic blindness Black describes but instead to reclaim vision as a means of textual empowerment or, to revise Chambers's terms, to bring the oppositional imagination *to the text*.

Both in the aesthetic realm and in the "ethical world" with which Black juxtaposes it, not to see violence or its effects is not to erase its existence but simply to ignore it. *Seeing into* violence, on the other hand, becomes a form of resistance when what is exposed before the eyes of the reader/viewer is not his or her own helplessness but the dynamics of violation; the critical reader in the scene of violence uncovers not just the vulnerability of the victim or the observer but the very power dynamics upon which the violator's force depends. The power of the reader to resist what Smith describes as the "force" of the text often parallels, in the representation of intimate violence, the power

of the reader to resist complicity—either through passive viewing or unconscious participation—in the act of violation represented therein.

By articulating the ways in which literary representations of violence construct and are constructed by the reader, this study attempts to provide a
critical perspective that allows the reader to resist the kind of intimate violence that certain texts would perpetuate through the act of reading. The
process of finding one's self in a scene of fictional violence is the first step
toward choosing a location rather than being located. Only by tracing the
way in which the reader responds to and participates in fictional scenes of
violence is it possible to empower ourselves as readers with the ability to
resist the pull of a textual representation of violation, to read ourselves out
of models of spectatorship or positions of aesthetic distance that themselves
imply a form of victimization.

I

READING RAPE

SANCTUARY AND
THE WOMEN OF BREWSTER PLACE

While the relationship between the violence of a culture and its representational counterpart in art is probed in many literary and artistic works, few deal with the issue with the immediacy of Marcel Duchamp's room-size artwork, "Etant Donnes: 1 la chute d'eau, 2 le gaz d'eclairage." "Etant Donnes" occupies one small room of the Philadelphia Museum of Art; the viewer's entrance into the room is marked by the absence of light and the looming presence of an actual wooden door that appears to have been taken out of a garden wall and set down in the museum intact. Although the door will not open, closer examination reveals that it contains two small holes through which it is possible to peer past the door itself, through the gap in a brick wall set about three feet behind the door, and into the world beyond. The backdrop of the scene that meets the viewer is artificially natural, a glitzy combination of fake trees, glittering lights, and mechanical waterfall that seems a poor imitation of an actual landscape. The glance of the viewer, however, is directed not toward that artificial backdrop but onto a life-size model of a woman's naked body, a body splayed out relentlessly before the viewer's eyes, a body that announces as its most prominent feature a hairless vagina that is cut into the woman like a wound. The woman lies as if abandoned after an act of violation, her legs spread painfully wide in a tangle of dark brush and autumn leaves. The peepholes in Duchamp's wooden door succeed in aligning the viewer's eyes with the glaring wound of the woman's sex; subtle techniques of focus that may be contradicted in a painting are replaced here by a physical alignment, a concrete limitation of sight, that is as effective as a strong pair of hands that jerk the viewer's head into position and hold it there. Having chosen to look, the viewer is held captive by the artwork, locked into the position of a voyeur without prelude or conscious choice. The degradation of the experience is heightened by the naked woman's forced participation in her own objectification. The victim, face obscured behind a wave of blonde hair, holds in her outstretched hand a gas lamp as if to illuminate every crack, crevice, and wound of the body that the viewer approaches as text. The violence to which the naked woman's body

17

bears testimony is reenacted in the guise of art; the viewer becomes a violator whose gaze perpetuates the violence of a crime that reduces woman to object.

I.

In deliberately blurring the boundaries between art and life, aesthetic and actual violence, Duchamp's study points to the way in which the conventions of art may both create and license the desire for violence. Art invites the audience's participation in its created worlds while offering that audience the comfort of aesthetic distance; that distance allows the reader or viewer to accept the work's invitation to titillation without appearing to become implicated in its trafficking with violence. Duchamp's work, in effect, upsets the fragile justification of aesthetic convention by undercutting the viewer's sense of the distinction between *studying* a scene of artistic violence and *participating* in an act of literal violation. "Etant Donnes" is shocking, not because it transgresses the boundaries that separate violence from the artistic *representation* of violence, but because it forces its viewers to recognize that transgression.

In Faulkner's *Sanctuary*, on the other hand, the reader's presence as not only an observer but a participant in the novel's violence is obscured by a literary screen that assures the reader of his or her distance from the act of violence even as it affords an entry into that violence. Faulkner exploits the conventions of literature to lure the reader past the boundaries of the printed page into the barn where Temple is raped. As *Sanctuary* pressures the reader not only to perceive the rape from the perspective of the violator but to assume the position of that violator, to anticipate, to plan, and to execute—in the arena of the imagination—the crime of rape, the novel continues to assert the purely literary nature of the violence enacted in the reader's mind.

The sensational crime around which *Sanctuary* revolves is never described in the novel. While the back cover of one Vintage paperback edition advertises that the novel's protagonist is "raped in a peculiarly horrible manner," the novel itself continually fails to satisfy the appetite for lurid description that it—and its advertisement—creates. By withholding any direct representation of the rape upon which it focuses, *Sanctuary* shifts the burden of creation away from Faulkner and toward the reader; while Faulkner invokes the conventions of high literature to authorize *Sanctuary* as a work of art rather than a piece of popular fiction, the novel relies upon its readers to create the scandalous story of violation that it only suggests. The reader's access to Popeye's horrendous act of violence is limited to a series of adumbrated narrative descriptions and a montage of speculations by the novel's characters; the novel itself provides no authorized version of the rape. With each tauntingly inadequate representation of the violence, each symbolic allusion to the crime, each purely imaginary conjecture of the rape by the novel's characters, the act itself becomes more visibly absent; the rape becomes a gaping hole in the text that the reader must fill.[1] In *The Act of Reading*, Wolfgang Iser describes such narrative gaps as "structured blanks." "Communication in literature," Iser states,

> is a process set in motion and regulated, not by a given code, but by a mutually restrictive and magnifying interaction between the explicit and the implicit, between revelation and concealment. . . . Hence, the structured blanks of the text stimulate the process of ideation to be performed by the reader on terms set by the text. (168–69)

Such blanks function as invitations to the reader to participate not only in the viewing but in the making of the novelistic universe; the gap in the narrative "turns into a propellant for the reader's imagination, making him supply what has been withheld" (Iser, 194). In *Sanctuary*, the narrative's withholding of the representation of Popeye's crime shifts the burden of creation away from Faulkner and toward the reader. The novel's refusal to write the rape jolts the reader into becoming the author of the crime.[2]

It is the reader who first articulates the possibility of rape in *Sanctuary*. The narrative's continual allusions to the danger that threatens Temple's sense of well-being are ambiguous and incomplete. Denied access to information that Temple herself possesses, the reader must name the threat that plagues the novel's protagonist. Even as Temple is about to communicate to Gowan (and the reader) the source and substance of her fear, her narrative is temporarily suspended; her recounting of her conversation with Ruby is interrupted by a crucial ellipsis that frustrates the reader's desire to pinpoint the exact nature of Temple's suspicions: "'Gowan, I'm scared. She said for me not to—You've been drinking again; you haven't even washed the blood—She says for us to go away from here. . . . . . .'" (51). The revelation that Temple appears about to deliver is immediately interrupted by her observation about Gowan's drinking. As a result, it is the reader who must fill in the gap marked by the narrative ellipsis. The reason for Temple's fear is never explicitly articulated; while the possibility of violence is suggested, the threat of rape is acknowledged by the reader alone.

While Temple's initial expression of her fear conceals more than it reveals, the anxious response that portrayal generates in the reader is kept alive through narrative ambiguity. Temple's elliptical comments feed the reader's suspicions of the threatened crime without actually confirming them.[3] Her disjointed sentences, ambiguous pronouns, and logical inversions create referential puzzles that the reader must take apart and reconstruct if Temple's remarks are to make sense: "'There are so many of them,' she said in a wailing tone, watching the cigarette crush slowly in her fingers. 'But maybe, with so many of them. . . . . . .' The woman had gone back to the stove" (57). Temple's comments appear as a type of idiosyncratic shorthand that bodies forth a more complete system of thought; in supplying the referential system for Temple's remarks, the reader remakes those remarks in accordance with his or her own assumptions. The narrative puzzle is never "solved"; instead, its pieces are reformed into diverse configurations that conform to the narrative patterns created by individual readers. The truncated nature of Temple's comments licenses the reader's imaginative foray into violence and sex by serving as an apparent narrative anchor for those explorations. In fact, however, Faulkner plays upon the ambiguity of the narrative's comments to transfer the responsibility for the creation of the novel's lurid plot to the reader.

The reader's active role in the construction of meaning blurs the conventional line between a novel and its audience, encouraging the reader's entrance into the fictional text. Temple's fragmented sentences and abrupt shifts of focus often emerge as if in response to an invisible commentator/reader who articulates her fears of violence. Having asked Ruby Lamar for a ride into town, for example, Temple suddenly breaks into a frantic speech that is supposedly directed at Ruby and her infant child. In fact, however, the monologue appears to be part of a dialogue begun somewhere outside the text; it opens with a response to what seems to be a missing question: "'I'm not afraid,' Temple said. 'Things like that don't happen. Do they? They're just like other people. You're just like other people. With a little baby. . . . What a cute little bu-ba-a-by,' she wailed, lifting the child to her face; 'if bad man hurts Temple, us'll tell the governor's soldiers, wont us?'" (59). Temple's unsolicited assertion—"I'm not afraid"—lacks apparent textual motivation, just as the demonstrative pronoun she employs—"Things like *that*" (emphasis mine)—lacks a visible referent. Her comments appear to be a response to an extratextual observation, a reply to the unvoiced concern of a reader who speaks from outside the novelistic world. Because the novel's characters fail to voice the threat of violence that haunts Temple, it is the reader who supplies the missing referent for her ambiguous words. While Temple's comments emerge as if in response to the reader's questions, they continue to conceal as much as they reveal. Her ominous reference to the unspoken fate that she fears—"Things like that don't happen. Do they?"—fuels the reader's imaginary fears even as it refuses to confirm the substance of those fears. The ambiguous imaging of the narrative assures, once again, that the only violence made explicit in the novel is a violence born of the reader's imagination; it is the reader's fearful anticipation of that violence that lends the rape imaginative form and brings it to life.

The early warnings of the rape that rumble through the novel without ever assuming articulate form tease the reader into a state of protracted sensitivity; in that state, the slightest movement, the least reported sound, triggers an avalanche of imaginative violences. Before the rape ever occurs, Faulkner plays upon the reader's understanding of literary conventions to ensnare the overeager reader in the web of his or her own expectations. As Iser points out, the function of the break between chapters in a novel "is not separation so much as a tacit invitation to find the missing link" (197); at the beginning of chapter 11, Faulkner invokes the convention of the chapter break to deliver such a "tacit invitation." He exploits the reader's expectation of the rape and understanding of the possibility of "off-screen" intra-chapter action to lure the reader into believing that the rape has already occurred: "Temple waked lying in a tight ball, with narrow bars of sunlight falling across her face like the tines of a golden fork, and while the stiffened blood trickled and tingled through her cramped muscles she lay gazing quietly up at the ceiling" (91). In this description, the sun becomes a weapon that rakes its tines across Temple's body to produce the trickling blood and cramped muscles that the reader—his or her anticipation heightened—automatically associates with rape. Faulkner plays upon the artificiality of metaphor to invoke the signs of rape in an alternative context. The narrative provides the raw materials of violent description, while the reader's heightened anticipation of the event constructs those materials into a representation of violence. Temple's physical discomfort, however, is soon traced to its undramatic origin in her cramped sleeping quarters; the rape to which the narrative seems to have alluded has occurred only in the reader's imagination.

Denied an explicit account of the novel's violence, the reader is tempted and frustrated, tempted and frustrated, until the process of reading begins to assume the rhythm of desire itself. The reader's absorption of warnings about the imminence of Temple's rape translates into an eagerness to peruse the spectacle that has been promised; his or her sensitivity to the subtle conventions of fiction is exploited by a narrative trap that invites the reader—if only momentarily—to envision and even create the promised violence. With the continued reiteration of hints and clues about the crime, however, the reader's horrified response to the projected rape may fade into a kind of numbed expectation. Through the sheer act of repetition, the novel's protracted inexplicit references to the rape rob the crime of its shock value; the reader's sympathy for the victim and the indignation inspired by the mere thought of the violent act become tinged with an impatience bred of familiarity. The desire for narrative closure turns the violent event that would provide that closure into a mere literary device as the reader is pressured into not only anticipating but impatiently awaiting the promised violence.

Like the reader, the little man who attempts to protect Temple from the advances of Goodwin and Popeye is also reduced to a state of dulled immunity to the impending rape. Throughout the first part of the novel, the physical postures of Temple's protector, Tommy, chart her increasing vulnerability and the reader's building agitation. Initially, Tommy reacts to Temple's impending violation with an indignation so violent that it overwhelms his own body: Tommy "began to think about Temple again. He would feel his feet scouring on the floor and his whole body writhing in an acute discomfort. 'They ought to let that gal alone,' he whispered to Goodwin. 'They ought to quit pesterin her'" (72). The "acute discomfort" that Tommy experiences as his "whole body writh[es]" not only points toward Temple's rape but metaphorically enacts it; his tortured empathy becomes a means of channeling his own unacknowledged and illicit desire. As the narrative progresses in its path toward the violence that both Tommy and the reader recognize as inevitable, the ineffectual protesting of Temple's protector generates a tension born as much of repressed desire as of moral frustration: "'Durn them fellers,' Tommy whispered, 'durn them fellers.' He could hear them on the front porch and his body began again to writhe slowly in an acute unhappiness. 'Durn them fellers'" (74). Tommy's distress echoes the discomfort of a reader forced to squirm in his or her seat while awaiting with frustrating slowness the inevitability of the rape that is to follow. Like the reader, Tommy follows Popeye's path back and forth, toward and away from Temple, unable to intervene as either protector or violator: "The third time he smelled Popeye's cigarette. Ef he'll jest keep that up, he said. And Lee too, he said, rocking from side to side in a dull, excruciating agony, And Lee too" (83). The "scouring feet" and "writhing" body that characterized Tommy's initial response to Temple's situation give way to what is now described as a "dull, excruciating agony." While that agony, like the other physical signs of his discomfort, is born of feeling for Temple, it is now a feeling tinged with resignation. The reader's pain, like Tommy's agony, is replaced by a "dulled" perception of the inevitability of Temple's violation.

As the prolonged anticipation of violence is finally confirmed, Faulkner downplays the reader's voyeuristic interest by emphasizing the apparently self-contained literary status of the rape. He uses the artifice of literary device—in this case, blatant symbolism—both to pique the reader's desire to view the forbidden act and to license that desire by clothing it in literary terms. As Popeye moves toward the cringing Temple, his approach is described as a type of symbolic and almost ritualistic dance in which the movement of his gun is clearly associated with the aggressive penis: ". . . he leaned out the door, the pistol behind him, against his flank, wisping thinly along his leg. He turned and looked at her. He waggled the pistol slightly and put it back in his coat, then he walked toward her" (107). Faulkner's choice of verbs exposes the discrepancy between literal vehicle and symbolic import; while the word "waggled" appears inappropriate for a gun, it is very appropriate for the symbolic counterpart of that gun. The mismatch of Faulkner's terms emphasizes the *process* through which violence is translated into literature, and encourages the reader to reenact that process in reverse, to trace the path from symbol to sign, from sign to signified. The reader participates in the creation of the rape scene by stripping away the layers of aesthetic mediation to unearth the crime beneath.

Like the symbolic imaging of Popeye's approach, the cryptic description of the violence that follows denies the reader a concrete representation that would take the place of the reader's own hazy formulations of the rape:

> She could hear silence in a thick rustling as he moved toward her through it, thrusting it aside, and she began to say Something is going to happen to me. She

was saying it to the old man with the yellow clots for eyes. "Something is happening to me!" she screamed at him, sitting in his chair in the sunlight, his hands crossed on top of the stick. "I told you it was!" she screamed, voiding the words like hot silent bubbles into the bright silence about them until he turned his head and the two phlegm-clots above her where she lay tossing and thrashing on the rough, sunny boards. "I told you! I told you all the time!" (107)

In this long-awaited "representation" of violence, the material dynamics of the rape are overshadowed by the function of the episode as a literary device; Temple's rape is communicated only as a *linguistic* event. The act is signified by a subtle motion of language, a shift of tense that marks the realization of narrative foreshadowing but not the demarcation of any visualizable incident. Temple's predictive remark, "Something is going to happen to me," is replaced by "Something is happening to me!"; in the infinitesimal space between the two phrases the rape is located but never defined, alluded to but never enacted. This confirmation of the reader's expectations of violence is less a resolution of tension than another invitation to narrative play that ends only in frustration. Like the old blind man who "witnesses" the rape, the reader is brought close to the scene only to be denied sensory access to it.

In fact, the old man "with the yellow clots for eyes" acts in many ways as the reader's double in the rape scene. Although he is close enough to the rape to reach out and touch Temple's writhing body, the old man remains "sitting in his chair in the sunlight, his hands crossed" in the posture of inaction. His handicaps appear to make his presence in the scene unproblematic; his blindness and deafness not only excuse his passive response but make intervention a sheer impossibility. The fundamental distance that separates the old man from the act that occurs in his presence affords him a unique status; he is exempted from the normal human responsibility for intervention. The reader, too, is present in the scene; while the old man "observes" the act blindly, the reader watches the violence unfold before his or her eyes, protected from the charge of voyeurism by an abstract representation that emphasizes the non-interventionist dynamics of the reading process. Temple's desperate accusation—"Something is happening to me!"—is directed at the old man who sits passively by as the rape unfolds; the *reader*, however, is clearly implicated by the remark as well. It is the reader, after all, who alone has been the recipient of Temple's frequent warnings of impending violence, the reader, as well as the old man, who sits silently, passively, watching without intervening. Even as the reader's imagination provides the details of a violence that the narrative has withheld, the hysterical young woman who is about to be raped screams out desperately: "I told you it was! . . . I told you! I told you all the time!"

Not surprisingly, then, in the metaphorical description of the rape that Faulkner *does* provide, it is the voyeur who perpetrates the ultimate crime. Faulkner's only description of the rape scene casts the violence as a struggle, not between Temple and Popeye, but between Temple and the old man with the phlegm-clotted eyes. During the rape, Temple screams desperately as a foreign body hovers over her own; it is not into Popeye's unresponsive eyes that she stares, however, but at "the two phlegm-clots above her where she lay tossing and thrashing on the rough, sunny boards." It is into the old man's blind eyes that Temple, at least in a metaphorical sense, looks as she thrashes on the boards; it is the old man, the voyeur, the reader, who assumes the posture of the rapist while Popeye himself stands on the sidelines, impotent.

At Miss Reba's, the endless parade of visitors through Temple's room reflects the desire of the novel's characters to look upon Temple's body—the object of rape—and to reconstruct through her presence the elusive details of that violence. Temple becomes an object of curiosity not only to Snopes (who is caught "peeping through the keyhole" of her door) and Benbow but to the reader as well. Her account of the rape, however, merely replaces the reader's fictional inventions with her own fantastic imaginings. As she weaves a story of rape that is actually a narrative of her own fantasies, Temple shocks Benbow into the realization that "she was recounting the experience with actual pride, a sort of naive and impersonal vanity, as though she were making it up" (226). Temple's relationship to her own experience of violation is defined by a detachment and a fascination not unlike that which governs the reader's literary experience of the rape. Like the naked woman in Duchamp's sculpture, she participates in her own objectification, offering herself up to the gaze of others as she peers at herself. Temple's account of the rape stimulates Benbow's own masturbatory fantasy, just as her lovemaking with Red arouses Popeye as he lingers panting and whinnying at the side of the bed. The light that Temple shines on her own experience thus implicates her, as well as the novel's characters and readers, in the pattern of obsessive looking that Faulkner establishes in the novel.

While both Temple and Benbow offer fantasy renditions of the novel's violence, it is not until the trial scene that the reader is offered any concrete information about the details of the rape. The information that is provided does not take the form of an eyewitness account or a straightforward recreation of the event; instead, the reader is offered yet another incomplete revelation, an invitation to speculation about an object that the reader must imaginatively place at the scene of Temple's rape: "The district attorney faced the jury. 'I offer as evidence this object which was found at the scene of the crime.' He held in his hand a corn-cob. It appeared to have been dipped in dark brownish paint" (298). The District Attorney's definitive proclamation of the corn-cob's relevance obscures the speculative nature of the reader's conclusions about the object. While the prosecutor invokes the testimony of a chemist and gynecologist to support his conclusions, the reader's access to those testimonies is blocked by the narrative's refusal to represent them; in the same way, the reader's access to the "evidence" that the prosecutor introduces is limited by the narrative's evasive description of the corncob. Although it seems clear that the stain on the cob is actually dried blood, the narrative insists on describing it as "dark brownish paint." Faulkner chooses the figure rather than the direct description because by indirect reference the reader is made to interpret the appearance of the cob, to transform paint into human blood; he or she has thus not read about a bloodied cob but has imaginatively created one. Having bloodied that cob, the reader has no difficulty in envisioning its function as the rape weapon; the narrative's failure to provide logical connections and accurate representations encourages the reader actively to construct the District Attorney's case. This technique of requiring the reader to image the violence, making the reader do his work for him, is characteristic of Faulkner's approach throughout *Sanctuary*.

It is this same approach that the prosecutor utilizes to convict Goodwin in the trial itself. The District Attorney's deliberate omission of details about the rape transfers the responsibility for imaging the event to the jury. The trial, then, serves as a reenactment of the reading process in which prosecutor and jury dramatize the interactive dynamics that govern the relationship between *Sanctuary* and its readers. The trial is sketched as a dialogue between the prosecutor—who provides only the barest of details—and the courtroom voyeurs who imaginatively participate in the construction of the rape scene:

> The District Attorney bowed toward the Bench. He turned to the witness and held her eyes again.
> "Where were you on Sunday morning, May twelfth?"
> "I was in the crib."
> The room sighed, its collective breath hissing in the musty silence. (301)

The "hissing" of the room's "collective breath" articulates the audience's voyeuristic fascination with the drama that the District Attorney promises to reenact. Temple's simple statement—"I was in the crib"—licenses imaginative speculation about the crime. It is in the imagination of "the room" that Temple is raped, for the District Attorney is careful never to solicit Temple's explicit testimony. Instead, he provides the imaginative impetus for the jury's construction of the event:

> The District Attorney returned. . . . [H]e caught [Temple's] gaze and held it and lifted the stained corn-cob before her eyes. The room sighed, a long hissing breath.
> "Did you ever see this before?"
> "Yes."
> The District Attorney turned away. "Your Honor and gentlemen, you have listened to this horrible, this unbelievable story which this young girl has told; you have seen the evidence and heard the doctor's testimony: I shall no longer subject this ruined, defenseless child to the agony of—" (302–303)

In fact, the "horrible . . . unbelievable story" that Temple has related has been no story at all. The District Attorney's questioning places Temple and Goodwin in the crib, confirms that Temple has seen the corncob . . . and goes no further. The anxious prosecutor interrupts Temple's testimony in mid-sentence on three separate occasions; at every point in her interrogation when she attempts to respond with more than a simple phrase, to fill in the story with details of her own, his "Wait" or "Just a minute" cuts off her narrative. It is the audience, the jury, that the District Attorney invites to fill in the ellipses of Temple's story, just as it is the reader whom Faulkner encourages to fill in the structured blanks of the narrative.

The dynamics of reading violence that underlie both the reader's and the jury's experience of Temple's rape are encapsulated in a casual conversation between out-of-town observers of the trial:

> "They're going to let him get away with it, are they?" a drummer said. "With that corn cob? What kind of folks have you got here? What does it take to make you folks mad?"
>   "He wouldn't a never got to trial, in my town," a second said.
>   "To jail, even," a third said. "Who was she?"
>   "College girl. Good looker. Didn't you see her?"
>   "I saw her. She was some baby. Jeez. I wouldn't have used no cob." (308–309)

The drummers' distance from the act allows them not only to deplore the rapist but to recreate the rape, not only to denigrate the method but to replace it with one of their own imagination. The self-righteous moralizing of these bystanders invites their imagination of the rape; in order to be appropriately horrified by the act they must reenact it mentally. In doing so, they create fictions of violence, casting *themselves* in the part of the rapist whose actions they so vehemently denounce.

For the reader, as for the drummer, the experience of Temple's rape is an imaginative one. Instead of obscuring the artifice inherent in fictional representation, Faulkner capitalizes on that artifice; the obvious literary quality of his representation invites the reader's creative voyeurism while offering the safety of a purely aesthetic manipulation. Reading appears to offer the opportunity for voyeuristic perception without actual participation; the distance between reader and text seemingly affords the reader the opportunity to enter imaginatively—and with impunity—into fictional universes of violence and sex. By emphasizing the literary quality of this rape, Faulkner invokes the distance of reading as a screen that obscures the reader's awareness of his or her own participation in the scene of violence. Although the knowing anticipation of another's rape lies dangerously close to an indulgence in voyeuristic pleasure, intellectual participation in a purely literary violence may appear to involve a manipulation of symbols rather than sexuality, of literary conventions rather than living bodies. While Duchamp's "Etant Donnes" blurs the boundaries that separate violence from the artistic representation of violence, then, Faulkner's *Sanctuary* exploits the reader's assumption of such boundaries even as it invites that reader to transgress them. Like the outraged drummers who go on to use Temple's rape as a springboard for a crime of their own creation—"I wouldn't have used no cob"—the reader, too, conspires in an act of imaginative assault that implicates that reader in the novel's violence not merely as a voyeur but as a violator.

II.

In "Visual Pleasure and Narrative Cinema," Laura Mulvey explores the way in which the "unconscious of patriarchal society" has structured film form (6). Applying the theories of Freud and Lacan to the conventional cinematic situation, Mulvey traces the spectator's visual pleasure to its origin in two "structures of looking." Scopophilia, the first aspect of viewing that Mulvey discusses, is defined by a voyeuristic dynamic in which the erotic identity of the viewing subject is clearly separated from the object (usually a woman) on the screen; the viewer derives pleasure from objectifying the screen persona and subjecting that persona to the power of the controlling gaze. The second and seemingly contradictory aspect of viewing allows the spectator to identify with the object on the screen (usually a male hero); through what Mulvey describes as "the spectator's fascination with and recognition of his like," the viewer participates vicariously in the screen protagonist's exploits (10). The process of identification with the screen hero depends upon the viewer's ability to transcend the barrier of the screen by entering imaginatively into the cinematic world. The voyeuristic outlook associated with scopophilia, on the other hand, is authorized by the sense of distance that governs the viewer's experience as he or she watches the large screen from the comfort and anonymity of the darkened auditorium. Because these processes of identification and objectification rely upon differing manipulations of the perceived distance between the audience and the cinematic world it observes, Mulvey describes them as the two "contradictory aspects" of viewing.

As *Sanctuary* reveals, however, these "structures of looking" only appear to contradict one another; in fact, the processes often occur simultaneously and function symbiotically. The processes of cinematic viewing that Mulvey describes operate in much the same way that the dynamics of reading operate in *Sanctuary*. While Faulkner's exaggeration of literary conventions distances the reader from the violence in the text, the structured blanks of the novel subtly undermine that distance by encouraging the reader's imaginative participation in that violence. In both Faulkner's novel and the films that Mulvey discusses, the reluctance of the viewer/reader to participate imaginatively in an artistic universe of sex and violence is defused by conventions of reading and viewing—be they the reiteration of literary symbols in the novel or the literal separation of audience and screen in the theater—that emphasize the distance separating that viewer/reader from the onscreen or intra-textual acts. Despite their contradictory origins, both voyeuristic viewing and imaginative identification "pursue aims in indifference to perceptual reality, creating the imagised, eroticized concept of the world that forms the perception of the subject and makes a mockery of empirical objectivity" (10).

In *Sanctuary*, the "empirical objectivity" of rape disappears altogether to be replaced by an imaginative construct created by the reader and endorsed by the text; within the frame of that construct, the reader identifies with (imaginatively becomes) the violator while the victim remains an object of imaginative manipulation, her body merely the text on which the crime is written. The reader who responds uncritically to the novel's structured blanks thus silently embraces the possibility of rape without pain, of violation without its attendant dehumanization. The juxtaposition of representations of rape in *Sanctuary* and *The Women of Brewster Place* brings the assumptions about violence implicit in both into relief. While *Sanctuary* exploits the processes of identification and objectification that Mulvey cites as central to the patriarchal gaze, Gloria Naylor's representation disrupts those processes to overturn the "imagised, eroticized" response to rape seemingly authorized by literary convention.

The rape scene in *The Women of Brewster Place* occurs in "The Two," one of the seven short stories that make up the novel. This story explores the relationship between Theresa and Lorraine, two lesbians who move into the run-down complex of apartments that make up "Brewster Place." Lorraine's decision to return home through the shortcut of an alley late one night leads her into an ambush in which the anger of seven teenage boys erupts into violence:

> Lorraine saw a pair of suede sneakers flying down behind the face in front of hers and they hit the cement with a dead thump. . . . [C. C. and the boys] had been hiding up on the wall, watching her come up that back street, and they had waited. The face pushed itself so close to hers that she could look into the flared nostrils and smell the decomposing food in its teeth. . . .
>
> [C. C.] slammed his kneecap into her spine and her body arched up, causing his nails to cut into the side of her mouth to stifle her cry. He pushed her arched body down onto the cement. Two of the boys pinned her arms, two wrenched open her legs, while C. C. knelt between them and pushed up her dress and tore at the top of her pantyhose. Lorraine's body was twisting in convulsions of fear that they mistook for resistance, and C. C. brought his fist down into her stomach.
>
> "Better lay the fuck still, cunt, or I'll rip open your guts."
>
> The impact of his fist forced air into her constricted throat, and she worked her sore mouth, trying to form the one word that had been clawing inside of her—"Please." It squeezed through her paralyzed vocal cords and fell lifelessly at their feet. Lorraine clamped her eyes shut and, using all of the strength left within her, willed it to rise again.
>
> "Please."
>
> The sixth boy took a dirty paper bag lying on the ground and stuffed it into her mouth. She felt a weight drop on her spread body. Then she opened her eyes and they screamed and screamed into the face above hers—the face that was pushing this tearing pain inside of her body. (170)

In Naylor's representation of rape, the victim ceases to be an erotic object subjected to the control of the reader's gaze. Instead, that gaze, like Lorraine's, is directed outward; it is the violator upon whom the reader focuses, the violator's body that becomes detached and objectified before the reader's eyes as it is reduced to "a pair of suede sneakers," a "face" with "decomposing food in its teeth." As the look of the audience ceases to perpetuate the victimizing stance of the rapists, the subject/object locations of violator and victim are reversed. Although the reader's gaze is directed at a body that is, in Mulvey's terms, "stylised and fragmented by close-ups" (14), the body that is dissected by that gaze is the body of the violator and not his victim.

The limitations of narrative render any disruption of the violator/spectator affiliation difficult to achieve; while sadism, in Mulvey's words, "demands a story," pain destroys narrative, shatters referential realities, and challenges the very power of language (14).[4] The attempt to translate violence into narrative, therefore, very easily lapses into a choreography of bodily positions and angles of assault that serves as a transcription of the violator's story. In the case of rape, where a violator frequently coopts not only the victim's physical form but her power of speech, the external manifestations that make up a visual narrative of violence are anything but objective. To provide an "external" perspective on rape is to represent the story that the violator has created, to ignore the resistance of the victim whose body has been appropriated within the rapist's rhythms and whose enforced silence disguises the enormity of her pain. In *The Accused*, a 1988 film in which Jody Foster gives an Oscar award-winning performance as a rape victim, the problematics of transforming the victim's experience into visualizable form are addressed, at least in part, through the use of flashback; the rape on which the film centers is represented only at the end of the film, *after* the viewer has followed the trail of the victim's humiliation and pain. Because the victim's story cannot be told in the representation itself, it is told first; in the representation that follows, that story lingers in the viewer's mind, qualifying the victim's inability to express herself and providing, in essence, a counter-text to the story of violation that the camera provides.[5]

While Naylor's novel portrays the victim's silence in its narrative of rape, it, too, probes beneath the surface of the violator's story to reveal the struggle beneath that enforced silence. Naylor represents Lorraine's silence not as a passive absence of speech but as a desperate struggle to regain the voice stolen from her through violence. "Power and violence," in Hannah Arendt's words, "are opposites; where the one rules absolutely, the other is absent" (56). The nicety of the polite word of social discourse that Lorraine frantically attempts to articulate—"please"—emphasizes the brute terrorism of the boys' act of rape and exposes the desperate means by which they rule. "Woman," Mulvey observes, "stands in patriarchal culture as signifier for the male other, bound by a symbolic order in which man can live out his phantasies and obsessions through linguistic control by imposing them on the silent image of woman still tied to her place as bearer of meaning, not maker of meaning" (7). In Naylor's description of Lorraine's rape "the silent image of woman" is haunted by the power of a thousand suppressed screams; that image comes to testify not to the woman's feeble acquiescence to male signification but to the brute force of the violence required to "tie" the woman to her place as "bearer of meaning."

While the distance that defines the experience of reading is exaggerated by Faulkner's constant invocation of literary conventions in *Sanctuary*, the illusion of distance is constantly undermined in Naylor's representation of rape. Rather than watching a distant action unfold from the anonymity of the darkened theater or reading about an illicit act from the safety of an armchair, Naylor's audience is thrust into the middle of a rape the representation of which subverts the very "sense of separation" upon which voyeurism depends. The "imagised, eroticized concept of the world that . . . makes a mockery of empirical objectivity" is here replaced by the discomforting proximity of two human faces locked in violent struggle and defined not by eroticism but by the pain inflicted by one and borne by the other:

> Then she opened her eyes and they screamed and screamed into the face above hers—the face that was pushing this tearing pain inside of her body. The screams tried to break through her corneas out into the air, but the tough rubbery flesh sent them vibrating back into her brain, first shaking lifeless the cells that nurtured her memory. Then the cells went that contained her powers of taste and smell. The last that were screamed to death were those that supplied her with the ability to love—or hate. (170–71)

The gaze that in Mulvey reduces woman to erotic object is here centered within that woman herself and projected outward. The reader is locked into the victim's body, positioned *behind* Lorraine's corneas along with the screams that try to break out into the air. By manipulating the reader's placement within the scene of violence, Naylor subverts the objectifying power of the gaze; as the gaze is trapped within the erotic object, the necessary distance between the voyeur and the object of voyeuristic pleasure is collapsed. The detachment that authorizes the process of imaginative identification with the rapist is withdrawn, forcing the reader within the confines of the *victim's* world.

Situated within the margins of the violator's story of rape, the reader is able to read beneath the bodily configurations that make up its text, to experience the world-destroying violence[6] required to appropriate the victim's body as a sign of the violator's power. Lurking beneath the image of woman as passive signifier is the fact of a body turned traitor against the consciousness that no longer rules it, a body made, by sheer virtue of physiology, to encircle and in a sense embrace its violator. In Naylor's representation, Lorraine's pain and not the rapist's body becomes the agent of violation, the force of her own destruction: "The screams tried to break through her corneas out into the air, but the tough rubbery flesh sent them vibrating back into her brain, first shaking lifeless the cells that nurtured her memory." Lorraine's inability to express her own pain forces her to absorb not only the shock of bodily violation but the sudden rupture of her mental and psychological autonomy. As the body of the victim is forced to tell the rapist's story, that body turns against Lorraine's consciousness and begins to destroy itself, cell by cell. In all physical pain, Elaine Scarry observes, "suicide and murder converge, for one feels acted upon, annihilated, by inside and outside alike" (53). Naylor succeeds in communicating the victim's experience of rape exactly because her representation documents not only the violation of Lorraine's body from without but the resulting assault on her consciousness from within.

In order to capture the victim's pain in words, to contain it within a narrative unable to account for its intangibility, Naylor turns referentiality against itself. In her representation of violence, the victim's pain is defined only through negation, her agony experienced only in the reader's imagination:

> Lorraine was no longer conscious of the pain in her spine or stomach. She couldn't feel the skin that was rubbing off of her arms from being pressed against the rough cement. What was left of her mind was centered around the pounding motion that was ripping her insides apart. She couldn't tell when they changed places and the second weight, then the third and fourth, dropped on her—it was all one continuous hacksawing of torment that kept her eyes screaming the only word she was fated to utter again and again for the rest of her life. Please.
>
> Her thighs and stomach had become so slimy from her blood and their semen that the last two boys didn't want to touch her, so they turned her over, propped her head and shoulders against the wall, and took her from behind. When they had finished and stopped holding her up, her body fell over like an unstrung puppet. She didn't feel her split rectum or the patches in her skull where her hair had been torn off by grating against the bricks. Lorraine lay in that alley only screaming at the moving pain inside of her that refused to come to rest. (170)

Recognizing that pain defies representation, Naylor invokes a referential system that focuses on the bodily manifestations of pain—skinned arms, a split rectum, a bloody skull—only to reject it as ineffective. Lorraine, we are told, "was no longer conscious of the pain in her spine or stomach. She couldn't feel the skin that was rubbing off of her arms. . . . She couldn't tell when they changed places. . . . She didn't feel her split rectum or the patches in her skull where her hair had been torn off. . . ." Naylor piles pain upon pain—each one an experience of agony that the reader may compare to his or her own experience—only to define the total of all these experiences as insignificant, incomparable to the "pounding motion that was ripping [Lorraine's] insides apart." Naylor, like Faulkner, brings the reader to the edge of experience only to abandon him or her to the power of the imagination;

in this case, however, the structured blanks that the novel asks the reader to fill demand the imaginative construction of the victim's pain rather than the violator's pleasure.

If Faulkner's reader is gendered male/violator, the reader of *The Women of Brewster Place* is gendered female and victim; Naylor's novel, then, effectively upsets Mulvey's model of patriarchal viewing. The freedom to navigate through the text of *Sanctuary* lends the reader the power of authoring his or her own crime. Like the violator who appropriates the victim's body to conform to the demands of his own violent script, Faulkner's reader treats Temple as an object of imaginative manipulation that may be safely invoked, altered, or destroyed to suit a particular scenario. That reader, then, possesses the autonomy of the rapist, the freedom to create a story of violence that the bodies of others are forced to substantiate. In *Against Our Will*, Susan Brownmiller describes the way in which the phenomenon of rape strips not only rape victims but all women of their freedom to act as autonomous persons. The ever-present vulnerability of women's bodies makes the possibility of rape a constant threat; by virtue of their physiology, women may be forced into a position of curtailed activity and psychological vulnerability that Brownmiller likens to enslavement. Describing rape as "man's basic weapon of force against woman, the principal agent of his will and her fear" (5), Brownmiller observes: "A world without rapists would be a world in which women moved freely without fear of men. That *some* men rape provides a sufficient threat to keep all women in a constant state of intimidation, forever conscious of the knowledge that the biological tool must be held in awe for it may turn to weapon with sudden swiftness borne of harmful intent" (229). The very possibility of rape serves as a cultural dividing line that enforces a hierarchy of autonomy in which the male, free to think, imagine, and act without fear of sexual violation, is always in a position of power. The very act of navigating through the texts of Faulkner and Naylor situates the uncritical reader on different levels within that cultural hierarchy.[7] While the experience of reading rape in *Sanctuary* is one of moving freely throughout the text, *The Women of Brewster Place* strips the reader of that freedom, pinning him or her to the victim's body and communicating an experience of rape that genders the reader—whatever sex he or she may be—female.

As Naylor disentangles the reader from the victim's consciousness at the end of her representation, the radical dynamics of a female-gendered reader are thrown into relief by the momentary reintroduction of a distanced perspective on violence: "Lorraine lay pushed up against the wall on the cold ground with her eyes staring straight up into the sky. When the sun began to warm the air and the horizon brightened, she still lay there, her mouth crammed with paper bag, her dress pushed up under her breasts, her bloody pantyhose hanging from her thighs" (171). In this one sentence, Naylor pushes the reader back into the safety of a world of artistic mediation and restores the reader's freedom to navigate safely through the details of the text. Under the pressure of the reader's controlling gaze, Lorraine is immediately reduced to the status of an object—part mouth, part breasts, part thighs—subject to the viewer's scrutiny. In the last sentence of the chapter, as in this culminating description of the rape, Naylor deliberately jerks the reader back into the distanced perspective that authorizes scopophilia; the final image that she leaves us with is an image not of Lorraine's pain but of "A tall yellow woman in a bloody green and black dress, scraping at the air, crying, 'Please. Please.'" (173). This sudden shift of perspective unveils the connection between the scopophilic gaze and the objectifying force of violence. The power of the gaze to master and control is forced to its inevitable culmination as the body that was the object of erotic pleasure becomes the object of violence. While Freud associated scopophilia with the idea of "taking other people as objects" (8), the same process of objectification underlies violence, in which violators "dehumanize their intended victims and look on them not as people but as inanimate objects" (Nagler, 12). By framing her own representation of rape with an "objective" description that promotes the violator's story of rape, Naylor exposes not only the connection between violation and objectification but the ease with which the reader may be persuaded to accept both. As the object of the reader's gaze is suddenly shifted, that reader is thrust into an understanding of the way in which his or her own look may perpetuate the violence of rape.

In that violence, the erotic object is not only transformed into the object of violence but is made to testify to the suitability of the object status projected upon it. Coopted by the rapist's story, the victim's body—violated, damaged, and discarded—is introduced as authorization for the very brutality that has destroyed it. The sudden interjection of an "objective" perspective into Naylor's representation traces that process of authorization as the narrative pulls back from the subtext of the victim's pain to focus the reader's gaze on the "object" status of the victim's body. Empowered by the distanced dynamics of a gaze that authorizes not only scopophilia but its inevitable culmination in violence, the reader that responds uncritically to the violator's story of rape comes to see the victim not as a human being, not as an object of violence, but as *the object* itself.

The "objective" picture of a battered woman scraping at the air in a bloody green and black dress is shocking exactly because it seems to have so little to do with the woman whose pain the reader has just experienced. Having recognized Lorraine as a human being who becomes a victim of violence, the reader recoils from the unfamiliar picture of a creature who seems less human than animal, less subject than object. As Naylor's representation retreats for even a moment to the distanced perspective that operates throughout *Sanctuary*, the objectifying pressure of the reader's gaze allows that reader to see not the brutality of the act of violation but the brute-like characteristics of its victim. To see Lorraine scraping at the air in her bloody garment is to see not only the horror of what happened to her but the horror that *is* her. The violation of her personhood that is initiated with the rapist's objectifying look becomes a self-fulfilling prophecy borne out by the literal destruction of her body; rape reduces its victim to the status of an animal and then flaunts as authorization the very body that it has mutilated. Insofar as the reader's gaze perpetuates the process of objectification, the reader, too, becomes a violator.

Naylor's temporary restoration of the objectifying gaze only emphasizes the extent to which *her* representation of violence subverts the conventional dynamics of the reading and viewing processes. By denying the reader the freedom to observe the victim of violence from behind the wall of aesthetic convention, to manipulate that victim as an object of imaginative play, Naylor disrupts the connection between violator and viewer that Mulvey emphasizes in her discussion of cinematic convention. If *Sanctuary* perpetuates the distanced dynamics that Duchamp exposes in "Etant Donnes," Naylor explodes those dynamics. Inviting the viewer to enter the world of violence that lurks just beyond the wall of art, Naylor traps the reader behind that wall. As the reader's gaze is centered within the victim's body, the reader, like the naked woman displayed in Duchamp's artwork, is stripped of the safety of aesthetic distance and the freedom of artistic response. In Naylor's representation of rape, the power of the gaze is turned against itself; the aesthetic observer is forced to watch powerlessly as the violator steps up to the wall to stare with detached pleasure at an exhibit in which the reader, as well as the victim of violence, is on display.

II

READING TORTURE
1984 AND AMNESTY INTERNATIONAL

In a world of constructed truths, fragmented subjects, and nonmaterial objects, the body emerges as an ever-present challenge to the abstract lessons of contemporary theories of knowledge. As modern physics replaces the idea of particles of matter with the concept of the electromagnetic field, the literal grounding of the physical universe seems to dissolve; the body, however, continues to anchor us to our own undeniable materiality through the immediacy of sensation.[1] Not surprisingly, then, as contemporary literary critics probe deeper and deeper into the intricacies of poststructuralist thought, references to the body emerge over and over again on the pages of professional journals, in the titles of critical works, in the listing of MLA conference sessions. While physical and metaphysical systems of grounding are challenged and their contingent natures exposed, the body—as bearer of sensation, as object of violence, as transmitter of pain—reasserts itself as a presence that demands accounting for in any critical theory. In contemporary literary criticism, then, continued excursions to the margins of critical discourse are complemented by a need to acknowledge the experience of embodiment through which subjectivity is in part constituted.

The representation of violence in *1984* serves as the locus for questions about the disembodied conventions of reading and criticism. Orwell's representations of torture expose the way in which the conventions of reading function to distance the reader from the body that is the object of torture. In lending the audience of a novel the freedom to respond to the victim's body as a text, such conventions obscure the material dynamics of violence beneath the dynamics of a reading process defined by mediation and distance. The enactment of the critical reading process, with its self-referential language and complicated linguistic and symbolic structures, implies a freedom from immediate physical oppression; the investigation of the nature of reality and of levels of fictionality can exist only when the investigator is not overwhelmed by the too-demanding-to-be-ignored complaints of his or her own body. In the process of torture, on the other hand, the body's pain constitutes such a monolithic reality that it overwhelms all distinctions of the nature of truth; to assent to a torturer's demands within what Elaine Scarry describes as "the thick agony of the body" is to testify to the absence of reality as it is known, to the total irrelevance of distinctions of intellect and mind (35). The representations of torture in *1984* both expose and problematize the gap between intellectual relativity and physical absoluteness. By blurring the lines that separate character and critic, perpetrator and reader, victim and observer, Orwell violates the conventions of reading. In the process of reading *1984*, the reader is thrust out of disembodiment and subjected not only to the representation but to the experience of torture.

The representations of violence in *1984* have led critics to question not only the success of Orwell's artistic techniques but the motivation underlying his novelistic enterprise, as one critic's response demonstrates:

> But when Orwell, in the most graphic way, writes about Winston's body being destroyed by various tortures, he crosses the line . . . from fact into fantasy. The torture scenes seem too lengthy, too vivid, occasionally too out of control, to serve only rhetorical or political functions; they do not seem mere warnings; rather they appear as an attempt by their author to catch up the reader in a whole series of fears and fantasies, fears and fantasies that in psychological terms seem persecuting and even paranoid. (Sperber, 219–20)

While Sperber begins his evaluation of Orwell's depiction of violence with specific comments on the novel's representations of torture, the critique itself soon gives way to psychological name-calling. Even as he seeks to undermine the impact of the novel's depictions of violence by labeling them "persecuting and even paranoid," Sperber's unusual choice of critical terms attests to the emotional power of the representations of violence that provoke such a personal response. Sperber's criticism offers not only a scholar's evaluation of *1984*'s shortcomings but an unsuspecting reader's self-righteous indignation at the novel's transgression of conventional artistic boundaries, its degeneration from "literature" into a form of psychological warfare. Inherent in Sperber's critique, then, is an assumption of the accepted limits of fictional representation and an implicit understanding of the conventions governing literary reading. While Sperber voices his outrage at Orwell's rejection of such assumptions, Sperber's critical outrage attests to the success rather than the failure of *1984*'s representations of violence. Orwell succeeds in communicating the victim's perspective on violence exactly because he overturns prescribed norms of reading and representation that mediate between the reader and the text.

Because violence in general and torture in particular depend upon the body's susceptibility to pain, any representation of the victim's experience of torture must recreate for the reader the sensation of an ever-present, ever-vulnerable body. Whether or not pain is actually inflicted upon the body in torture, it is the threat of that pain, the constant awareness of its potential to intrude upon and destroy the self, that lends the torturer his power. As Elaine Scarry observes in *The Body in Pain*, "The objects of consciousness . . . are swept through and annihilated" in the process of torture (32). In their place emerges a body that expands to fill the victim's empty universe, a body defined by vulnerability to a pain that overwhelms the outer world and the inner self until it appears to subsume all. Torture, then, "has at its center the single, overwhelming discrepancy between an increasingly palpable body and an increasingly substanceless world" (Scarry, 30). In *1984*, Orwell documents the emergence of such a discrepancy between Winston's body and the outside world. After enduring session after session of Big Brother's torture, Winston "became simply a mouth that uttered, a hand that signed whatever was demanded of him" (200). The violent world that Winston enters in the last section of the novel is a world in which pain overwhelms thought, emotion, and perception. "In this place," Winston observes, "you could not feel anything, except pain and the foreknowledge of pain" (197).

For Orwell and other novelists, the representational challenge posed by violence and its attendant pain is complicated by the dynamics of the literary reading process. While torture reduces its victims to mere bodies, the act of reading reduces the reader to sheer consciousness. Regardless of the degree of his or her sympathy for the victim, the reader approaches the novel of violence not as a body without consciousness but as a consciousness without body. The reader's participation in the novelistic universe is a purely imaginative experience; insofar as that reader enters into the scene of violence, he or she leaves behind the self that sits, book in hand, in a library, on a porch swing, or in a living room armchair. Because it is the reader's body that anchors him or her to an actual material universe, the loss of that body is the price paid for entry into the fictional world. The reader's disembodiment, however, implicitly contradicts the *experience* of violence, an experience defined by the increasingly urgent and overwhelming presence of the body.

As violence becomes the subject of the reading process, the element of distanced observation that distinguishes the act of reading from its experiential counterpart assumes not only a formal but a substantive role. Because the dynamics of reading necessarily involve the reader's distance from the fictional content of the novel, the reader maintains a sense of coherence that counteracts the chaotic, fragmented experience of the victim of violence. Even when the reader's viewpoint is aligned with that of the victim, the reader perceives the act of violence from a perspective outside the text, a perspective mediated through the fictional frame that brackets the novel's violence. When that frame situates violence within aesthetic forms that lend it an artificial coherence, the novel itself offers the reader a sense of control over the violence about which he or she reads. Even in the absence of a manipulatory frame, however, the reader's relationship to fictional violence is defined by the reader's ability to suspend, at any time, his or her participation in the activity of reading, to put down the novel when the violence that it contains becomes too threatening. For an actual victim of violence, on the other hand, there is no frame through which to view the act of violation, no opportunity to interrupt the act of violence that claims him or her as its victim.

The conventions of reading thus conspire to make the novelist's task of representing the victim's experience of violence an extremely problematic one. In *1984*, however, Orwell attempts to meet the representational challenge that violence poses by gradually undercutting the reader's traditional role in the fictional text. While the novel begins by emphasizing the reader's sense of bodiless invulnerability and distanced perspective, both are slowly eroded in the process of the novel. The experience of reading *1984 is*, as Sperber so passionately observes, an experience of violation; that experience, however, is one that the novel cultivates in order to convey to the reader the victim's perspective on violence.

In the first two sections of the novel, Winston's perspective on the violence that he witnesses is surprisingly detached; he reacts to the violence around him less as a participant implicated in its effects than as a distanced observer, a reader. While the first representation of violence in the novel is communicated to the reader through Winston, the violence that Winston recalls is not an actual war in which he participates but a war film that he views with other audience members in a large auditorium:

> then you saw a lifeboat full of children with a helicopter hovering over it. there was a middleaged woman might have been a jewess sitting up in the bow with a little boy about three years old in her arms. little boy screaming with fright and hiding his head between her breasts. . . . then the helicopter planted a 20 kilo bomb in among them terrific flash and the boat went all to matchwood. then there was a wonderful shot of a childs arm going up up up right up into the air a helicopter with a camera in its nose must have followed it up. . . . (11)

Winston's reading of the film's violence is defined by a detachment that propels the reader through the horror of the experience described to the technical means by which that experience is captured in film. As a sophisticated "reader" of the film, Winston's concern with camera angle and technical innovation is expressed at the expense of a more immediate response to the violent scene. When he describes the film's representation of the boy's severed arm flying into the air as a "wonderful shot," Winston's language remains free of irony; his recollection of the film encourages the reader to experience the destruction of the little boy's body as a cinematic event. Although other viewers of the film respond with horror to the film's violence—"a woman down in the prole part of the house suddenly started kicking up a fuss and shouting"—Winston is distanced not only from the on-screen violence but from the unsophisticated reaction of the other viewers: "nobody cares what the proles say typical prole reaction they never—" (11).

The reader of *1984* is thus first introduced to violence in a passage that may be described in Gerald Prince's terms as a "reading interlude," a moment in which the text provides clues as to the way in which its subject—in this case, violence—should be read. Reading interludes, in Prince's words, display "the stance taken by the narrative with regard to its own communicability and readability, as an indication of how it ostensibly wants to be read and a cue to the kind of program it considers most useful for its decoding, and as a factor determining to some extent the response of any reader other than itself" (237). In the case of *1984*, the narrative's detached perspective on violence is rendered less harsh by the circumstances of the reading interlude itself. Because the novel begins with a representation of a representation of violence, the reader of the novel is distanced from the physical immediacy of a violence alluded to in the story within the story; he or she comes to assent to a paradigm of reading violence that might, in a less mediated representation, be difficult to embrace.

When Winston, later in the novel, finds himself in the midst of a real war, an explosion that destroys buildings and rips human bodies to pieces, his reaction to actual violence is a carryover from his aestheticized response to the film. As Winston glimpses "a human hand severed at the wrist" lying in "a little pile of plaster," "He kicked the thing into the gutter, and then, to avoid the crowd, turned down a side street to the right" (72). While the callousness of Winston's act is undeniable, the reader's response to that act is qualified by the recollection of the novel's earlier reference to another severed body part; the transition from the novel's representation of a cinematic representation of violence to the novel's own representation of violence is accomplished with ease. While Winston's response to the severed human hand is an extension of his aesthetic response to the cinematic representation of a severed arm, the reader's response to this second incident is also dictated by a pattern of reading established in the earlier episode.

Although the reading interlude that first introduces the issue of violence is the most blatant example of Winston's role in directing the reader's response to the novel, Winston continues to function as the narrative vehicle through which the reader is situated in the novel's scenes of violence. As Julia is beaten in front of Winston's eyes at the end of the novel's second section, Winston embodies the reader's response to the scene:

> One of the men had smashed his fist into Julia's solar plexus, doubling her up like a pocket ruler. She was thrashing about on the floor, fighting for breath. Winston dared not turn his head even by a millimeter, but sometimes her livid, gasping face came within the angle of his vision. Even in his terror it was as though he could feel the pain in his own body, the deadly pain which nevertheless was less urgent than the struggle to get back her breath. He knew what it was like: the terrible, agonizing pain which was there all the while but could not be suffered yet, because before all else it was necessary to be able to breathe. Then two of the men hoisted her up by knees and shoulders and carried her out of the room like a sack. Winston had a glimpse of her face, upside down, yellow and contorted, with the eyes shut, and still with a smear of rouge on either cheek; and that was the last he saw of her. (184)

In this scene, as in the war film scene, Winston steps out of his body and into the disembodied status of the reader; he remains an observer rather than an actor, an eye rather than a body. While Winston remains locked into his rigid stance, bodies fly around and about him without ever seeming to touch his own. Like the reader in the scene of violence, Winston remains invisible in the reported action as his consciousness—and not his body—responds to the physical violence that rages around him. The emotion that he feels for Julia as he glimpses her "livid, gasping face" is not betrayed through even the slightest motion toward her suffering body; almost as if propelled from the plot into the narrative, from the story into the diegetic universe of the novel, Winston responds to Julia's plight by *reading* her experience rather than intervening in it. His reaction to the inevitable brutality of Big Brother heightens the reader's distanced apprehension of the scene, reinforcing the assumptions of a noninterventionist reading process. As Julia's pain is described, enunciated by Winston, his intellectualization of her agony testifies to his physical separation from that pain even as it reflects his imaginative participation in it; his exemption from the victimization that he reports allows him to translate the violence that Julia herself cannot express into a series of words, into a chronology of deadly pain and stolen breath. While he reduces Julia's experience into words for the reader, her body —the site of her agony—is reduced to an object, "a sack" that the torturers carry out, a figure marked not by humanity but by a "yellow and contorted" face that seems to belong to a frightening monster rather than to Winston's own lover.

As Winston is arrested and imprisoned, he clings to the status of bodiless observer that has defined his attitude toward violence throughout the earlier sections of the novel. At this point in *1984*, Winston's noninterventionist response to violence becomes a survival tactic; his attempt to remain absolutely still in the midst of atrocity is, in part, an attempt to rid himself of the body that would make him vulnerable to pain. As the skull-faced prisoner enters Winston's cell, clearly suffering from starvation, Winston, emotionally moved but physically motionless, observes the events that follow:

> The man sat down on the bench at a little distance from Winston. Winston did not look at him again, but the tormented, skull-like face was as vivid in his mind as though it had been straight in front of his eyes. Suddenly he realized what was the matter. The man was dying of starvation. The same thought seemed to occur almost simultaneously to everyone in the cell. . . . The eyes of the chinless man kept flitting toward the skull-faced man, then turning guiltily away, then being dragged back by an irresistible attraction. Presently he began to fidget on his seat. At last he stood up, waddled clumsily across the cell, dug down into the pocket of his overalls, and, with an abashed air, held out a grimy piece of bread to the skull-faced man. (194)

As the chinless man, shocked out of his observer status, stirs from his seat, his act of offering is represented primarily as a motion amid stillness; while Winston and the other prisoners remain watching, locked in the frozen stance of disembodiment, the chinless man rises into his body, into the clumsy waddle of motion that allows him to navigate through the space between himself and his fellow sufferer. The sheer physicality of the chinless man's act is set off by the aura of hushed stillness in which it occurs. The humanity of that act is figured in the very inelegance of his gesture as he digs deep into his pocket, in the awkward shuffling that lays bare the vulnerable human body, in the grimy piece of bread that he so ungracefully offers. The reader's sympathy for such an act of humanity is, however, indulged only momentarily in the narrative; in the scene that follows, the clumsy tangibility of the human body is rewritten not as a sign of humanity but as a mark of vulnerability:

> [The guard] took his stand opposite the chinless man, and then, at a signal from the officer, let free a frightful blow, with all the weight of his body behind it, full in the chinless man's mouth. The force of it seemed almost to knock him clear of the floor. His body was flung across the cell and fetched up against the base of the lavatory seat. For a moment he lay as though stunned, with dark blood oozing from his mouth and nose. A very faint whimpering or squeaking, which seemed unconscious, came out of him. Then he rolled over and raised himself unsteadily on hands and knees. Amid a stream of blood and saliva, the two halves of a dental plate fell out of his mouth.
>
> The prisoners sat very still, their hands crossed on their knees. The chinless man climbed back into his place. Down one side of his face the flesh was darkening. His mouth had swollen into a shapeless cherry-colored mass with a black hole in the middle of it. (194–95)

This representation of the guard's assault against the chinless man emphasizes the way in which violence reduces the prisoner to an object that falls prey to the influence of gravity and force. The account of the chinless man's body flying across the cell emerges as a study in physics, an experiment in the effect of certain angles of assault on physical mass. In the shadow of violence, the body that had testified to the chinless man's humanitarianism betrays his very humanity; the prisoner appears as an object that may be thrown, an animal that squeaks, a robot constructed of blood, saliva, and dental plates—in short, as anything but a person. The identity of the victim is stripped away by violence until even the face, the mark of individuality, becomes no more than "a shapeless cherry-colored mass with a black hole in the middle of it." The reader's previous sympathy is replaced by a mingled curiosity and aversion to the ugliness of the object that is destroyed before his or her eyes. Whereas the clumsy physicality of the act of compassion seems to draw the reader in, to locate him or her somewhere directly adjacent to or behind the shoulder of the chinless man as he engages in the process of sharing, the precise, scientific representation of this act of violence causes the reader to pull back; as he or she views from across the room the geometrical arcs of motion created by the impact of the guard's fist on the chinless man's body, the reader is disassociated from the violence enacted in the novel. It is the still, bodiless presence of Winston, through whose perspective that violence is seen, that offers the reader this locus of distanced security, and it is the sudden, abrupt withdrawal from the body of the victim in the scene of offering to the locus of secure observation in the scene of violence that demonstrates the reader's conventional freedom. As Winston describes the source of violence, its implementation and its effect on the victim, the reader, like the rest of the prisoners, sits "very still," "hands crossed" in the posture of bodiless nonintervention (196).[2]

While the reader's observation of the novel's violence is shaped by Winston's attribution of cause and effect and the novel's fictional frame, the victim's experience of violence is defined by the very loss of such intelligibility, the very sacrifice of coherence. In an act of violence, as defined in my introduction, the familiar form of the self is forcibly altered and sometimes destroyed; the violator usurps the victim's body, translating its familiar form into a new shape and forcing it to assume the configurations of the violator's own decree. As the literal points of reference by which the self is known are obliterated by the violator's force, the very conventions of self-knowledge must be redefined. Violence, then, has the capacity to destroy not only the form of the victim's body but the familiar forms of understanding through which that victim apprehends both self and world.

In the final section of *1984*, the forms of understanding created by Winston—and passed on to a reader who employs them to navigate through the text—disappear as Winston himself becomes the victim of violence. As Winston is stripped of the conventions of self-knowledge, as he falls from bodilessness into embodiment, the reader is denied the comfort of a stable narrative frame and stripped of the luxury of traditional conventions of reading. While Winston's presence up to this point in the novel had served to exaggerate the dynamics of a distanced and bodiless reading experience, Winston's sudden victimization thrusts the reader into an unfamiliar fictional universe in which he or she is stripped of traditional reading conventions even as Winston is stripped of bodily control. The reader, losing the detached perspective that would distance him or her from the novel's violence, is shocked into embodiment.

1984 begins to undercut the conventions of reading at the very point at which Winston first becomes the victim of violence. "With that first blow on the elbow," Winston later recalls, "the nightmare had started" (198). By denying the reader distance from the victim's body, the novel's representation of Winston's victimization communicates, for the first time in the novel, the victim's experience of violence. The alliance that the novel had created between Winston and the reader—an alliance that allowed the reader to indulge in the distanced perspective of the bystander of violence—explodes in the reader's face as Winston himself is stripped of all points of reference. The blow to Winston's elbow that functions as his initiation into torture also functions as the reader's introduction to a world of muddled referentiality and narrative confusion:

> All [Winston] had eyes for was the truncheon in the guard's hand. It might fall anywhere: on the crown, on the tip of the ear, on the upper arm, on the elbow—
> The elbow! He had slumped to his knees, almost paralyzed, clasping the stricken elbow with his other hand. Everything had exploded into yellowlight. Inconceivable, inconceivable that one blow could cause such pain! The light cleared and he could see the other two looking down at him. (197)

As the indeterminacy that governs Winston's experience of the event overwhelms the reader's perception of violence, the reader, like Winston, is denied the comfort of intelligibility. While Winston begins the scene in the reader's position—speculatively imagining the possible violence that may follow—that kind of abstract rumination is interrupted by a violence the immediacy of which renders Winston's intellectual survey irrelevant and representation itself impossible. As Winston's imaginative focus on a blow to the elbow is interrupted by the physical immediacy of that very blow, Winston is stripped of language as well as temporal and spatial organization; under the shadow of his own agony, he is able only to repeat the word "inconceivable." Similarly, the reader is denied an image of the incident and is forced instead to share Winston's perspective, a perspective in which fragmentary knowledge is overwhelmed by the panicked awareness of vulnerability. As Winston's own body becomes the theater on which violence is enacted, his ability to read and to narrate that violence for the reader is suspended.

The perspective on violence that *1984* naturalizes in its first two sections is undercut in the novel's final scenes as the limitations of Winston's point of view become more and more apparent. While any point of view provides only a selective perception of novelistic events, the conventional narration of the book's first two sections masks the issue of narrative standpoint that surfaces immediately as Winston becomes not only the observer but the victim of violence. In the third section of the novel, Lynette Hunter claims, "the reader is closer to Winston . . . than at any other time because we are only given access to the same bases for assessment as he has" (215). Denied the vision of an omniscient narrator or a knowledgeable character, the reader must rely upon Winston's severely limited perspective to guide him or her through the novel's final scenes. The reader's desire for a clear vision of the novel's violent events is frustrated again and again as Winston's body—a body almost always bound, imprisoned, or in pain—becomes the only narrative entrance to the experience of torture. As the novel progresses, the body that the reader had clung to as an anchor for a clear perspective on the novel's earlier scenes of violence becomes a prison in which the reader is trapped. While that body becomes larger and larger, the world surrounding it loses all definition; returning from an episode of torture, Winston "did not remember any ending to his interrogation. There was a period of blackness and then the cell, or room, in which he now was had gradually materialized around him" (201–202). Instead of offering the reader a stable world in which Winston is situated variably, the narrative now withdraws all conventional points of reference. Winston's body—itself in a state of painful flux—becomes the only constant in the narrative. Under the force of Winston's pain, the material world loses its solidity, appearing and disappearing as Winston is able to recognize its existence.

As the novel progresses, every assault on Winston's body also emerges as an attack on the reader's increasingly contracted field of vision. The angle of Winston's tortured body, for example, limits the reader's access to an accurate description of Winston's torturer. Any illusion of narrative omniscience is shattered as O'Brien is described again and again from the limited perspective of Winston as he lies on the torture table looking up at his violator:

> Winston was almost flat on his back, and unable to move. His body was held down at every essential point. Even the back of his head was gripped in some manner. O'Brien was looking down at him gravely and rather sadly. His face, seen from below, looked coarse and worn, with pouches under the eyes and tired lines from nose to chin. He was older than Winston had thought him; he was perhaps forty-eight or fifty. (202)

The distanced, disembodied perspective of the earlier narrative here collapses as the limitations of Winston's physical vision distort the conclusions passed on from narrative to reader. As O'Brien bends over Winston, we are told, "His face looked enormous because of its nearness, and hideously ugly because it was seen from below. Moreover it was filled with a sort of exaltation, a lunatic intensity" (209). The hideous ugliness of O'Brien's face may or may not be a matter of proximity; for the reader, however, there is no point of reference against which to measure that perception. Orwell undercuts the reader's seemingly disembodied perspective by attaching that reader to a body in the text; over and over, Winston's physical suffering asserts itself between the reader and the novelistic world.

The violence inflicted on Winston, then, seems designed not only to reprogram him as a character but to demonstrate his unreliability as a narrative anchor. As he is tortured before the reader's eyes, Winston's vision falters beneath the weight of his own pain. Eventually, even his simplest testimonies become unreliable; the four fingers that O'Brien holds before Winston's eyes become five, six, seven—"a forest of fingers" that "seemed to be moving in a sort of dance, weaving in and out, disappearing behind one another and reappearing again" (207). As Winston is tortured, the reader is forced into a perspective that is limited not only by the consciousness of one character but by the fragmented consciousness of a character whose body is overwhelmed by pain.

In the novel's final torture scenes, then, the narrative frame that had mediated between the reader and the novel's violence is stripped from the reader just as Winston's control over his own body is stripped away by the torturers. As Winston is subjected to the agony of torture, the only description of violence that the reader is offered is one in which the sourcelessness of Winston's pain is its defining characteristic:

> Without any warning except a slight movement of O'Brien's hand, a wave of pain flooded his body. It was a frightening pain, because he could not see what was happening, and he had the feeling that some mortal injury was being done to him. He did not know whether the thing was really happening, or whether the effect was electrically produced; but his body was being wrenched out of shape, the joints were being slowly torn apart. (202)

While the reader, like Winston, watches O'Brien turn the knobs on the torture machine, the connection between that act and Winston's pain remains uncertain. The sense of referentiality that defines the novel's earlier representations of violence is eroded as the reader's vision shrinks to the confines of Winston's sight. While the guard's drawn fist formed a clearly defined angle of assault against the chinless man's head, O'Brien's hand never comes near Winston in this scene; while Julia's doubled-up form registered the response of her body to the impact of a soldier's fist, Winston's pain seems to move from the inside out, emanating from the very joints that hold his body together. In this scene, then, Orwell registers the victim's experience of pain, an experience made "frightening" exactly because it refuses to yield to the demands of referentiality and the limits of agency. "Physical pain, unlike any other state of consciousness," Elaine Scarry observes, "has no referential content." In discussing the "sense of self-agency visible in many dimensions of torture," Scarry goes on to state, "In physical pain, then, suicide and murder converge, for one feels acted upon, annihilated, by inside and outside alike" (53). The novel's depictions of the torture inflicted upon Winston recreate the victim's experience of violence even as they frustrate the reader's desire for coherent representation.

As the novel progresses, the reader is not only denied the comfort of an omniscient narrative perspective but is forced to watch helplessly as that perspective is stolen away from the narrator by O'Brien himself. The torturer not only asserts his control over Winston but goes on to usurp the position of the narrator, claiming an omniscience that extends into the diegetic universe of the work:

> [Winston's] body was being wrenched out of shape, the joints were being slowly torn apart. Although the pain had brought the sweat out on his forehead, the worst of all was the fear that his backbone was about to snap. He set his teeth and breathed hard through his nose, trying to keep silent as long as possible.
> "You are afraid," said O'Brien, watching his face, "that in another moment something is going to break. Your especial fear is that it will be your backbone." (202)

The reader's privileged access to narrative information is eroded as Winston's control over his own body is undermined. Almost as though he were stepping away from his role as character to infiltrate the narrative space of the novel, the torturer mysteriously gains access to Winston's thoughts, thoughts articulated only in the space of the novel's pages:

> "You will be annihilated in the past as well as in the future. You will never have existed."
> Then why bother to torture me? thought Winston, with a momentary bitterness. O'Brien checked his step as though Winston had uttered the thought aloud. His large ugly face came nearer, with the eyes a little narrowed.
> "You are thinking," he said, "that since we intend to destroy you so utterly . . . in that case, why do we go to the trouble of interrogating you first? That is what you were thinking, was it not?"
> "Yes," said Winston. (210)

While O'Brien's ability to penetrate Winston's mind is clearly part of the horror of Winston's torture, the torturer's penetration into the arena of privileged reader information constitutes a violation of the reader's expectations, as well. The reader's distance from the novel's scenes of torture depends upon his or her knowledge of the clearly demarcated line between the characters' experiential world and the novelistic universe in which that world is captured. As O'Brien transgresses that line, he seems to move from his role in the story into the written pages of the novel; the conventions of reading that allow the reader access to information never articulated in the characters' world are disrupted as O'Brien comes to share in the reader's privileged access to that information. By deliberately flaunting established reading conventions, Orwell upsets the careful dynamics of the reading process and subjects the reader to the *experience*, as well as the intellectual apprehension, of violent disorientation. In *Interpretive Conventions*, his study of the reader in American fiction, Steven Mailloux distinguishes between the apprehension and the experience of novelistic themes; in certain novels, Mailloux states, the work's central idea is "not simply a theme that hovers over the narrative giving it holistic coherence; rather it is an ambivalence that is elaborated in the reader's experience, through a temporal structure of response provided by the text" (78). When the "theme" of a novel is the total disintegration of the conventions of selfhood through violence, the experience of that theme demands the destruction of the conventions of reading as well.

While O'Brien infiltrates the narrative to gain access to information known only to Winston and the reader in the initial scenes of Winston's torture, the torturer usurps the narrator's role even more fully in Room 101. O'Brien not only has equal access to the information that the narrator offers the reader; he seems to know more than the narrator, the reader, and Winston combined. While the narrator shares Winston's fragmented, limited perspective, O'Brien not only participates in the torture scene but frames that scene for the reader;

like a narrator, he enters to introduce the characters, set the tone, and provide background information that might otherwise be unavailable to the reader. The novel's narrator introduces the torture scene with a few sparse details already familiar to Winston, who, from his limited field of vision, strains to discern more. As O'Brien grabs the reins of narration away from the narrator, however, the torturer holds forth like a psychopathic Thackeray, indulging in extended authorial intrusions that convey information to the reader as well as to Winston:

> When [O'Brien] spoke it was in the schoolmasterish manner that he sometimes affected. He looked thoughtfully into the distance, as though he were address-ing an audience somewhere behind Winston's back.
> "By itself," he said, "pain is not always enough. There are occasions when a human being will stand out against pain, even to the point of death. But for everyone there is something unendurable—something that cannot be contem-plated. Courage and cowardice are not involved. If you are falling from a height it is not cowardly to clutch at a rope. If you have come up from deep water it is not cowardly to fill your lungs with air. It is merely an instinct which cannot be disobeyed." (234)

O'Brien's "schoolmasterish" discourse is clearly directed not only at Winston but at the reader who, however invisible, is also located in the scene of violence. As the torturer looks past Winston "into the distance," the "audi-ence" that he finds there is the reader, a reader drawn into the scene of torture as an almost physical presence. The tension between the narrative's descrip-tion of Winston's unrelenting pain and O'Brien's endless theoretical specu-lation on torture places the reader in the scene of violence with frightening immediacy. As O'Brien becomes the reader's primary source of information, the narrator upon whom the reader relies ceases to be an objective ally, a kind of civilized friend, and becomes instead an extraordinarily intelligent and ruthless adversary willing to trap the reader as well as Winston in his violent plot. In Room 101, O'Brien, the torturer/narrator, addresses both Winston and the reader; as he does so, the boundaries that separate plot and narrative collapse, trapping the reader as well as Winston in the scene of violence.

As the reader is trapped in that scene, his or her perspective is limited to the visual space of Winston's gaze. Winston is "strapped upright in a chair, so tightly that he could move nothing, not even his head. A sort of pad gripped his head from behind, forcing him to look straight in front of him" (233). Later in the scene, Winston's vision is even more restricted as he is made to wear a mask-like attachment that forces him to confront immediately the violence that is about to be inflicted upon him; as the torture scene progresses, the narrative itself serves a similar function as it jerks the reader's head into place, forcing him or her to focus with unmitigated intensity upon a violence from which there is no narrative escape. Throughout the torture scenes, then, neither the reader nor the narrator is able to move outside of

Winston's limited perspective; it is O'Brien, and O'Brien alone, who navigates freely through both the room and the narrative. When the guard carries the instrument of torture into the room, Winston, and the reader, have only a brief glance of "a box or a basket of some kind. . . . Because of the position in which O'Brien was standing, Winston could not see what the thing was" (233). While the torturer's literal position in the room blocks Winston's vision, O'Brien's unwillingness to narrate to the reader the contents of that box frustrates the reader's struggle for perception in a similar fashion. Instead of revealing the instrument of torture, O'Brien offers an extended commentary that heightens Winston's sense of anxiety even as it denies the reader the knowledge that would distance him or her from Winston's situation:

> "The worst thing in the world," said O'Brien, "varies from individual to individual. It may be burial alive, or death by fire, or by drowning, or by impalement, or fifty other deaths. There are cases where it is some quite trivial thing, not even fatal."
> He had moved a little to one side, so that Winston had a better view of the thing on the table. It was an oblong wire cage with a handle on top for carrying it by. Fixed to the front of it was something that looked like a fencing mask, with the concave side outwards. Although it was three of four meters away from him, he could see that the cage was divided lengthways into two compartments, and that there was some kind of creature in each. They were rats.
> "In your case," said O'Brien, "the worst thing in the world happens to be rats." (233)

O'Brien stalls the delivery of the information that the reader seeks, speculating with agonizing slowness on the possibilities of torture even as Winston's vision gradually picks out the shape and form of the torture vehicle. Only as Winston's blurry vision focuses into acute perception does O'Brien's seemingly pointless diatribe move into revelation. As the plot and the narrative converge, the repetition of the word "rats" falls on the reader's ear like a gun that double fires; as narrative time and story time converge, the experience of reading conforms to the building rhythms of Winston's anxiety.

While Winston willed himself into a disembodied stillness as he, like the reader, observed the initial violence of the novel, his motionlessness in Room 101 is anything but a sign of bodilessness. As he awaits the inevitable pain of torture, Winston's enforced stillness is one in which the vulnerable body is urgently present:

> O'Brien picked up the cage, and, as he did so, pressed something in it. There was a sharp click. Winston made a frantic effort to tear himself loose from the chair. It was hopeless: every part of him, even his head, was held immovably. O'Brien moved the cage nearer. (235)

Unlike the frozen stance of disembodiment that Winston assumed as Julia and the chinless man were beaten, Winston's enforced stillness in this scene is a sign that he is *locked into* his own body, unable to escape the vulnerability of the victim of violence. Winston's apparent immobility masks his "frantic effort" to break free; the urgent struggle of the vulnerable body is merely heightened by the restrictions of the violator. In this scene, as elsewhere in the novel, the reader is also denied the ability to move, to intervene, to act. Because Winston's immobility in the face of violence has always marked him as the reader's envoy in the text, the reader's position of disembodied detachment from the novel's violence is undercut when Winston's immobility is rewritten as a sign of bodily vulnerability. Although Winston's presence earlier in the novel had functioned to emphasize the conventional distance of reading, that distance is suddenly collapsed. As Winston is thrust out of disembodiment, the reader's bodiless status is also rewritten; the reader's inability to intervene physically in the narrative action becomes a mark of vulnerability rather than a sign of imaginative immunity. Locked into the immobility that he once willingly embraced, Winston shares the reader's inability to intervene in the novel's unfolding action. While the narrative forces the reader to confront the violent content of *1984* without the buffer of formal mediation, the mask that Winston wears gradually blocks his vision of everything except his own impending violation: "The circle of the mask was large enough now to shut out the vision of anything else" (235). Although the threat of violence that O'Brien communicates is never directly realized, both Winston and the reader *are* violated; in both cases, it is the stripping away of the victim's sense of autonomy that constitutes the act of torture.

Denied the possibility of physical intervention in the novel's unfolding series of events, Winston is forced to resort to the one method of participation to which he—and the reader—have access; as he struggles desperately to avoid the fate that seems inevitable, Winston turns away from his body to move into his imagination:

> The cage was nearer; it was closing in. Winston . . . fought furiously against his panic. To think, to think, even with a split second left—to think was the only hope. . . . There was a violent convulsion of nausea inside him, and he almost lost consciousness. Everything had gone black. For an instant he was insane, a screaming animal. Yet he came out of the blackness clutching an idea. There was one and only one way to save himself. He must interpose another human being, the body of another human being, between himself and the rats. (235)

In the immediacy of his vulnerability, locked into a body stripped even of its power to move itself, Winston clutches at an *idea*. In order to remove himself from the threat of violence, he must distance himself, must thrust something between his vulnerable body and the bodies of the bloodthirsty rats that threaten to attack. The object of mediation that he lights upon is not merely another human being but "the *body* of another human being," a body that, like his own, is susceptible to violence because it is vulnerable to pain. Unable to tear himself free from the chair into which he is strapped, Winston pulls in a body in the only way available to him, through the power of the imagination:

> But he had suddenly understood that in the whole world there was just *one* person to whom he could transfer his punishment—*one* body that he could thrust between himself and the rats. And he was shouting frantically, over and over:
> "Do it to Julia! Do it to Julia! Not me! Julia! I don't care what you do to her. Tear her face off, strip her to the bones. Not me! Julia! Not me!" (236)

Although the sacrifice of Julia's body is enacted only on a *mental* theater, the narrative description of Winston's surrender to torture belies the purely imaginative dynamics of his betrayal; as Winston searches through the materials of his imagination, he struggles to find a "body that he could thrust between himself and the rats." While the narrative's qualification of the word "person" by the use of the more concrete term "body" calls attention to the materiality of the self that Winston would sacrifice, the verb "thrusts" emphasizes the physicality of Winston's imaginative interposition of another body between his own and that of the rats. Initially, *1984* indoctrinates its readers into a distanced perspective on violence by prefacing its own representation of violence with a representation of a representation of violence; in these final scenes, that technique is reversed. After being forced to read passage after passage in which Winston is tortured, the reader is suddenly introduced to Winston's imaginative enactment of torture on another human being; as a result, the words of Winston's command—"Tear her face off, strip her to the bones. Not me! Julia! Not me!"—assume an equivalency in the narrative with the words describing Winston's own torture. The act of imaginative violence perpetrated in Winston's mind blends with the acts of imaginative violence that the reader has enacted in his or her own mind throughout the novel; the distinction between a fiction and a fiction within a fiction blurs as the reader seizes gratefully upon Winston's solution to stopping a torture that is directed against the reader as well as Winston. The relief that the reader registers as Winston successfully stops the narrative's inevitable progression of violence is a sign of that reader's participation in the act of imaginative violation that Winston commits.

The blurring of imaginative levels that results as Winston betrays Julia is reflected in a narrative that loosens its grasp on realism, conflating the inner world of imaginative experience with the outer world of material reality:[3]

> He was falling backwards, into enormous depths, away from the rats. He was still strapped in the chair, but he had fallen through the floor, through the walls of the building, through the earth, through the oceans, through the atmosphere, into outer space, into the gulfs between the stars—always away, away, away from the rats. (236)

This description of Winston's imaginative flight from his material universe might also pass for a description of the literary reading process; the chair in which Winston sits as he falls into a world of imaginative release has become the same chair in which the reader sits as he or she reads the novel. In the process of reading *1984*, the reader becomes attached to a material body in the text while Winston disassociates himself from that body to assume the imaginative freedom of the reader. As the conventions separating reader and character erode, Winston's imaginative participation in the scene of fictional violence implicates the reader in the act of violation as well. The distinction between imaginative and actual violence that would allow the reader to maintain a distance from the novel's torture scenes dissolves, forcing the reader into the scene of violence with an immediacy that overwhelms the mediating power of language and subverts the distancing conventions of reading.

It is to his own sudden vulnerability as reader, then, that Sperber reacts as he condemns the novel's representations of violence as "persecuting and even paranoid." Insofar as *1984* undercuts the sense of bodiless detachment that would allow the reader to approach the novel without becoming implicated in or vulnerable to its violence, its representations are both persecuting and paranoid. Ironically, it is only by destroying the familiar conventions of literature that Orwell is able to liberate the novel as an effective medium of representing violence. In *The Enormous Room*, his own novel about the horror of torture, e. e. cummings articulates the connection between creation and destruction in a literature of violence:

> for an educated gent or lady, to create is first of all to destroy—that there is and can be no such thing as authentic art until the bon trucs (whereby we are taught to see and imitate on canvas and in stone and by words the so-called world) are entirely and thoroughly and perfectly annihilated by that vast and painful process of Unthinking which may result in a minute bit of purely personal Feeling. Which minute bit is Art. (224)

The disembodied response of a reader prepared to react intellectually to a representation of violence—to respond, as Winston did, by describing a scene in which a child's body is mutilated as a "wonderful shot"—can be undone only insofar as the very conventions of perception defining that reader's vision are unraveled. In the story that Orwell tells, Winston's distanced response to violence is subverted through the most immediate form of destruction—the destruction of Winston's own body. While that destruction is not one to which Orwell's readers could—did he wish it—be subjected, Orwell's novel enacts its own form of persecution as it destroys, one by one, the literary conventions upon which the reader's access to the novelistic world depends. As the dynamics of the reading process are subverted, the reader of *1984* is left stranded in a text that offers no obvious points of reference and no clear means of negotiating through the violence of its fictional universe.

The literary strategies used in *1984* to manipulate the reader's imaginative response to violence are revised and extended in nonliterary portrayals of torture created and circulated by Amnesty International, the Nobel Prize-winning human rights group that has launched a worldwide campaign for the abolition of torture. The television commercials designed by Amnesty International to promote viewer participation in the organization's campaign represent several diverse strategies for portraying torture, each of which responds in a different way to representational tensions that also surface in *1984*. As the conventions of reading that define response to novelistic representations of torture give way to the conventions of commercial viewing, the uneasy balance between the representation and the reality of torture, between imaginary participation and embodied experience in a scene of violence, is rendered visible.

Unlike most television advertisements, Amnesty commercials on torture frequently undercut their visual quality to elicit the type of imaginative response more often associated with the act of reading. In order to create such a response, recent Amnesty commercials manipulate their visual text to restore the power of imaging to the audience; by undercutting the visual dimension of the commercial medium, these advertisements force the viewer to imaginatively create a violence that he or she cannot see on the screen. A recent Amnesty commercial, for example, begins with a shadow that quickly focuses into a pair of legs—seen only from about the knee down—and a pair of black leather shoes that are soon surrounded by many pairs of official-looking military boots. The voice-over of the commercial is accompanied by the sound of these boots on a tile floor as the prisoner marches down hallway after hallway in a dark basement, accompanied by guards. Once again, the camera shoots the scene from mid-leg down, so that it is only a series of feet that we see as we hear the following voice-over:

> After having spent over four years in an East European prison, this man was arrested again—his crime, participating in a peaceful demonstration for a martyred student. He's just one of tens of thousands of men, women, and children in prison for their beliefs—beaten, tortured, and often killed because of the color of their skin, their religion, or even their sex. Since 1961, Amnesty International has worked on behalf of over 42,000 such prisoners. By writing thousands of letters and putting pressure on governments, Amnesty members are giving prisoners like him not just hope but freedom.

As the voice-over establishes the fact of the prisoner's arrest, this commercial works hard to restore the freedom of imaging to the viewer. To do so, it must return the body of the victim to the position of text, manipulate the camera to render invisible that which would normally be visible on the screen. Despite its visual component, this representation does not allow the viewer to focus on a specific body as it is tortured; instead, it shows us only a pair of legs that we imaginatively attach to the body of the prisoner.

The commercial, then, operates not through an explicit portrayal of a man being tortured but through the invocation of what might be described as the typology of torture. The shadowy basement through which the prisoner marches is readily identified by the viewer as the conventional location of a torture scene and is made even more sinister by virtue of the fact that it is filmed in black and white. The sound of heavy boots pounding rhythmically on a tile floor ominously exaggerates every movement of the marching feet. Even the familiar is endowed with symbolic threat by brief shots that render ordinary objects—such as exposed water pipes—full of sinister portent. In this commercial, not only the victim's body but every aspect of his surroundings become part of a text that the reader must interpret; the angle of the camera disrupts the viewer's visual response until the act of viewing is itself a process of interpreting that involves active imaging rather than passive assimilation. Our fears are unleashed through a representation that lends us the signs and symbols of a torture that we see only in our imagination.

In the conclusion of the commercial, however, those fears are quickly contained. The typology of torture is rewritten as the shoes that we have imaginatively attached to the prisoner's body leave the boots behind to march slowly up a flight of stairs. Suddenly, the background music of the commercial bursts into crescendo and the camera cuts to a scene shot in full color. Instead of following the prisoner to the torture room we have created in our imagination, we witness a man identified in a caption as Vaclav Havel waving to a cheering crowd of supporters from a balcony as a voice-over states: "Raise your voice. Call 1-800-55 Amnesty."

The cleverness of "Prisoner to President" lies in its ability to manipulate the viewer into misreading visual signs, to encourage him or her to imagine the possibility of a prisoner being tortured only to discover that what is really being shown is an ex-prisoner—now an important government official—being escorted to his podium by a group of security men. In the beginning of the commercial the near absence of Havel's body requires the reader to imagine its presence; the viewer must actively construct the situation, the nature of the victim's political crime, the tortures he has and will endure, because so little information is given. That act of imagination, however, is suddenly and gloriously followed by the transformation of the absent and mentally constructed victim into a visually present free man; the energy of imagining the victim is instantly rewarded with the victim's freedom. Only at the end of the commercial, when Havel's identity is revealed, do we perceive the full body of a politically empowered person rather than the fragmented and anonymous body of a victim. The commercial thus moves us out of the victim's experience of violence without having fully transported us there. While the experience of torture reduces a victim, in Scarry's terms, to sheer bodily presence, in this commercial the victim's body is absent during torture and only appears when the threat of torture has disappeared. A person doesn't exist, in effect, until he or she is saved.

Amnesty's representation of torture in this commercial thus raises questions about the role of the imagination, the issue of embodiment, and the relationship between representation and response in portrayals of torture. Like *1984*, Amnesty's "Prisoner to President" blurs the boundary between imagination and reality, between mental and physical worlds. Whereas *1984* strips the reader of imaginative freedom to locate him or her within the confines of a textual body, however, this commercial enacts an opposite reversal. Even as it appears to trap the viewer within a scenario of bodily imprisonment and torture, "Prisoner to President" goes on to affirm the power of the imagination even in a world of bodies. The viewer's fear of torture is not only contained but removed; instead of legitimizing our imaginative excursion into terror, this commercial releases our worst nightmares only to awaken us to a reality created by the group that we are asked to support.

The message that a mental or verbal imaginative act has the power to free a physically oppressed person appears not only in this commercial but in several other Amnesty advertisements. In the "Talking Heads" series, several segments feature celebrities attributing the success of Amnesty International to the ability of its supporters to "care" or to "speak out." Rather than mentioning the importance of sending money or distributing pamphlets, the commercials emphasize small symbolic actions, such as raising a glass "to freedom." In one segment an inmate in a realistically presented prison is freed when letters typed by the disembodied hands of Amnesty volunteers pile up outside the window and burst through the bars. Another commercial ends with the celebrity reader claiming, "You'll never forget the first prisoner you free." The implication that the imaginative acts of viewers have the ability to create a free, safe person out of nothing is made almost explicit here; the saved victim is "yours" once you have expended the energy to create him. By tracing the origin of charity to its source in the viewer's imagination, such Amnesty commercials redefine the conventional limits of imagination to cite the disembodied status of the viewer as a source of empowerment rather than a mark of detachment and distance. In *1984*, the illusion of imaginative freedom is undercut by the reality of bodily imprisonment; in "Prisoner to President," the reality of bodily imprisonment is revealed as an illusion both created and overturned by the power of the imagination. Ironically, Amnesty's effort to render torture immediate involves an appeal to the very kind of imaginative convention that Orwell attempts to undercut in his novel. Even as Orwell's literary portrayal attempts to capture the physical and emotional dynamics of the victim's experience of torture, Amnesty invokes those dynamics only to offer the viewer imaginative avenues of escape from them.

"Prisoner to President" represents a recent Amnesty advertising strategy that the group's New York communications officer characterizes as an attempt to be "strong" but not "threatening."[4] In straddling what Helen Garrett describes as "the line between quasi-pornography and being impactful," the organization attempts to expose the horror of torture without horrifying its audience. Because the subject of torture is so repugnant, because the reality in which Amnesty International deals is so unpleasant, it is important, Garrett claims, not to produce a representation so shocking that it simply makes the viewer turn away. In exploring the possibility of representing torture without alienating a potential audience, she speaks of diverse representational strategies that include, for example, the idea of caricatured rather than realistic pictures of violence in newspaper advertisements and a recent Amnesty International calender filled with beautiful pictures that cushion the horror of the literary and nonfictional texts that caption them.

Such an advertising campaign seeks to avoid the sort of violating representation that might offend viewers much as the representation of violence in *1984* offends certain critics. Previous Amnesty commercials, however, have taken a different approach; several of them expose the viewer to representations that, like the torture scenes in *1984*, limit the audience's imaginative freedom to translate words into pictures of reality. Whereas Orwell effects such a limitation through the destruction of literary convention, earlier Amnesty commercials accomplish a similar effect by exaggerating the conventions of visual representation. Commercials such as Amnesty's "Drowning" confront the audience with the act of torture and its impact on the victim by offering the viewer a body present not only in the imagination but on the screen.

In the "Drowning" commercial, which public service directors of many television stations have refused to air, a man is forcibly submerged and held in a pool of water by a uniformed guard who ignores the victim's frantic struggle to rise to the surface for air. The camera is placed at the bottom of the sink or toilet in which the man is immersed so that the viewer is forced to confront the presence of the victim's body; the man's straining, horrified face is literally jammed against the camera. As he struggles desperately for breath, huge bubbles burst out of his mouth into the viewer's face and a voice-over announces, "In certain countries, a police interrogation can be rather relentless. In fact, they don't even give you a moment to catch your breath. . . . Torture hurts everyone. To stop it, write Amnesty International, USA."

The experience of reading is defined by the freedom to image; even the most careful description requires the imagination of a reader to lend it form and substance. By forcing the viewer to witness every motion of the victim's body as he is tortured, however, this visual representation situates the viewer in the position of image receiver rather than image creator. The viewer's freedom to imagine, create, or deny the scene of violation is checked by a visible representation that resists easy imaginative manipulation. The viewer's powerlessness is further emphasized by the television audience's inability to change the pace of the representation or to skip over it. Short of turning it off, the viewer has no choice but to perceive what seems to be the unnecessarily lengthy portrayal of a drowning man's gasping and gurgling struggle for breath.

This direct visual representation strips the viewer of the kind of imaginative freedom that would allow him or her to deny the presence of the victim's body; in this commercial, Scarry's definition of torture is graphically and immediately portrayed as the torture victim is reduced to a purely physical presence. While the commercial does not place the observer within the victim's body and consciousness to the extent that Orwell's literary portrayal does, the middle-class viewer's identification with the victim is emphasized by the features and attire of the drowning victim, who looks like a white, middle-class businessman rather than a uniformed soldier or a foreign citizen.

The discomfort experienced by a viewer accustomed to the pleasing smoothness of most commercial images is increased by a commercial voice-over that is both authoritative and strangely jocular as it proclaims: "In certain countries, a police interrogation can be rather relentless. In fact, they don't even give you a moment to catch your breath." The commercial's play on the literal versus the figurative meanings of the familiar phrase "catch your breath" represents humor based on a disjunction not only of language but of worlds. Like O'Brien's voice in 1984, the words of the commercial narrator seem to enlist the victim and the viewer in the intensification of their own pain through a kind of cruel humor. Many of Amnesty's documentary descriptions of torture point out the tendency of torturers to engage in a humor based on using puns and double meanings to compare the victim's pain to normal or pleasurable activities.[5] Scarry, in discussing the same phenomenon, observes that the torturer's words, as well as his actions, "reach out, body forth, and destroy more distant and more numerous manifestations of civilization" (42); familiar words assume new meanings as violators appropriate terms such as "the telephone," "the birthday party," and "the submarine" not to name familiar objects and events but to define acts of torture. Whereas the narrator of "Prisoner to President" intercedes to rescue not only the apparent victim but the viewer from the possibility of torture, the voice that guides us through the "Drowning" commercial subjects the viewer to the torture of a wordplay that signifies at best the ironic perspective of a detached observer and at worst the cruel linguistic manipulation of the torturer himself.

What is emphasized in this portrayal of torture, as in 1984, is the viewer's inability to interrupt or to evade the act of violation in any form, imaginative or otherwise. The text that confronts the viewer in this commercial is one created and controlled by an unseen torturer who manipulates the victim unchecked and unaffected by the viewer's repulsion, protestation, or imaginative participation. Helen Garrett describes Amnesty International's more recent commercials as part of an attempt to initiate a "more constructive approach" to advertising that not only moves people but "gives them a sense that they can do something" about the horrors of torture. The "Drowning" commercial, on the other hand, gives the viewer a sense of what it feels like to be unable to do anything; both here and in 1984 the conventions of viewing/reading are manipulated to entrap the audience in the discomfort of looking or reading, just as in torture the conventional language of domestic life is manipulated to heighten pain rather than produce pleasure.

Amnesty's commercials represent two very different strategies of representation, both of which manipulate not only the portrayal of bodies on the screen but the viewer's relationship to the scene of violence. Inherent in both strategies is the assumption that a viewer's experience of torture relies upon not merely the text of a commercial but the role the imagination plays in responding to, participating in, and even creating that text. Whereas Amnesty's "Prisoner to President" encourages the viewer to experience the dynamics of rescue, imaginatively enacting the operation of the organization, the "Drowning" commercial frustrates the viewer's effort to intercede— imaginatively or otherwise—in the violation of the victim. The experience of reading *1984* pushes the progression toward disempowerment a step further; as it both enlists the reader's imagination in the act of violation and traps the reader within the role of torture victim, it appropriates the freedom of the imagination as a weapon used to enlist the reader in his or her own violation. The risk that Orwell's novel assumes in alienating potential readers is documented not only by the response of critics such as Sperber but in the concerns suggested by Amnesty International officials about their own representational campaigns against torture. Ultimately, however, such a risk must be weighed against the potential of *1984* and other literary works to introduce their readers imaginatively to a kind of intimate violation that demands acknowledgment of the victim's experience by defining it as the reader's own.

III

SWEET PAIN AND CHARRED BODIES
FIGURING VIOLENCE IN *THE WHITE HOTEL*

In "The Rhetoric of Temporality," Paul de Man defines and challenges a tradition of literary criticism that has valued symbolism over allegory. "The supremacy of the symbol, conceived as an expression of unity between the representative and the semantic function of language, becomes a common-place," de Man observes, "that underlies literary taste, literary criticism, and literary history" (189). While Coleridge praises the symbol for its "translu-cent" quality, its potential to body forth the eternal in the temporal, de Man calls attention to the way in which that illusory "translucence" culminates in what he describes as "the seductiveness . . . of a symbolical diction" (206). Whereas allegory flaunts its own artifice, symbolism reflects a romantic epis-temology in which meaning appears to emanate from an object rather than being projected onto it by a human mind. Unlike its allegorical counterpart, then, the symbol obscures the formal manipulation that it enacts: "Whereas the symbol postulates the possibility of an identity or identification, allegory designates primarily a distance in relation to its own origin, and, renouncing the nostalgia and the desire to coincide, it establishes its language in the void of this temporal difference" (207). De Man's willingness to embrace allegory over symbolism is a response to what he describes as the "tenacious self-mys-tification" inherent in the symbolic mode of representation (208).

D. M. Thomas's *The White Hotel* adopts the symbolic mode of representation that de Man defines only to expose its "seductiveness." By uncovering the way in which the symbolic imagination can shape the perception of violence, Thomas's novel offers a radical critique of conventional forms of understand-ing violence. Initially, the novel adopts symbolic forms the authority of which, to use Alan Singer's terms, "masks the contingencies of their linguistic power" (44). Having drawn the reader into the powerful linguistic world created through the symbolic imagination, *The White Hotel* uses its explosive subject matter to expose the contingent nature of its own claim to authority. In de Man's terms, *The White Hotel* indulges in the symbolic imagination only long enough to reveal itself as an allegory in disguise. In so doing, it forces the reader to question not only the particular definitions of violence that the text appears to endorse but the very process through which fiction simultaneously creates and disguises its own ideologies.

The novel's explosive critique of the symbolic imagination relies to a large extent upon Thomas's appropriation and manipulation of Sigmund Freud as a character. In *The White Hotel*, Thomas exploits issues of language and meaning suggested by the body of Freud's writings as background for his own fiction. Jean Laplanche has pointed out the way in which Freud's discourse constantly blurs the line between what Jakobson terms metaphor and metonymy, relying upon the conclusions generated by linguistic continuity as well as actual contiguities of reality and perception to extend claims of discourse into the domain of the real.[1] In *The Rule of Metaphor*, Paul Ricoeur also suggests the necessary connection between Freudian theory and issues of linguistic hermeneutics; psychoanalysis, he observes, is "directly linked to linguistic perplexities due to its own use of symbolic structures" (317). It is not surprising, then, that Thomas invokes the figure of Freud and the language of psychoanalysis as a means of exploring the manipulative power of the symbolic imagination.

Through his fictional characterization of Freud, Thomas joins in the contemporary debate of literary authors, critics, and theorists who use the body of Freud's writings to discuss not only the value of psychoanalysis but the questions it raises about the nature of interpretation and the process of representation. Peter Brooks's "Fictions of the Wolf Man" initiates one such line of debate as it appropriates Freud's case history as a "radically modernist" text that resists closure, "destabilizes belief," and self-consciously assesses its own process of constructing meaning.[2] In the more recent "Withholding the Missing Portion," Stanley Fish revises Brooks's revision, claiming that Freud's is not a "post-modernist narrative" revealing the contingent nature of its own claim to authority but a manipulative text that seduces the reader by naturalizing its own rhetorical claims.[3] Thomas's characterization of Freud, like Fish's more recent critical assessment of Freudian narrative, emphasizes the seductive rather than the self-conscious Freud. My concern in the argument that follows will be to explore the issues of interpretation and representation raised by the figure of Freud as he appears in Thomas's fiction.[4]

In *The White Hotel*, Lisa's pain serves as the variable that generates a hermeneutical contest; the narrative documents opposing interpretations of Lisa's symptoms that vie for authority in the text. While it initially appears to endorse Freud's psychoanalytic model of understanding that pain, the novel goes on to expose the degree to which Freud's critical forms misrepresent Lisa's experience by recasting it in purely symbolic terms.[5] By probing the operation of metaphor and tracing the way in which symbolic forms may be used to contain and transform violence, Lisa's poem and narrative expose the limitations of Freud's hermeneutics. As the representations of violence in the Babi Yar section of the novel demonstrate, the symbolic structures employed by Freud not only obscure but exploit the violence that is subsumed within their abstract systems of understanding.

The symbolic forms through which Freud approaches Lisa's situation blind him to the reality of her pain; within his psychoanalytic system of understanding, the immediacy of Lisa's suffering is denied as her pain is relegated to a purely symbolic status:

> In a sense, too, her mind was attempting to tell us what was wrong; for the repressed idea creates its own apt symbol. The psyche of an hysteric is like a child who has a secret, which no one must know, but everyone must guess. And so he must make it easier by scattering clues. Clearly the child in Frau Anna's mind was telling us to look at her breast and her ovary: and precisely the left breast and ovary, for the unconscious is a precise and even pedantic symbolist. (115)

Given the limitations of his interpretive model, Freud's misguided assessment of Lisa's pain is inevitable. After ruling out any physiological source for Lisa's suffering, Freud transforms his patient's body into a text and proceeds to interpret the pain that is written on that body in symbolic terms. He concludes that Lisa's suffering is the result of several psychological factors, including repressed homosexuality and a "profound identification with her mother, preceding the Oedipus complex" (135). It is later, in Lisa's letter to Freud, that the reader receives the first inkling of the inadequacy of his psychoanalytic reading. In that letter, Lisa corrects Freud's reduction of her experience to sexual terms, claiming that her trauma "had very little to do with sexual problems" (225). She traces Freud's conclusions about her vexed relationship with her mother to their origin in his own obsession with maternal influence; the issue of her mother's sexual transgression, she claims, is manufactured and sustained by Freud's psychoanalytic concerns: "In a way you *made* me become fascinated by my mother's sin. . . . I don't believe for one moment *that* had anything to do with my crippling pain" (226). Instead, Lisa anticipates the true origin of her pain by relating her own symptoms to the omnipresent suffering that she senses around her: "I have always found it difficult to enjoy myself properly, knowing there were people suffering 'just the other side of the hill'" (225). In the Babi Yar section of the novel, that "hill" assumes a literal presence, while the true origin of Lisa's pain—in all its violent immediacy—is revealed.

As Lisa's response to Freud suggests, Freud's interpretive framework is responsible for dictating not only his reaction to her situation but the substance of her commentary on that situation as well. Freud's choice of questions channels the conversations between patient and analyst, confining their discourse to the narrow categories of his own understanding. In her letter, Lisa protests against such manipulative "inquiry": "Frankly I didn't always wish to talk about the past; I was more interested in what was happening to me then, and what might happen in the future" (226).

Lisa's letter to Freud criticizes his models of analysis and initiates a skepticism in the reader that is born out when it is revealed that Lisa's pain *is* real rather than merely symbolic, that it is the literal mark of an event to come in the future rather than a symbolic trace of an incident in the past.[6] In Mary F. Robertson's words, Lisa's "belated responses show that Freud had not 'imagined the real' Lisa, but rather, without quite realizing it, had subordinated her to the imperatives of his own narrative" (469). Clearly, Freud's psychoanalytic perspective precludes his recognition of the very categories of experience in which Lisa's situation is based; Freud's limited forms of understanding lead him to read Lisa's suffering as a symbolic manifestation (rather than a literal demarcation) of a past event (rather than a future occurrence). As the Babi Yar section of the novel later demonstrates, the true import of Lisa's pain refuses to be contained within the dichotomous assumptions that underlie Freud's assessment. If her pain is symbolic, it is also literal; if her consciousness bears the traces of past trauma, it also bears the marks of future violence.

Although the tension between the violent subject matter of Thomas's novel and the symbolic forms in which Freud attempts to contain that subject matter does not fully manifest itself until the Babi Yar section of the novel, *The White Hotel*'s sustained inquiry into the nature of the symbolic imagination is first apparent in its thematic concentration on the subject of metaphor. Lisa's poem and prose narrative anticipate the dangers of symbolic representation by tracing the limitations of the metaphorical hermeneutics that govern the perceptions of Lisa's protagonist. In these subtexts of the novel, metaphor functions to distort Anna's understanding of her surroundings in much the same way that Freud's symbolic imagination distorts the reader's understanding of the novel's violence.

The operation of metaphor establishes a representational paradigm that is useful in exploring the type of formal critique that is effected in *The White Hotel*. Metaphor, in Alan Singer's words, "offers a model for fictive production—insofar as fiction is conceived as a rupture of the contextual seams binding established discourse" (25). While de Man utilizes his theory of the seductive power of representation to distinguish between symbol and allegory, his insight may be applied to a theory of metaphor as well. Metaphor may reflect a symbolic rather than an allegorical imagination when it effectively obscures the artificial relationship between its vehicle and tenor.[7]

Because the relationship between the literary vehicle and its symbolic tenor is defined by "sustained oscillation or 'play'" (Singer, 40) rather than linear progression, metaphorical representation has the potential to revise radically its literal subject, a potential that the conventionality of its forms often masks. Metaphor depends upon the yoking of two different notions of experience; in order for metaphor to work, according to Paul Ricoeur, "the everyday reference to the real must be abolished in order that another sort of reference to other dimensions of reality might be liberated" (145). In the case of violence, replacing "the real" with "other dimensions of reality" quite often means obliterating the horror associated with "real" violence by replacing it with the alternative reality of the metaphorical tenor; that tenor frequently overwhelms the narrative violence by relegating it to the realm of literary vehicle. In "The Metaphorical Plot," Patricia Parker describes Du Marsais's comparison of the metaphorical tenor to an imposter that not only invades but completely reorganizes its "borrowed home":

> The *exemplum* of the "imposter" in Du Marsais is followed by an explicit metaphor for metaphor, that of dwelling in "a borrowed home" . . . a familiar image of domestication, or of the "naturalising" of the "alien," which can, however, as easily suggest usurpation or appropriation, a transfer in which the guest becomes host. (136)

Du Marsais's metaphor documents the way in which metaphors are read not only forward but backward; the metaphorical act depends upon a dynamics of resignification in which the artifice of linguistic translation is frequently obscured by the ease with which the symbolic import of an image subsumes and transforms the vehicle that is its mode of access. Metaphor, in other words, has the potential to "naturalize" its impact by obscuring its own rhetorical processes and encouraging the reader to ignore the "alien" status of its self-constructed meaning. By probing the vexed relationship between violence and the metaphors that both represent and transform it, *The White Hotel* denaturalizes the metaphorical process and exposes the mechanisms of captivation that dictate the reader's response to fictional violence.

Metaphor, in I. A. Richards's words, is "a transaction between contexts." In *The White Hotel*, Thomas exposes the dynamics of metaphor—and the symbolic imagination underlying it—by exploring the effect of conflating two essentially incompatible contexts of experience. Lisa's prose narrative bears the traces of Freud's symbolic imagination; in that narrative, the narrator's obliviousness to the violence around her and failure to communicate both stem from a tendency to apprehend metaphorically a realistic world that refuses to be contained within the bounds of symbolic form. Thomas paves the way for the novel's critique of Freud's forms by having Lisa portray a heroine (hereafter known as Anna) whose vision of reality—and especially violence—is mediated by a symbolic imagination that transforms every word she hears into metaphor.

Lisa's prose narrative is directed toward an audience composed solely of Freud; it is not surprising, then, that the "linguistic perplexities" resulting from the use of symbolic structures of understanding become a crucial concern in the narrative. Lisa's protagonist assimilates a metaphorical perspective on reality that distances her, like Freud himself, from more immediate realities; Anna's misreading of her lover's simple statement, like Freud's misreading of Lisa's pain, is based on the process of metaphorical recontextualization:

"What a lot of crows there are on the wires," he found himself saying. It sounded—to him—boyish, uncertain, stupid; his maladroitness disturbed him.

But the young woman smiled a joyful agreement, saying, "It's a very difficult passage. *Vivace.*" And she broke into a husky, pleasant hum. . . . (39)

Anna's symbolic outlook allows her to equate the black birds that her lover glimpses out the window with the musical notations on her score; her "agreement" with his statement is, of course, an agreement to the metaphorical import of words that originated in a literal context. Because her lover's words bear no sign of the way in which they are to be read, they, like all language, are susceptible to a literal/metaphorical confusion. In *Knowledge, Fiction and Imagination*, David Novitz suggests that "by itself, standing free of any context, a sentence or sentence-type cannot properly be said to be a metaphor. There are no syntactical or grammatical markers that declare a sentence metaphorical. This must always be discerned in context" (147). By ignoring the context in which her lover's remark originates, Anna transforms the very substance of that remark; the slippery nature of representation allows her license to wander as she retraces the path from the linguistic signifier to its material origin.

The instability of language that underlies such misinterpretation is doubly complicated by the lack of grammatical perspicuity in everyday speech. The vexed issue of linguistic referentiality extends to the arena of grammar and syntax, as the conversational non sequiturs exchanged between the two lovers reflect; in the dialogue that follows, an ambiguous "it" functions as a hermeneutical crux:

The wind flailed against the window. He took his lips from her breast to say anxiously, "I hope it won't break." She directed her nipple again into his mouth and said, "I don't think so. It swelled like this when I was feeding my son." (46)

Anna's comically inappropriate response points to the obvious shortcomings of her self-referential interpretive scheme. She takes advantage of the ambiguity of language to mold a discourse that revolves solely around her own experience; that discourse serves as a buffer between Anna and the universe of violence and chaos that constantly threatens to intrude on her pleasure.

The interpretive frame within which Anna responds to others' discourse dictates the path she traces between signifier and signified. As those around her comment on the immediate, external world that they view, Anna continually resituates their remarks in a symbolic framework that transforms the import of the words by stripping them of their original context:

Their fellow travellers were in high spirits, gasping their wonder as the train pulled them slowly higher and higher into the mountains. "There's plenty of

snow still!" chattered the lady who sat opposite. . . . "I think so." The young
woman smiled back. "I don't feel sullied in the least." (43)

Anna not only applies metaphorically a comment of literal origin but directs
that comment toward herself rather than toward the external world. Through
exchanges such as this one, the conventions of Anna's hermeneutic framework are revealed; she ignores the literal to read symbolically and revises any
reference to the external world in self-referential terms. In so doing, she
rewrites the world to assure that it conforms to her own model of understanding, ignoring documented reality by reinscribing it within a symbolic
framework that transforms its most basic import.

The implications of the symbolic imagination become fully apparent in
Lisa's poem, which probes the effect of apprehending violence in purely
metaphorical terms. In this fantasy rendition of her experience with Freud's
son, Lisa adopts the psychoanalyst's tendency to conflate totally different
contexts of experience by translating reality into symbolic form. The poem
bears witness to her protagonist's attempt to appropriate the violent tragedies
that occur at the White Hotel within a personal psychological landscape that
reduces violence to a metaphorical extension of her sexual pleasure.

The poem's immediate juxtaposition of public suffering and personal pain
reflects Anna's willingness to level the distinctions between violence and
sexuality: "in the gloom / bodies were being brought to shore, we heard / a
sound of weeping, his finger hurt / me jammed right up my arsehole . . ."
(19). The shift here from the pain of the outsiders—the grief resultant upon
the violent death of their friends—to Anna's painful pleasure-seeking situates
both types of pain in the same arena, appearing to equate what are in fact
very different dimensions of experience. There is even a suggestion that Anna
and her lover exploit the pain of others by employing that pain as a means
of heightening their own sexual pleasure:

> . . . It wasn't till
> the sun drew in, that their gaze turned away,
> not to the crimson sunset but the blaze
> coming from our hotel, again in sight
> between the tall pines. It outblazed the sky. . . .
> So, pulling me upon him without warning,
> your son impaled me, it was so sweet I screamed
> but no one heard me for the other screams
> as body after body fell or leapt
> from upper storeys of the white hotel.
> I jerked and jerked until his prick released
> its cool soft flood. Charred bodies hung from trees,
> he grew erect again. . . . (21)

The violence of sexual impalement is implicitly equated with the violence
occurring around the lovers, and both, in turn, are made to seem "sweet."

While the lovers ignore the violence around them by relegating it to the realm of objective correlative for their own sexual play, the narrative recreates in aesthetic terms the symbolic imagination in which the lovers indulge. The lovers' obliviousness to the raging flames of the devastating fire is sanctioned through literary forms that deny the expression of the horror of violence by relegating violence itself to a purely symbolic realm. While there is no metaphorical bridge that yokes the pleasurable experience of the lovers with the painful experience of the victims, the poem's parallel treatment of these two disparate contexts reduces both to the same literary plane. Screams of agony and pleasure blend together as the "charred bodies hung from trees" come to serve, not only as symbolic equivalents of the limp phallus, but as the rejuvenating force that stirs the lovers' sexual excitement. While the facts of violence and sexual excitement are aligned through their assignment to parallel clauses in the same sentence unit, the placement of those clauses, coupled with the building rhythms of the passage, suggests a causal relationship between the two.

Violence is not only relegated to the same level of experience as the lovers' passion; it emerges—through the manipulation of form—as the instrument that sparks their continued desire for one another. Although that desire culminates in the release of the male lover's "cool soft flood," that metaphorical flood has no capacity to put out the white-hot flames that simultaneously reduce human beings to charred bodies. While Freud subsumes all evidence of violence within a psychoanalytic paradigm that stresses the primacy of sexuality, the lovers in Lisa's poem literalize that response; their clear indifference to the violence around them allows them to ignore its consequences and actually adopt that violence as fuel for their lovemaking. Thomas's characterization of the lovers thus emphasizes the danger of subsuming violence within a metaphorical context that obscures its material dynamics.

Metaphor is not simply a one-way path of transcendence from vehicle to symbolic tenor; Singer, along with Eco and Deleuze, has successfully questioned what he describes as "the causal imperative on which orthodox metaphoric logic appears to be based" (163). Although violence is evoked as a symbolic agent in *The White Hotel*, it refuses to be relegated to the status of literary catalyst; instead, it functions as an active force in the creation of narrative meaning. While the reader may be directed away from the violence to its symbolic import, his or her vision of violence is not obliterated but transformed. Because the symbolic framework of the novel is accessed only through an immediate perception of the work's violence, the process of reading involves an act of redirecting the gaze, not away from violence entirely, but *through* violence to its symbolic meaning; unless the artificiality of the literary process is emphasized, that symbolic meaning soon becomes entangled in the thorny arena of violence itself. The metaphorical tenor transgresses the boundaries of the symbolic network to permeate the literal universe of the vehicle. The workings of metaphor, then, do not confine themselves to a separate transcendent sphere but instead reflect back upon and qualify the reader's mimetic understanding. The fictional representation of violence, whether intended as a form of mimetic depiction or as a type of aesthetic tool, necessarily invokes the reader's awareness of violence as an empirical reality.

By adopting metaphors that obscure the strictly literary source of their authority, the speaker of Lisa's poem invents an artificial world that immediately denies its created nature. Metaphor becomes a strategy that encourages the reader to see violence without registering its material dynamics, to absorb its symbolic impact without, frequently, absorbing its horror. The lovers' immersion in their own context of experience makes them read the world through the eyes of their own lovemaking; as a result, the very real violence occurring around them is reduced to a play of forms seemingly created for their added enjoyment:

> . . . my light
> head felt him burst up through, the cable car
> hung on a strand, swung in the wind, my heart
> was fluttering madly and I screamed, the guests
> fell through the sky, his tongue drummed at my breast,
> I've never known my nipples grow so quickly,
> the women fell more slowly, almost drifting . . .
> the women seemed to rise not fall, a dance
> in which the men were lifting in light hands
> light ballerinas high above their heads. . . . (28)

The linguistic yoking of these two experiences—Anna's lovemaking and the cable car disaster—implicitly reduces them to the same context. The pain of the victims' experience is defined against the lover's pleasure; only in comparison to the nipples growing "so quickly" are the women seen to fall "more slowly." The speaker's conflation of the two realms of experience stalls the women's violent flight, suspending them in space; instead of plummeting to their death, the women appear to "drift" effortlessly through the air. By removing violence from the world of narrative time in which its immediacy rests, the speaker of Lisa's poem moves toward spatial form, freezing the women's bodies in a moment of time that draws attention away from the victims' horrific predicament and toward the intricate visual pattern that their drifting bodies create before the reader's very eyes. In *The Forms of Violence*, Leo Bersani and Ulysse Dutoit describe the creation of a similar effect in Assyrian palace reliefs, reliefs that both portray violence and adopt "formal relations which distract the viewer from the violent subject":

> Such formalization could be thought of as repressing differences crucial to a narrative reading of the scene, and as thereby encouraging us to emphasize what might be called counternarrative organizations and identifications. . . .

One's interest moves between the geometric and the anecdotal at the very point at which the anecdotal center of the scene is being most strongly emphasized. The force of this violent subject is, then, contravened by visual abstractions which disrupt the spectator's reading of the subject. (9)

The success of the "counternarrative" in *The White Hotel*'s presentation of the cable car disaster is marked by the extent to which the "geometric" rendering of the victims' falling bodies comes to overwhelm the reader's apprehension of the disaster itself. The lovers' sexual encounter, rather than any natural disaster, appears to orchestrate the scene of plummeting bodies; the rhythms of lovemaking provide background music that transforms the women who plunge tragically to their death into "light ballerinas" performing a dance in the hands of their partners. The literal imperative of violence is rewritten in figural terms and relegated to the background of the scene, where it functions as a form of mood music that encourages the lovers' sexual play.

Through literary device, the violent tragedy at the White Hotel is thus appropriated as a mere sign or symbol of Anna's sexual encounter. The reader who falls prey to the narrative's translation of violence into a play of forms is swept away from the "facts" of violence into a metaphorical apprehension that denies the implicit horror of the scene. Under the force of metaphor, experience is leveled; public and personal worlds are conflated while interior and exterior flow together in a seamless blending of contexts. The full import of such a radical conflation of worlds is revealed at the end of Lisa's poem, when her protagonist's interior pours out and colors the world; as the milk from her breast thickens into cream and then butter, the speaker literally transforms the landscape with her presence: "the falling light / spread butter suddenly on the trees outside / the great french windows, butter on the lake . . ." (25). Anna's vision of the world is filtered through the forms of her own experience to the point where that world itself is remade in the image of Anna's body. The price of such limitless subjectivity, in which the stuff of the self subsumes and transforms the world, is the sacrifice of any type of sensitivity to a shared historical reality; the cultural dialogue between the self and its world is reduced to a self-referential monologue that excludes all but the most solipsistic arenas of thought and action. The epigraph from Yeats that Thomas invokes at the beginning of *The White Hotel* suggests the cost of severing that dialogue: "We had fed the heart on fantasies, / The heart's grown brutal from the fare. . . ."

While Anna's sexuality overwhelms and redefines the landscape, the obsession with sexuality that she shares with Freud colors her vision of the world at large, forcing her to see natural forms as sexual symbols. Staring down from the lake at gold and silver fish swimming below her, Anna is reminded of "the sperm seeking my womb," and stops to question her own transposition of forms: "Am I too sexual? I sometimes think / I am obsessed by it" (28). Indeed, Anna's Freudian obsession with sex relegates everything else—even immediate violence—to secondary status.

It is not surprising, then, that the dream in Lisa's poem—a dream that clearly prefigures the violence that is to come—cloaks that violence in images of penetration that are at once violent and sexual. The surrealistic fantasy of the poem extends a clear invitation to the reader to approach its violent subject matter only as a code that must be broken and discarded in favor of the "real" content that lurks beneath. The dream is a mass of blatant sexual imagery that cries out for Freudian interpretation; in that dream, the speaker figures as both penetrator and penetrated, mother, whore, and child. She is the figurehead of a boat named *Magdalen* that is "plunging in deep seas" as the figurehead is "impaled / upon a swordfish." The passage is defined by a deceptively easy motion between pain and pleasure, softness and sharpness, and the exterior and interior of bodies:

> The ice was soft at first, a whale who moaned
> a lullaby to my corset, the thin bones,
> I couldn't tell the wind from the lament
> of whales, the hump of white bergs without end.
> Then gradually it was the ice itself
> cut into me, for we were an ice-breaker,
> a breast was sheared away, I felt forsaken,
> I gave birth to a wooden embryo
> its gaping lips were sucking at the snow
> as it was whirled away into the storm,
> now turning inside-out the blizzard tore
> my womb clean out, I saw it spin into
> the whiteness have you seen a flying womb. (22–23)

Initially, the speaker is cradled in the "soft" embrace of the ice, listening to the "lullaby" of a whale/mother. That soothing crooning is soon transformed, however, as the rhythms of the whale's song fade into the sexual humping of ice bodies and the whale's body is fragmented into the whale bones of the corset; the soft embrace of the mother metamorphoses into the constricting grip of Anna's rigid stays. Love itself turns violent; the movement of the figurehead through "soft" ice—the "plunging" of the icebreaker into the vulnerable sea—is reversed as the ice tears at the figurehead, ripping her breast, inverting her body in the act of birth. Throughout there is no clear victim, no clear violator, and no proclamations of pain. The only emotion the speaker registers is that she "feels forsaken." The violations of her body, as well as her collisions with others, seem exhilarating and powerful, moving the poem forward in a transcendent blend of bodies and elements, an orgiastic montage of tenderness, sex and violence. The surrealistic content of the dream transforms violence into liberation; while the narrator's body is invaded and parts of it forcibly torn out, the violence reported results not in a mutilated form—a body deprived of an essential part—but in the creation of a new form: "a flying womb," a body part liberated into a being of its own.

The effect of such metaphorical masking is fully apparent only when viewed in comparison to the violence of the novel's Babi Yar section; while the dream prefigures that violence very closely, the mere juxtaposition of the two scenes exposes their crucial differences. Like the dream vision in the poem, the description of Lisa's experience at Babi Yar is rife with the imagery of penetration, the collision of bodies, the physical dynamics and textures of violence and sex. Rather than sailing through the frigidly beautiful arctic sea, however, Lisa is here immersed in "a sea of bodies covered in blood" (291). The "whale who moaned / a lullaby to my corset" disappears, replaced by a brutal soldier who "started hitting her with his club, on her back and shoulders" because "she couldn't unhook her corset fast enough" (284); in this concrete depiction of a violence that defies the mediation of metaphor or symbol, "the thin bones" of the image-laden poem take on literal form and become recognizable as part of Lisa's own fragile body. The falling embryo defined in the poem by its "wooden" lifelessness is transformed here into the flesh and blood of Lisa's child; the metaphorical embryo's flight into space prefigures but in no way prepares the reader for the little boy's chilling leap into the death pit.

While other imagistic details from the dream, as well as from the poem as a whole, are invoked in the novel's depiction of the violence at Babi Yar, the jarring juxtaposition of contexts in the slaughter scene only emphasizes the horrific gap between this violence and its metaphorical antecedent. As Lisa's bones are broken, her body torn, her womb pierced with a bayonet, echoes from her painless dreamworld of whales and ice resound eerily beneath the brutal details. In the end of the section, Lisa—still alive—is discovered amid the pile of dead bodies by a Nazi soldier:

> Then she heard people walking near her, actually on the bodies. They were Germans who had climbed down and were bending over and taking things from the dead and occasionally firing at those who showed signs of life.
>
> An SS man bent over an old woman lying on her side, having seen a glint of something bright. His hand brushed her breast when he reached for the crucifix to pull it free, and he must have sensed a flicker of life. Letting go the crucifix he stood up. He drew his leg back and sent his jackboot crashing into her left breast. She moved position from the force of the blow, but uttered no sound. Still not satisfied, he swung his boot again and sent it cracking into her pelvis. Again the only sound was the clean snap of the bone. (292–93)

While the narrator laments that "There are things so far beyond belief that it ought to be possible to awake from them" (279), it is clear that this is no dream. In contrast with the earlier aestheticized violence of the novel, the violence in the Babi Yar section is immediate and undeniable; the reader is offered no alternative sight at which to gaze and no obvious mediating framework through which to assess the violent experience that the novel describes. Instead of witnessing the victim's agony through the blur of sexual excitement, the reader accompanies Lisa to the very edge of violence; the reader shares Lisa's perspective and listens to her voice until that voice, like the reader's consciousness, is assaulted by an act so harsh that it fragments the mediating forms of the novel as clearly as it destroys Lisa's own body. While the act of violence finally reveals the true cause of Lisa's excruciating pain, the stark description of that violence displaces once and for all Freud's abstract symbolism and the metaphorical forms in which that symbolism cloaks the facts of violence.[8]

Like the violence reported in Lisa's poetic rendering of her heroine's experience at the White Hotel, the violence of the Babi Yar section is also tied up with sex. In the latter case, however, that violence refuses to be contained in purely metaphorical terms. The collision of lovemaking and violence—unlike the collision of sex and metaphorical, aestheticized violence—is horrific rather than exciting, as the description of Lisa's rape and murder reveals:

> With Semashko's assistance he found the opening, and they joked together as he inserted the bayonet, carefully, almost delicately. The old woman was not making any sound though they could see she was still breathing. Still very gently, Demidenko imitated the thrusts of intercourse; and Semashko let out a guffaw, which echoed from the ravine walls as the woman's body jerked back and relaxed, jerked and relaxed. But after those spasms there was no sign of a reaction and she seemed to have stopped breathing. Semashko grumbled at their wasting time. Demidenko twisted the blade and thrust it in deep. (294)

Thomas carries to a logical extreme the implications of Freud's elision of the differences between lovemaking and violence. Having used violence to re-create forcibly the superficial manifestations of sexual pleasure, Demidenko and Semashko respond gleefully to the apparently sexual writhing of Lisa's body without concerning themselves with other interpretations for her motion. The two soldiers use violence to coopt the text of Lisa's body and then proceed to read that text in purely sexual terms; having molded Lisa's physical form so that it submits to the configurations of pleasurable lovemaking, they ignore the role that their own violence has played in creating the spectacle they witness. While they naturalize the violent "metaphor" that they create, the literal vehicle upon which the violators' theater of violence depends hovers painfully in the background of the scene. When, in her dream, Anna is "impaled / upon a swordfish," her womb torn "clean out" by the blizzard, the unself-conscious reader is tempted to respond solely to the sexual possibilities of the images; Thomas's brutal depiction of Lisa's murder, however, qualifies such a response. Through his representation of sexualized violence in the Babi Yar section of the novel, Thomas condemns Freud's metaphorical perception of Lisa's agony; in the shadow of the violence at

Babi Yar, Freud himself becomes a Demidenko figure, passing over real pain for the gratification of his own sex-obsessed theorizing.

The White Hotel, then, ultimately critiques the symbolic forms of understanding in which it initially appears to indulge, calling attention to the allegorical or constructed nature of those forms. The novel, like de Man's theory of the symbol, calls into question a romantic model of symbolism, one which begins with the "literal" and moves naturally and necessarily into teleological plenitude. While romantic thinkers such as Coleridge concentrate on the truth found in symbolic multeity, Thomas adopts as his concern the space between the literal and the symbolic, the assumptions inherent in (and obscured by) any process of totalizing perception. *The White Hotel* exposes the artificiality of such a process by reversing Coleridge's order, by beginning with symbolic plenitude—the endless sexual connotations of Lisa's pain— and moving toward the violent "literal" reality that is both the source and the consequence of that plenitude. In so doing, the novel also locates the source of Lisa's pain in a future rather than a past event, challenging the retrospective methodology that accompanies Freud's analytical models. Thomas's novel manipulates chronology to unveil the illusion of symbolic totality, reversing past and future as it inverts the move from literal to symbolic and questions the ideological assumptions underlying the symbolic act of perception.

Thomas's brutal representation of the violence at Babi Yar is unmediated by any obvious interpretive scheme; in its painstaking, literal detailing of atrocity after atrocity, it defies any facile metaphorical interpretation. While Freud's explanation of Lisa's pain relegates it to the realm of psychological symbol, the description of Babi Yar converts that pain into fact. In Mary F. Robertson's words,

> Surely the readers of the chapter on Babi Yar in *The White Hotel* will agree that it portrays a "reality that drives out the [psychoanalytic theory]" which dominates the first part of the book. The rhetorical force of that chapter is greater than that of the rest of the novel put together. A hush settles over one's reading like that of stunned conferees. And the force seems to depend a great deal precisely on that simple clear-sighted difference between fact and fantasy accepted by the modernists but rejected by the surfictionists. (460)

Thomas's representation does not move out of language and into the realm of unmediated experience; nor does it suggest the theoretical possibility of doing so. As the novel critiques its earlier totalizing perspective, however, it appeals to the authority of historical experience to loan it a less seductive voice. Thomas's appropriation of an antecedent text as the basis for his representation of Lisa's rape and murder has generated, in the years since the novel's publication, a passionate critical controversy.[9] While Thomas's unacknowledged "borrowing" from a Holocaust victim's text may be problematic, his use of the historical account is yet another reflection of the novel's concern with the issue of intellectual mediation. Although Thomas cannot avoid representing and thus to some extent formalizing violence, his appeal to a first-person account of Holocaust experience represents a nod toward grounding his postmodern text in an experiential framework that acknowledges rather than disguises the facts of violence.[10] The details of the massive slaughter at Babi Yar serve as the ultimate critique of all systems of interpretation that obscure those facts beneath fantastical or symbolic forms; the inability of Freud's forms to account for the immediate horror of that violence points to the need to reevaluate the conventional frameworks within which violence is understood and communicated.

The White Hotel, then, denaturalizes its own myths of violence by exposing what Patricia Parker describes as the "plot" of metaphor: "If we view metaphor as a kind of 'plot'—whether as a space of encounter or as a *mythos* with its own 'sense of an ending' (Kermode)—we can also see it as a 'plot' in the sense of 'conspiracy'. . ." (153). The compelling power of metaphor, as Parker observes, rests upon its potential to transcend the narrow framework within which it asks to be read:

> Metaphors are "arresting"; they compel as well as invite us to enter their figurative ground in order to "grasp" them. But it is often difficult, in this process of "play," for the reader to perceive that he himself has been "grasped," or "occupied". . . . Metaphor both opens up and forecloses. (154–55)

In *The White Hotel*, the reader is coopted by a metaphorical plot that denies its own complicity in the novel's acts of violence. By "grasping" Freud's symbolic interpretation of Lisa's pain, the unself-conscious reader participates in an act of imaginative violence paralleling that of the soldiers who grasp Lisa's body and the Nazis who occupy her country. Once the reader is firmly locked within the text's symbolic framework, however, the novel draws back from its self-created universe to reveal the extent to which the reader has been entrapped by the subtle persuasions of literary form. The reader's acquiescence to the work's formal mechanisms of captivation bestows unconditional authority on the novel's narrative voice; by unconsciously affirming the absolute power of the text to serve as a mediator between the reader and the world, that reader enters into an intimate alliance with the text that, in the Babi Yar section of the novel, explodes in his or her face. Ted Cohen observes:

> Intimacy sounds like a good thing, and I have been urging attention to the use of metaphor in its cultivation. It is not, however, an invariably friendly thing, nor was it intended to be. Sometimes one draws near another in order to deal a penetrating thrust. When the device is a hostile metaphor . . . it is all the more painful because the victim has been made a complicitor in his own demise. (11–12)

The White Hotel relies upon the hostile metaphor to entrap the naive reader within a psychoanalytic system of understanding violence that the novel itself goes on to critique; while the narrative retreats from its symbolic stance, the unself-conscious reader is implicated—along with Freud—in the very system that the narrative has come to renounce. Stripped of the external sanction that lured him or her into viewing the narrative violence in purely metaphorical terms, the reader remains suspended between what Singer describes as the "literal and figural imperatives" of metaphorical representation (27). As the tenuous bridge between these two representational contexts collapses, the reader is left to negotiate the resulting narrative gap; the "fantasy" born of metaphor erodes, leaving the reader face to face with a brutality that his or her unself-conscious approach to literary form has helped to create.

IV

ENVISIONING VIOLENCE
SEEING/SELLING THE BODY
IN *LAST EXIT TO BROOKLYN*

The issue of the body made visible through representation is articulated most clearly in the visual arts, in works which rely upon an audience's sight to construct meaning. Matisse's *Carmelina*, for instance, questions the terms of its own representational strategies as it both translates the female form into art and pauses to reflect upon the terms of that translation. Matisse's studio painting captures not only the female model but the artist in the process of painting her. The viewer who first turns to look at the study is confronted with the naked form of Carmelina's body. The woman before us is not draped or sensuously enfolded or enticingly cast into shadow; instead, she is seated four-square on a table staring straight ahead at the viewer. The front of her body is part of a single plane perpendicular to the line of the viewer's sight; shoulders back, legs and feet hanging, her eyes, nose, mouth, breasts, and belly greet us straight on. Although she holds a piece of material on her leg, it is not draped enticingly or protectively; the hand that holds it neither covers nor reveals her crotch. Matisse's model is stripped of the allurement of angle and the suggestiveness of shadow and granted instead a face that is harsh with subjectivity. As she stares at us, her nose flat and her mouth closed in a tight line without smile, her features assert neither beauty nor desirability but the sheer fact of her presence. The force with which her body refuses to bend or soften into curve lends it a hostile stance that not only resists the viewer's gaze but makes it uncomfortable.

The nude that we as viewers would consume aesthetically becomes a woman—Carmelina—who overwhelms Matisse's work with her presence; only a small mirror placed on a table behind and to the right of Carmelina marks the presence of the artist and *his* creation. That mirror captures the artist not only in the act of looking but in the act of creating his nude. In that picture within the picture, his red shirt overwhelms the pale body of the nude, a body now seen from the back and to one side. In the mirror, her form is curved, her hair draped, not only her features but even her right ear missing. Smoothed into convention and seen from this angle, her body signifies her female-ness and nothing more. The subject attached to that body is written out of the frame, suspended in the shadowy areas of the painting.

In questioning the relationship between subject and body, presence and absence, reality and representation, Matisse's *Carmelina* raises issues crucial to understanding what is at stake in representing the female body, not only in art in general, but especially in artistic representations of violence. It is the materiality of the human body that makes it susceptible to violence, while it is the presence of the human subject in that body that makes it susceptible to violation. In contrasting the female body with the embodied female, *Carmelina* exposes the way in which an artistic representation may present the body without acknowledging its presence.

Such a distinction becomes crucial in the fictional scene of violence; representations that render the female victim's body invisible even as they claim to acknowledge her subjective presence render that presence absent as clearly as do representations that sketch the victim's body but obscure the subjectivity that it bodies forth. Both by elevating the female form to abstraction and reducing it to the purely material, representations of violence may push the reader away from the consequences of violation and into a situation in which the act of reading becomes itself a form of consuming.

"Tralala was 15 the first time she was laid" (93). "Tralala," Hubert Selby's narrative of a Brooklyn teenager in *Last Exit to Brooklyn*, begins with Tralala's sexual initiation and ends a few months and twenty pages later with Tralala's gang rape and murder. Although Tralala's body quite literally constitutes the setting for the narrative's events, the reader's response to that body is manipulated by a text that only gradually lends it narrative visibility. In the story's initial representations of sex and violence, Tralala remains a purely literary figure whose body, like the image of Carmelina in the mirror, is present only as a conventional form. In gradually rendering that form visible to the reader, Selby reveals not only Tralala's embodied presence in the narrative but the cost and consequences of the reader's interpretation of her absence.

Although she never comes to own her own desire, Tralala is quick to assert ownership of the body that she deems commodity and sells for profit. While her friends giggle and gossip about their romantic encounters, "Tralala shrugged her shoulders. Getting laid was getting laid. Why all the bullshit?" (93). In her sexual encounters, Tralala exchanges her body not for the intangible rewards of romance but for goods and money. As the men who sleep with her fulfill their desire, Tralala also "got what she wanted. All she had to do was putout. . . . Lay on your back. Or bend over a garbage can. Better than working" (94). Tralala's matter-of-fact attitude reflects her sense of her body as a commodity that she owns rather than an extension of herself. In such a way, Tralala forges a magical economy in which she reaps reward without labor—"Better than working"—at no apparent cost to herself. The female body becomes the great capitalist resource, a commodity that can be sold again and again without ever being used up. Tralala, as controller of that body, can thus be compared to Marx's dis-embodied capitalist. In *The Body in Pain*, Elaine Scarry discusses the relationship between economics and bodies in Marx's work; in doing so, she defines the capitalist as a person who "has a relation to the system of production that allows him to survive without risking his own embodied psyche, will, and consciousness in that survival" (265). As long as she is able to exchange her body without risking her embodied self, Tralala participates in the magical economy of the capitalist. Opposed to this magical economy is the embodied status of the worker, whose material existence Marx traces in excruciating detail. "Marx's own exhausting labor," Scarry observes, "is the work of restoring the original referent, not just pointing to the human authors again and again, but carrying their portraits forward into the analysis, so that the sentient origins of the made world stay visible and accompany the progressively spiritualized or sublimated reappearances of that object world" (272). As a prostitute, Tralala is both author and text, creator and commodity. Rather than making visible the connection between her laboring body and the subject who not only controls but inhabits it, however, Tralala obscures that connection. Tralala denies her own embodiment when she detaches herself from the physical form she exchanges in return for money; she denies her status as a laborer when she opposes prostitution to work.

Selby's narrative would seem to substantiate such a view insofar as it represents Tralala as bodiless. Although the narrator introduces us to Tralala's idiom, her fiercely casual attitude, her actions and exploits, he seldom allows the reader to see the body that Tralala so willingly trades for profit. Feminist film theorists have explored in depth the problematics of turning the female body into an object of the male gaze;[1] Selby's narrative, however, reveals the process of objectification at work even in the absence of representation. In this story, what is not shown is as problematic as what is. The reader is locked into a narrative that, like Tralala, casually assumes the presence of a body that is invisible even during sex: "You aint going no where now. She shrugged and they went to bed. The next afternoon they went to the Greeks for coffee . . ." (99). In a narrative that focuses almost exclusively on sex, Tralala's body is almost entirely absent: "She stood there drinking and smiling and eventually left with a drunken soldier. They screwed most of the night, slept for a short time then awoke and started drinking and screwing again. She stayed with him for a day or two . . ." (108). The absence of any representation of Tralala's body or emotion during sex allows the reader to place Tralala in the scene without imagining her place in it. Tralala remains the disembodied capitalist who seems to reap the reward of a magical economy without sacrificing the labor of her own body.

Lea Melandri posits a link between the invisible female body and the concealment of labor power when she claims that "Idealism, the oppositions of mind to body, of rationality to matter, originate in a twofold concealment:

of the woman's body and of labor power. Chronologically, however, even prior to the commodity and the labor power that has produced it, the matter which was negated in its concreteness and particularity . . . is the woman's body. Woman enters history having already lost concreteness and singularity . . ." (in de Lauretis, *Alice Doesn't*, 30). Melandri's analysis parallels the woman's body with labor power, both of which are concealed historically. Prostitution, it would seem, could make visible both the body and the labor power that might normally be hidden, for as a prostitute the woman participates in the commodification of a body made not only visible but public; for this reason, Marx defines prostitution as "a specific expression of the general prostitution of the laborer" (133).[2] In denying the reader vision of Tralala's body, however, Selby's narrator obscures the surface on which the marks of labor are written. "Tralala" permits the reader to acknowledge Tralala's consciousness without recognizing its connection to the body that contains it; in doing so, the narrative contributes to an illusion of woman as disembodied even as it seems to empower the disembodied woman. "Female experience," Muriel Dimen observes, "is often one in which mind and body, mind and matter, are joined and, jointly, are ripped off. And at times we collude in this evisceration of our subjectivity, even as we resist" (37). In asserting herself as bodiless, as disembodied reaper of an economic exchange, Tralala colludes in an act of severing that the narrator reinforces through representation.

The narrator disembodies Tralala not merely by refusing to represent her body but by invoking it in purely conventional terms. Although the narrative sometimes lends Tralala a form, it is the abstract form of woman rather than what Melandri describes as the concrete and particular form of the individual. The narrator tells us that Tralala "had big tits. She was built like a woman," but leaves the reader without a specific body to assume the shape of that vague feminine ideal (93). We as readers do not know the texture or the color or the smell of Tralala's body but only the familiar gestures with which she offers it to others as she pulls the top of her dress down, sticks her chest out. In response to a customer who "pushed a bill from a thick roll and dropped it on the counter," Tralala "pushed her chest out" (95); when a seaman approaches her in a bar she "smiled and pushed her chest out" (105); in the process of looking for customers she "pulled her dress tight and forced her shoulders back" (106). Her body's presence in the story manifests itself in a series of conventional gestures that afford that body no distinguishing mark, no personal characteristics; it has as little connection with the character about whom we read as the nude in the mirror has with the portrait of Carmelina in Matisse's painting. Insofar as Tralala's body exists for the reader, it exists only as a convention, as the object of the reader's imaginative creation of the female form. Tralala's figure, then, emerges only as a literary figure, an image that announces itself to the reader as art.

The absence of Tralala's specific body in the narrative obscures the toll that her "laborless" exchange takes on her and denies the vital connection between body and subject. It also, however, reveals that prostitution—which would seem to expose publicly the female body upon which such commerce depends—actually functions through the obscuring of individual bodily characteristics. In offering her body for sale, the prostitute capitalizes on its desirable attributes (as Tralala capitalizes on her breasts); her commercial success will depend upon the specific contours of her physical form. Rather than serving as testimony to the "concreteness and particularity" of her body, however, the prostitute's conformity to the ideal shape of female-ness testifies to the ease with which she slips into the position of female signifier, seemingly erasing any trace of her existence as individual subject. In his study of prostitution, *Figures of Ill Repute*, Charles Bernheimer parallels the figure of the prostitute and the figure of the artistic nude: "The nude, like the prostitute, is an erotic commodity. Her nakedness is valuable not for its particular individuality, the marks of one woman's fleshly embodiment, but for its transcendence of these marks in a formalized language intended to feed male fantasies while it erases any potentially threatening signs of woman's desiring subjectivity" (105). To offer a concrete and human body to the prostitute would be to remove her from the realm of erotic commodity and expose her status as embodied worker and desiring human being. Bernheimer's comparison between the prostitute's body and the body of the nude points to the way in which the painter enacts in artistic terms the commodification of the female form. Like such painters, Selby's narrator uses the conventions of art to reinforce the essential assumption of prostitution. By relegating Tralala to the status of a purely literary figure whose body exists only as a series of conventions supplied by the reader, Selby's narrator—adopting his cue from Tralala herself—effectively markets his protagonist as commodity to an audience of readers.

As the narrative continues, Tralala extends her capitalist ventures to include a different kind of bodily exchange. Like prostitution, violence emerges in "Tralala" as a means of converting bodies into easy capital. Although the bodies traded in this exchange are forcibly appropriated, the victims of violence remain as disembodied as Tralala herself:

> The guys had what [Tralala] wanted. Especially when they lushed a drunk. Or pulled a job. She always got something out of it. Theyd take her to the movies. Buy cigarettes. Go to a PIZZERIA for a pie. There was no end of drunks. Everybody had money during the war. The waterfront was filled with drunken seamen. And of course the base was filled with doggies. And they were always good for a few bucks at least. Sometimes more. . . . If they were too big or too sober theyd hit them over the head with a brick. If they looked easy one would hold him and the other(s) would lump him. A few times they got one in the lot on 57th street. That was a ball. It was real dark back by the fence. Theyd hit him until their arms were tired. Good kicks. Then a pie and beer. And Tralala. She was always there. . . . Theyd make the rounds of the bars and spot some guy with a roll. When he left theyd lush him. Sometimes

Tralala would set him up. Walk him to a doorway. Sometimes through the lot. It worked beautifully. They all had new clothes. (94)

The emphasis of this paragraph is on the ease with which Tralala's friends are able to generate capital without labor, the simplicity, sometimes even the pleasure, involved in transforming a wandering drunk into new clothes, a pie and a beer, a good time. The short, simple sentences emphasize this easy equivalence. "Theyd hit him until their arms were tired. Good kicks. Then a pie and a beer." The absence of transition between the violence and the party suggests both that they are equally enjoyable ("the guys had a ball") and that, except for the violators' tired arms, there is no mess or inconvenience involved in mugging. The slangy euphemisms for violence—"lushed a drunk," "Drop them," "Good kicks"—and victims—"doggies" "drunks" "seamen"— obscure the acts so fully from the reader that he or she is not even sure what sort of crime (burglary, armed robbery, mugging, pickpocketing) the violators are committing, much less what its consequences for the victim might be. Although the expressions used here acknowledge violence as a kind of work (the men "pulled a job"), the materials of labor—the bodies of seamen and soldiers—are seemingly inexhaustible, instantly replenishable with others: "The waterfront was filled with drunken seamen. And of course the base was filled with doggies." Doggies, drunks, and seamen collapse finally into the nameless, bodiless identity of a person marked only as victim: "A few times they *got one* in the lot on 57th street" (emphasis mine). The narrative lends us a full sense of the magical ease these men, and Tralala, see in their way of life, without a complicating awareness of who their victims are and what pain they might endure.

In the passage above, Tralala's body figures as a reward for the men's hard work, something to be taken in and taken for granted: "Good kicks. Then a pie and beer. And Tralala. She was always there." As he parallels her with the post-event snack, the narrator names "Tralala" but not her body, while the reader reduces that name—the sign of subjectivity—to the mark of sexual presence. The individual body being exchanged in this transaction is only as real to the reader as the pie or the beer to which the narrator refers. Even as Tralala distances herself from the body she offers in commercial transaction, the narrator's representations perpetuate a world governed by the radical dislocation of bodies from selves. As the disembodied subject collapses into the undifferentiated body, the split between body and consciousness that Tralala herself helped to create turns against her. In severing the connection between subject and object, the narrative marks Tralala only as the anonymous object of male desire.

Rather than rebelling against its dangerous implications, Tralala embraces the subject/object split; to recognize its problematic assumptions would be to expose herself, in Marx's terms, as a form of living capital rather than a capitalist. Tralala is able to market her body with ease only because she sees it as a detachable possession, an inexhaustible resource that, like Marx's commodity, exists as "an object outside" the self (*Capital*, 41). Although always willing to exchange her body for profit, she refuses to engage in any transaction in which she is the subject of emotional exchange as well as the object of physical satisfaction. When an enlisted soldier she picks up begins to tell her the story of his war experience, Tralala reacts with anger and resentment at his breaching of the contract into which she believes she has entered:

> He kept talking. About the war. How he was shot up. About home. What he was going to do. About the months in the hospital and all the operations. . . . He said he just wanted to be near her for a while. Talk to her and have a few drinks. She waited. Cursed him and his goddamn mother. If hed fucker maybe she could get the money out of his pocket. But he just talked. The hell with it. She hit him over the head with the bottle. She emptied his pockets and left. . . . Never had this much at once before. Shouldve gotten more though. Listenin to all that bullshit. Yeah. That sonofabitch. I shoulda hittim again. A lousy 50 bucks and hes talkin like a wheel or somethin. (95–96)

As the audience of the soldier's story, Tralala finds herself written into a narrative defined by shared subjectivity rather than sexual commerce. In subject-ing her to his talk, demanding that she see him as more than an anonymous body, the soldier asserts a mind/body connection that implicates Tralala as well as her customer in a new form of exchange. As Tralala's response makes clear, this form of commerce would extract from her a burden for which his "lousy 50 bucks" is small recompense. Even as the soldier's complaints center around his identification with his own body—an identification brought home through the wounds of warfare—Tralala demands that he detach that body from consciousness and fall into the familiar motions of sex. When her attempt to return the interaction to familiar terms, to get him to "fucker" so that she could take his money and be gone, fails, she uses violence to sever forcibly the connection between the speaking subject and his suffering, desiring body. As the magical economy of prostitution is threatened, Tralala resorts to the equally magical commerce of violence, aided and abetted by a narrative that makes the equation between violence and reward simple and clean, uncomplicated by a lingering attention to the victim. "To hell with it. She hit him over the head with the bottle. She emptied his pockets and left" (95).

Although the pattern established by the narrative leads the reader to believe that the victim will be written out of the text, discarded narratively as he is abandoned physically, the threat of individual embodiment that the soldier represents is not so easily banished. This soldier returns to the Greeks to plead not for the money in his wallet but for the return of his ID card; it is the loss of the victim's identity that propels him to confront Tralala with the visible signs of bodily violation: "[T]he doggie came in. He was holding a bloodied handkerchief to his head and blood had caked on his wrist and cheek" (96). The results of an act of violence return to the violator, and to the reader, for the first time in the story. Confronted with this bleeding body and the sentient subject attached to it, Tralala attempts to assert once again the purely financial basis of her exchange with the soldier: "A lousy 50 bucks and he was cryin. And anyway, he shouldve had more. Ya lousy fuckin creep. She kicked him in the balls. He grabbed her again. He was crying and bent over struggling to breathe from the pain of the kick" (96–97). As Tralala attempts to focus on commercial exchange, the soldier's very presence asserts the connection between body and subject; even his words are embodied by the heaving attempts at breath that punctuate his plea for help. His reference to his war wounds ("I've been all shot up") asserts his physical vulnerability as his emotional outburst asserts his psychological need: "Please, PLEASE. Just the wallet. Thats all I want. Just the ID Card. PLEASE PLEASE!!! The tears streaked the caked blood . . ." (97). The victim's body, temporarily reduced to silent anonymity through violence, *now* accuses and threatens Tralala as effectively as do his words.

Although Tralala and her friends resort once again to violence to silence the soldier and deny the presence of his wounded body, the continued visibility of that body marks the reader's uneasy initiation into a world of consequences:

> He was still crying and begging for his ID Card and trying to tell them he wanted to go home when Tony pulled his head up by his hair and Al punched him a few times in the stomach and then in the face, then held him up while Tony hit him a few times. . . . [T]hey dropped him and he fell to the ground on his back. Before they left Tralala stomped on his face until both eyes were bleeding and his nose was split and broken then kicked him a few times in the balls. (97)

As it marks the presence of the suffering body, the narrative moves the reader outside a magical economy to reveal the cost of violence. With the narrator's sudden focus on the soldier's bleeding eyes—we later discover that he was blinded in the act—violence is linked to its consequences and the seemingly inexhaustible material on which the magical economy of violence is based is revealed to be the vulnerable human body.

Although the sudden presence of the victim's body allows the reader an understanding of the cost of violence, Tralala continues to deny not only the consequences of her violence for others—"he may go blind in one eye. Ain't that just too bad" (97) —but the personal cost of her decision to detach, commodify, and exchange her own body for profit. While it is physical pain that reestablishes the connection between subject and body in the first case, it is physical desire that leads Tralala to reappropriate her own body. Because it depends upon the constant resale of her body to generate capital, Tralala's magical economy is "better than work" only insofar as she can detach herself from the physical body that she commodifies. Tralala's successful marketing and manipulation of her own body allows the narrative to image penetration without violation, to represent Tralala as the disembodied capitalist rather than the embodied laborer. Tralala's detachment signals her separation from a body on which male desire is erased even as it is written; her own freedom from desire affords her a control that the desiring body lacks. The prostitute, as Bernheimer observes, "is somehow impenetrable even as she gives herself to be penetrated, opaque just when she should be readable. She asserts her independence of the male plot at the very moment when the male thinks he is inscribing her body into it" (88). Tralala escapes the "male plot" as long as she lends her form but not her content, her body but not her desire.

In embracing the absolute separation of subject and body, Tralala empowers herself as a capitalist but relinquishes the power of female desire. Tralala's magical economy relies upon a detachment from her own body that reinforces and extends an early refusal to envision herself as the subject—rather than the object—of physical desire: "She said yes. In the park. 3 or 4 couples finding their own tree and grass. Actually she didnt say yes. She said nothing. Tony or Vinnie or whoever it was just continued" (93). The representation of Tralala's first sexual encounter emphasizes the absence of female agency rather than the presence of female desire. Not saying no is as close to saying yes as Tralala will come; in the absence of her speech, the boys enact their own desires, using her body as a means to their pleasure. Desire is figured here, as it is in the discourse of Lévi-Strauss which Teresa de Lauretis discusses in *Alice Doesn't*, as "a property of men, property in both senses of the word: something men own, possess, and something that inheres in men, like a quality" (20). Tralala cleverly turns dispossession into capital as she manipulates a body free of the demands of personal desire into a property that she is able to sell. In buying into the notion of her body as detached object, however, Tralala not only frees herself for capitalist profit but locks herself into a kind of self-estrangement experienced by the laborer. As Marx states in his manuscripts of 1844, "Estrangement is manifested . . . in the fact that my means of life belong to someone else, that my desire is the inaccessible possession of another . . ." (156). In embracing the commodification of her own body, Tralala uses patriarchal oppression for capitalist gain; in doing so, however, she asserts a distance between self and body that dispossesses her not only of her physical self but of her very right to physical desire.

When that desire emerges in the narrative, therefore, it undermines Tralala's professional status as broker of a detached body and disrupts the system of commerce she has so carefully created. The cycle of bodiless sex that generates Tralala's capital is interrupted by a three-day interlude with an officer who forces Tralala out of the bank and into her body:

> When they got to his room she went right into the bathroom, smoothed out
> the bills a little, and counted them. 45. Shit. Fuckit. She folded the money, left

the bathroom and stuffed the money in a coat pocket. He poured two small drinks and they sat and talked for a few minutes then put the light out. Tralala figured there was no sense in trying anything now so she relaxed and enjoyed herself. They were having a smoke and another drink when he turned and kissed her and told her she had the most beautiful pair of tits he had ever seen. He continued talking for a few minutes, but she didnt pay any attention. She thought about her tits and what he had said and how she could get anybody with her tits and the hell with Willies and those slobs, she/d hang around here for a while and do alright. They put out their cigarettes and for the rest of the night she didnt wonder how much money he had. (102–103)

Tralala's first encounter with the officer is framed in commercial terms; the passage both begins and ends with references to money, while the prolonged encounter between the two is justified in purely pragmatic terms: "there was no sense in trying anything now so she relaxed and enjoyed herself." The carefully veiled subtext, however, marks Tralala's movement away from the commodification of her own body. In the process of accepting the officer's praise of her breasts—"he turned and kissed her and told her she had the most beautiful pair of tits he had ever seen"—Tralala figures her response in the familiar terms of economy, speculating about the value of what is affirmed as a particularly desirable commodity. Although the officer goes on to praise Tralala's emotional support as well as her physical form, Tralala is unable to acknowledge the officer's expression of emotion in any form except praise for the body that she offers in exchange. Her proud acknowledgment of his praise, however, is also an acknowledgment of her pride in and connection to the body that she manipulates for profit. Her reaction to his words signals the first time in the narrative that she even implicitly affirms an essential relationship between herself and her body. That unspoken acknowledgment leads Tralala to distance herself from the crowd at Willies and allows the narrator to frame the sexual exchange of bodies in a new light: "for the rest of the night she didnt wonder how much money he had." Although the details of the two bodies engaged in sex are still absent, the narrator's casual comment removes what happens in bed that night from the realm of commercial exchange, asking the reader—as well as Tralala—to explore a new way of reading and responding to her body.

When morning comes—and with it, the time for Tralala to accept payment and move on to the next commercial exchange—her excuses for staying with the officer are framed in the vocabulary of commerce but lapse into the language of desire:

she said sure. What thefuck. This is much better than wresslin with a drunk and she felt good this morning, much better than yesterday (briefly remembering the bulls and the money they took from her) and he might even give her his money before he went back overseas . . . and with her tits she could always makeout and whatthehell, it was the best screwin she ever had. . . . (103)

Tralala's discomfort with her own embodiment manifests itself in the quick, uneasy motion between the languages of economy and desire in this passage. In a rare moment of self-reflection, Tralala reveals that "she felt good this morning"; immediately, however, she must resignify what might be a sign of her personal pleasure into a mark of commercial success by juxtaposing today with the economic disaster of yesterday. Because this particular encounter has left her no richer in terms of capital, she marks it as an investment for the future: "he might even give her his money before he went back overseas." It is only after weaving into and out of this commercial discourse that she lapses momentarily into an admission of the sexual pleasure she has found: "whatthehell, it was the best screwin she ever had."

Having acknowledged her body as the source of personal desire, Tralala falters in the attempt to return it to the status of pure commodity. The officer's disappearance seems to force Tralala into a frenzy of commercialism as she searches for a more lucrative exchange of a body of newly assessed value; her search for customers, however, is now as much an assertion of personal pride as a quest for professional gain:

> She went to a bar in Times Square and sat at the bar. It was filled with servicemen and a few drunken sailors smiled at her as she looked around, but she ignored them and the others in the bar ignored her. She wanted to be sure she picked up a live-one. No drunken twobit sailor or doggie for her. O no. Ya bet ya sweetass no. With her clothes and tits? Who inthehell do these punks think they are. I oughtta go spit in their stinkin faces. Shit! They couldnt kiss my ass. (105)

The presence of Tralala's rhetoric of pride—"They couldnt kiss my ass"—reveals the sudden intrusion of ego and personality into the commerce of the body. The blurring of boundaries between subject and object, consciousness and body, spells disaster for Tralala's commercial success. In accepting the praise of her body as affirmation of herself, Tralala loses the advantage of the shrewd property manipulator. Clumsily, she attempts to repossess her own desire, to reappropriate her body as an extension of her subjectivity as well as an object of economic manipulation; in doing so, she tailors her commerce not only to the demands of the market but to the shape of emotional need. Her "clothes and tits" have always marked the value of her body as commodity; in claiming them as evidence of her individual worth, however—"No drunken twobit sailor or doggie for her"—Tralala sacrifices the empowerment of the disembodied capitalist and the independence of the undesiring prostitute. By reading the exchange of bodies as more than a business transaction, Tralala moves out of the realm of professional prostitution: "The bartender refilled her glass and marked her for an amateur" (106).

Tralala's downward spiral from successful capitalist to desperate whore is marked by the gradual intrusion of her body into the text. For the first time, Selby's narrator not only refers to but represents sex. While Tralala once "went to bed" with men or "was laid" by them, she now spreads her legs to receive their lunges:

> She bounced from one bar to another still pulling her dress tight and occasionally throwing some water on her face . . . and sometimes never seeing the face of the drunk buying her drinks and rolling on and off her belly and slobbering over her tits; just drinking then pulling off her clothes and spreading her legs and drifting off to sleep or a drunken stupor with the first lunge. (108)

With the intrusion of represented bodies into the text, the narrative begins to unveil the commodity on which the magical economy of prostitution depends. Marx defines money as "the external, common medium and faculty for turning an image into reality and reality into a mere image" (168). In this representation, the reader begins to glimpse the reality of sexual exchange that lurks beneath the narrative's veiled images. The inexhaustible resource that Tralala sells loses its magical quality as it becomes visible in the text. Although this representation of Tralala's body still renders it faceless and in some sense anonymous, its blurred outline *is* attached to an identity by a narrative that emphasizes the connection between subject and body through the repetition of the possessive pronoun: "her belly" is rolled on, "her tits" covered with saliva, "her legs" spread wide. Although Tralala's perception of this exchange may be blurred by sleep or drunkenness, this passage initiates the reader's movement into narrative vision; the myth that Tralala has sold to herself and her customers, that the narrator has perpetuated for the reader, begins to dissolve under the clumsy physicality of a representation that moves away from magic into blunt crudeness, finally collapsing into the jarring consonants of "the first lunge."

The expression of her own desire initiates a movement toward embodiment that undercuts Tralala's successful commodification of her body and results in the undesirability of the physical self that she now not only sells but offers desperately to others. Even as Selby's narrative allows the reader to see more and more of Tralala, to witness her fall into embodiment—"she flopped from one joint to another growing dirtier and scabbier" (108)—Tralala herself becomes invisible to the men who would once have paid dearly for her: "The honeymoon was over and still she pulled the sweater tight but there was no one there to look" (108). Although the narrator documents the loss of the desiring, possessive male gaze—and with it, Tralala's financial and personal collapse—his statement that "there was no one there to look" applies to everyone but the reader. The reader, who did not see the body that was the object of male desire, sees now only when no one is looking.

As Tralala returns to Willie's in the final scene of the story, she thrusts her body before a seaman in much the same way that the narrator has thrust it before the reader. Tralala's success as a prostitute depends upon her ability to control her image; she markets not herself but the body that she images as an object of male desire. In this sense, the body of the prostitute is not only opaque but reflective. When the male gaze is turned upon the female body, what it sees is an image while what it experiences is an act of imaging; the female form effaces itself to mirror male desire. When her body ceases to command that desire, Tralala must forcibly direct what she no longer imagistically controls. Whereas her body once sold itself by assuming the conventional gestures of sexuality, Tralala is now forced to supplement the image with the act. Leaning against the seaman she targets and rubbing her breasts against his arm, Tralala thrusts herself into the reluctant customer's face, forcing the male gaze onto her body:

> Tralala . . . leaned against the seaman and rubbed her tits against his arm. . . .
> [She] lifted her drink and said chugalug and banged her glass on the bar and
> she rubbed her tits against Jacks arm and he looked at her wondering how
> many blackheads she had on her face and if that large pimple on her cheek
> would burst and ooze and he said something to Annie then roared and slapped
> her leg and Annie smiled and wrote Tralala off and the cash register
> kachanged. . . . (110)

By forcing the look, Tralala unknowingly disrupts the circle of male desire instead of completing it; for the first time, the male gaze confronts a body that is more than image, a face not empty and reflective but marked by embodiment. As Tralala's pimples and blackheads are exposed, the act of unveiling exaggerates her body's alterity rather than its desirability. Instead of contributing to the male plot, Tralala's pimpled face disrupts it as effectively as the presence of Carmelina's body in Matisse's painting disrupts the faceless image of the nude in the mirror. When Jack looks at Tralala, the story that he creates is defined not by his desire but by the individual characteristics of her body. Instead of absorbing, exaggerating, and returning his look, Tralala's body threatens to burst and ooze its way into Jack's physical space, claiming an agency of its own. The image of the female form gives way to a reality that is anything but salable; as Tralala's body erupts from the mold into which the desirable female form is cast, the look of desire is made uncomfortable.

The reader's way of looking is also made uncomfortable, not only because of the proximity of the object that he or she interprets, but because of the reader's forced conspiracy in the act of looking. As a prostitute, Tralala offers the customer poetic license to shape her body according to the parameters of his own desire; she, in turn, converts the look of desire into capital. As readers, our tendency to re-create the absent body as object of desire is made comfortable by the illusion that it is Tralala who *lends* control of her body, who ultimately authors a magical economy through which she benefits without being inscribed in the male plot. In this scene, however, the reader is confronted with the consequences of reading, forced to participate in and witness a scene in which Tralala commands neither her body nor its interpretation. As Fred stares at Tralala's pimpled form, "wondering . . . if that large pimple on her face would burst and ooze," the magical economy *of reading* —the power to share the insights and the consciousness of more than one character at a time—turns against the reader. Even as the reader's desire to author the absent body is undermined by the presence of the interpretive object, Tralala's false interpretation of the gaze that interprets her unveils as illusion her ability to create and control male desire; what Tralala reads as a sign of male desire is, as the reader is painfully aware, nothing more than a look of disgust.

As readers, we read too well in this scene, finding ourselves participants in an act of looking that we—and not Tralala—must register as violation. The gaze of the consumer that Tralala once translated into capital here becomes a consuming gaze that she misreads as a look of desire; forced both to look and to register the consequences of our look in a way that Tralala does not, it is the reader who is denied the comfort of illusion in this scene. The audible kachang of the cash register that punctuates the scene marks not the profit but the cost of the exchange for both Tralala and a reader forced to mark her participation in an economy no longer magical.

In her essay on the representation of women's bodies in surrealist art, "Ladies Shot and Painted," Mary Ann Caws asks,

> Is there some way of looking that is not the look of the intruder, some interpretation from which we could exempt ourselves as consumers? . . . Here the dimension of desire appears, and . . . returns the contemplator and participator in Surrealist art back to the very subject: how might we desire to function so as not to be implied in the *incorporation* and *embodiment* of the desire of another. . . ?" (269–70)

The reader's "way of looking" in the early sections of the narrative is a process of not seeing, of not accessing the body that is traded in the text. This obstruction of sight, rather than exempting the reader from the position of consumer, places him or her exactly in that relationship to the absent body. The disembodied Tralala of the early text is assigned a figure by the reader, whose interpretation is itself a form of desire. "Desire and the desire to know," Julia Kristeva observes in "Psychoanalysis and the Polis," "are not strangers to each other . . ." (88). In apprehending Tralala as a purely literary figure, we absorb her within the parameters of convention that we bring to the narrative; she becomes the absent object of our desire to interpret, the empty signifier to whom we lend meaning. The reader's creation of Tralala thus operates within what Kristeva describes as a discourse of delirium:

> Desire, the discourse of desire, moves toward its object through a connection, by displacement or deformation. The discourse of desire becomes a discourse of delirium when it forecloses its object . . . and when it establishes itself as the complete locus of *jouissance*. . . . In other words, no other exists, no object survives in its irreducible alterity. (88)

As readers, our desire to know Tralala is fulfilled rather than frustrated by the absence of her body in the narrative; unchecked by a form that restricts or circumscribes our interpretation, we write rather than read her body, creating rather than confirming her presence.

In doing so, we implicate ourselves, along with Tralala's customers, as consumers. Our participation in the commerce of the body is revealed only when we as readers are confronted by the absent object of desire. At the very point when Tralala's customers no longer look at her, her sudden embodiment in the text forces the reader to see a body quite different from the literary figure that we have known, a body defined not by its submission to convention but by its "irreducible alterity." Kristeva states: "Whatever *object* one selects (a patient's discourse, a literary or journalistic text, or certain sociopolitical behavior), its interpretation reaches its full power, so as to tip the object toward the *unknown* of the interpretive theory or, more simply, toward the theory's *intentions*, only when the interpreter *confronts* the interpretable object" (86). It is only when we are brought close to the object we interpret—when we are forced to see Tralala's wet breasts, her pimpled face, her spread legs—that we become aware of the implications of the interpretive process in which we are engaged. Having formed and formulated her based on our own desire, we are now forced to acknowledge the extent to which we have assumed authorship of the very text we choose to interpret. As the distanced perspective that allowed the reader to see Tralala only as a literary figure collapses, the reader is trapped in a self-conscious glance that frustrates rather than perpetuates desire.

As Tralala begins to undress before the men in the bar, the conventional gestures of sexuality are replaced by an awkward, revealing motion that marks her attempt to get to what lies beneath, to assert the subject beneath the object that she unveils. Her striptease generates ridicule rather than desire because her motivations for exposing herself are personal rather than professional: "Tralala pulled her sweater up and bounced her tits on the palms of her hands and grinned and grinned and grinned and Jack and Fred whooped and roared and the bartender told her to put those goddamn things away and getthehelloutahere . . ." (111). As she displays her body for public view, offering her breasts first to Jack, then the bartender, then the entire bar, both the narrator and Tralala address those breasts in words of praise first offered by the officer who sparked Tralala's desire: Tralala "slowly turned around bouncing them hard on her hands exhibiting her pride to the bar and she smiled and bounced the biggest most beautiful pair of tits in the world on her hands" (111). Tralala "exhibit(s) her pride," not only in displaying the objects that are her breasts, but in proclaiming her body as her own. In demanding assurance of the value of her breasts, Tralala exposes the connection between the physical self she flaunts so carelessly and the emotional and psychological self she struggles desperately to maintain. Tralala uncovers her most intimate thing, not because she bares her body to men (she has done this constantly throughout the narrative) but because she exposes her emotional need. In his essay "Striptease," Roland Barthes distinguishes between professional and amateur stripping. Amateur striptease is defined by what he calls a "technical awkwardness" which "gives to the gestures of unveiling an unexpected importance, denying the woman the alibi of art and the refuge of being an object, imprisoning her in a condition of weakness and timorousness" (86). As Tralala acknowledges the connection between herself and her body, the object that Tralala once used as a tool of commercial empowerment becomes a mark of her subjectivity; the conventions of art dissolve, turning a textual figure into an individual body.

As Tralala's striptease lapses into what Barthes might define as a "genuine undressing," the much-too-loud laughter of her audience reveals the extent to which their desire has been made uncomfortable. Their constant questioning—"someone yelled is that for real" (111) and "he poked them with a finger and said I guess theyre real" (110)—echoes the reader's response to a body that has emerged from the realm of literary convention to assert the "irreducible alterity" of its presence. Confronted with the unmediated objects of their desire, the men that surround Tralala find themselves poking and prodding real human flesh. Tralala's body assails customer and reader alike; no longer merely a sign subject to physical and imaginative manipulation, it becomes abrasively real. What is unveiled as Tralala undresses is not only object but subject, not merely the body but what Scarry defines as the "embodied psyche, will, and consciousness" (265).

In responding to Tralala, the men in the bar attempt to sever the connection between the female body and the embodied female. They demand that Tralala verify herself as reality rather than image; their definition of reality, however, reduces the real to the physical, the subject to the object. Tralala responds to the men's skepticism not by changing their terms but by agreeing to unveil herself further and further. In doing so, she pushes herself into a spiral that moves away from the physical and the verifiable, placing her outside the only categories that her interpreters wish to acknowledge. After thrusting her breasts before them to be poked and prodded, Tralala is pushed to provide further substantiation of her bodily reality: "someone yelled all tits and no cunt . . . Tralala told him to comeon and find out" (112). In the scene that follows, Tralala has sex with man after man after man, attempting to affirm not only the reality of her invisible cunt but the presence of a subjectivity invisible to the men that surround her.

The story's representation of rape suspends the reader between presence and absence as it asks him or her to interpret what seem to be two different textual bodies. In one reading, Tralala offers her body to the men who have sex with her as a way of pushing them to acknowledge her presence; in another, the men in the bar rape Tralala repeatedly, using sexual violence as a means of obscuring her status as embodied individual. Initially, the narrator seems to conspire with the men's way of looking by reasserting the bodiless forms of interaction prevalent early in the story. The opening moments of the rape scene are reminiscent of the early parts of the story; there is the same carnival atmosphere, the same concentration on the peripheral pleasures resulting from violence, the same absence of a victim's body. With Tralala's invitation to "comeon and she/d fuckim blind" the crowd in the bar picks her up and drags her to a wrecked car in an abandoned lot, where they

> pushed her inside and a few guys fought to see who would be first and finally a sort of line was formed everyone yelling and laughing and someone yelled to the guys on the end to go get some beer and they left and came back with cans of beer which were passed around the daisychain and the guys from the Greeks cameover and some of the other kids from the neighborhood stood around watching and waiting and Tralala yelled and shoved her tits into the faces as they occurred before here and beers were passed around . . . and guys left the car and went back on line and had a few beers and waited their turn again and more guys came . . . and more beer was bought. . . . (112–13)

The jostling bodies in this description are not those of Tralala and her sexual partner but of the men who jockey for position in line. Once again, sex with Tralala is equated with the pleasure of beer drinking, intercourse with her body framed by the exchange of beers that, like her, are "passed around," bought and consumed. The magical economy is disrupted, however, by the slightest of glimpses of Tralala's presence in the scene. Although Tralala's yell is overwhelmed by the laughter and the screams of the men who surround her, the brief moment in which she asserts her embodiment, literally thrusting her breasts into the men's faces, returns the reader not only to her body but to her subjectivity. Tralala's desperate attempt to assert her reality in the face of the male gaze pushes her to expose first the outside and then the inside of her body; the capitalist who disconnected herself from the laboring body here asserts that body as a way of asserting herself. As Tralala brings the men closer and closer to her body, she pushes them to acknowledge her presence; as they penetrate her again and again, they relegate her to absence. The reader is caught not only between two bodies—an absent and a present one—but between two interpretations of Tralala's sexual exchange. The rape that occurs in the final scene of the story occurs only in the space between those two interpretations; it is the reader, and not Tralala, who is forced to recognize that the act to which Tralala consents is not the act in which the men around her engage.

Even as the men attempt to reduce Tralala to a passive receptacle of their desire, momentary glimpses of Tralala's presence force the reader to acknowledge what is at stake in this way of looking. The text no longer conspires to perpetuate her absence, but instead forces us to look even as we recognize the consequences of looking:

> they screwed her and went back on line and had a beer and yelled and laughed and someone yelled that the car stunk of cunt so Tralala and the seat were

taken out of the car and laid in the lot and she lay there naked on the seat and their shadows hid her pimples and scabs and she drank flipping her tits with the other hand. . . . (113)

The violence with which the men re-cover Tralala's diseased body, forcing it to assume the shape of their own desire, is recast as a shielding of her ugliness, a covering of that which was exposed: "their shadows hid her pimples and scabs." The narrative, however, unveils Tralala's presence in the act of representing its transformation into absence. The men's attempt to return Tralala's body to a mere figure, a conventional form, highlights the process of obscuring rather than the thing obscured. Even as Tralala's body is described as hidden, it becomes increasingly visible to a reader forced to image that body stripped not only of clothing but of shelter. The image of Tralala's naked body laid in the middle of an empty lot forces the reader to see without mediation, to visualize a body foregrounded against emptiness. Although Tralala's nakedness is soon qualified in the narrative, the representation of shadows does not block the vision of the reader; trapped in a narrative unveiling that neither the reader nor Tralala controls, the reader sees that which is unveiled *and* that which is covered, looking through the men's bodies to Tralala's pimples and scabs. We see Tralala's body not only from a distance, as a naked form exposed to the elements and to the view of every passerby, but immediately, from a perspective so close that we recognize her public display as an unusually painful kind of humiliation. Even as the men force Tralala into the conventional shape of desire, conventions are stripped away from the reader; forced to watch as a literary figure assumes the outlines of a human form, we are caught in the act of looking at a victim both exposed and vulnerable.[3]

As the representation continues, Tralala's body emerges from the shadow of male desire; as it does so, its wounds testify to the body's failure to remain pure image:

> Tralalas back was streaked with dirt and sweat and her ankles stung from the sweat and dirt in the scrapes from the steps . . . and she drank flipping her tits with the other hand and somebody shoved the beer can against her mouth and they all laughed and Tralala cursed and spit out a piece of tooth and they all laughed and yelled and the next one mounted her and her lips were split this time and the blood trickled to her chin and someone mopped her brow with a beer soaked handkerchief and another can of beer was passed to her and she drank and yelled about her tits and another tooth was chipped and the split in her lips was widened and everyone laughed and she laughed and she drank more and more and soon she passedout. . . ." (113)

Although the reader is able to trace the visible effects of violence on Tralala's body—broken teeth, split lips, a bloody chin—her own response belies her connection to that body once again: as her body is wounded, Tralala drinks beer, yells about her tits, and laughs along with those who assault her. Tralala's estrangement from her body is reflected in a process of misplaced signification that the reader must actively correct. Even as the reader wants to retreat from knowing, to escape from a text no longer pleasurable, he or she is forced to register the consequences of Tralala's magical economy. The grotesque enumeration of men having sex with her—"and someone asked if anyone was keeping score and someone yelled who can count that far . . . and more came 40 maybe 50 and they screwed her and went back on line" (113)—coupled with this enumeration of wounds suggests, as does Marx's representation of labor, a precise attention to the economy of pain that underlies the commodification of the body—a commodification enacted, in this case, through violence and prostitution. Having accepted the narrative's vision of Tralala as a disembodied capitalist, we are now forced to recognize her as a laborer bearing the cost of her transactions on her own body. Rendering in imagistic terms the distinction between the embodied worker and the disembodied capitalist, Scarry states:

> Two men crossed the plain, approached the commodity, and stood on either side of it. The one extended his arm and touched the artifact and, as he did so, his body grew larger and more vivid until all attention to his personhood or personality or spirit was made impossible by the compelling vibrancy of his knees, back, hands, neck, belly, lungs: even the interior of his body stood revealed in small cuts and larger wounds. Simultaneously, the other extended his arm and touched the artifact and as he did so, his body began to evaporate, grow airy: he was spiritualized, and disappeared. A name was given to each of the two: in his bodily magnification, the first was called by the name "worker"; in his bodily evaporation, the second was called by the name "capitalist." (275)

Whereas the narrative disappearance of Tralala's body had allowed the reader to name her as capitalist benefiting from her manipulation of the commodity, the final scenes of the story return us to that body in all its "compelling vibrancy." The wounds on Tralala's body testify to its involvement in an act of labor. Before Tralala's body had seemed to disappear as she touched the artifact that emerged as the magical source of capital. Now, as she touches the artifact, she touches herself; her body not only registers the wounds of the laborer but reveals itself as the site of labor. As it does so, the once absent body grows larger and larger, assuming an immediacy not only in the narrative but in the reader's mind.

In this final scene, Tralala's magical economy turns against her. Now, instead of generating infinite capital without labor, she labors infinitely for no return as the apparently inexhaustible commodity of her body is violently exhausted:

> soon she passedout and . . . they couldnt revive her so they continued to fuck her as she lay unconscious on the seat in the lot and soon they tired of the dead piece . . . the kids who were watching and waiting to take a turn took

out their disappointment on Tralala and tore her clothes to small scraps put out a few cigarettes on her nipples pissed on her jerkedoff on her jammed a broomstick up her snatch then bored they left her lying amongst the broken bottles rusty cans and rubble of the lot. . . ." (114)

In revealing Tralala's body completely, the narrative also completely reveals the nature of the violence that, at the beginning of the story, it so effectively concealed. The fiction of the victim's bodilessness is obliterated as the nature of the "kicks" so often alluded to at the beginning of the story becomes clear. The short, simple sentences that suggest easy equivalences and allow for visual absence in what is left unsaid are replaced by the endless prose of physical presence and pain. The parallels that Selby has hinted at between the magical economies of prostitution and violence become explicit here. With Tralala's lapse into unconsciousness, the possibility of consensual sex disappears. As the men rape the unconscious Tralala, the alarming fact that confronts the reader is not the difference between this act and the ones before it but the similarity. Through violence, the rapists forcibly sever the connection between Tralala as subject and as object, reducing her from an embodied female to "the dead piece" on which they inscribe their desire. Although her lapse into unconsciousness appears to signify the sudden absence of her will, it merely makes visible the problematics of consent underlying all of Tralala's sexual exchanges in the narrative. "To be able to give or to give oneself," Mary Ann Caws observes, "one must know oneself to be free. To be given in free exchange, to be willingly kept in ocular circulation, to serve as object for readerly and visual reception . . . is surely an act of generosity, if not forced. We have to be able to refuse it . . ." (284–85). The narrative that seizes on Tralala's body, claiming it as an "object for readerly and visual reception," pushes the reader toward an uncomfortable acknowledgment of the way in which Tralala is forcibly coopted both by the men who rape her and the text that lays her bare. Such obvious violation, however, merely renders visible the dynamics of exchange operative throughout the narrative. Tralala's magical economy relies upon bartering a body that she never knows herself to possess, through which she never functions as the subject of desire. Her willingness to disembody herself is no more "an act of generosity" than her apparent consent to rape; as long as it renders her body invisible, however, the narrative allows the reader to interpret Tralala as the beneficiary of free exchange without recognizing her entrapment in both a system that denies her ownership of her own desire and a body that bears silently the cost of prostitution and violence.

As Tralala's lapse into unconsciousness makes tangible and public the violation of her will in what appeared to be free sexual exchange, a gradual and climactic escalation into perception also makes the violation of Tralala's body visible to the reader. Whatever small privacy was left in the sex act as Tralala was pulled from the car is peeled back; male sexual response is openly

displayed in visible masturbation, and the sexual battering of Tralala's vagina, previously distanced to her ankles and lips, is made grotesquely visible
with the broomstick. As the absent body that appeared inexhaustible to the
consumer is itself consumed, the reader's desire to interpret is used up as
well. Splayed out before us, Tralala's physical presence deadens our desire.
We find ourselves face to face with an interpretive commodity no longer
receptive to facile resignification. In this scene, the boys who lurked on the
sidelines imagining the fulfillment of their pleasure now move close enough
to Tralala to confront her magical sexuality; having "jammed a broomstick
up her snatch," however, they quickly turn away. As readers, our own desire
to interpret quickly becomes a wish to turn away as we find ourselves in the
midst of a story we no longer wish to read. Our desire to know entraps us
in a knowledge of our desire as Tralala's battered body lies revealed before
our eyes; finding ourselves alone in an abandoned lot with the dead body of
a brutally raped woman, we realize with a shock that our total perception of
Tralala's body is coterminous with her death. What should be an affirmation
of presence gives way to the production of absence; as the force of violence
reduces the embodied female to the female body, the reader's look registers
her as the product of male violence rather than the producer of her own
subjectivity. Having distanced ourselves from the men's desire for Tralala and
our own desire for interpretation, we find ourselves forced to know the body
that desire has created. In unveiling the wounds disguised by the narrator's
refusal to represent her body and the reader's desire to manipulate it as
interpretive object, the text places the reader with uncomfortable force in the
scene of violence. Our way of looking becomes connected not with pleasure
but with pain as the object of our narrative vision becomes not a creative
absence waiting to be filled with a story but a destroyed presence speaking
the story of its own loss.

In Selby's narrative, then, the reader is neither victim nor violator but an
observer suspended uneasily in the scene of violence. "Tralala" unveils not
only the price that Tralala's body pays for participating in her magical economy but the cost of such an economy to the reader whose way of looking is
itself a form of consuming. The final image of the story emerges in the form
of a tableau witnessed through the back window of a moving car as Jack,
Fred, Ruthy, and Annie drive past Tralala:

> and they leaned toward the window as they passed the lot and got a good
> look at Tralala lying naked covered with blood urine and semen and a small
> blot forming on the seat between her legs as blood seeped from her crotch and
> Ruthy and Annie happy and completely relaxed now that they were on their
> way downtown and their deal wasnt lousedup and they would have plenty
> of money and Fred looking through the rear window and Jack pounding his
> leg and roaring with laughter. . . . (114)

In this passage, getting "a good look" at Tralala's wounded body becomes another form of sport, yet another way of consuming a spent commodity. Tralala's loss of control over her body becomes painfully apparent as she is literally fixed as an object before the moving gaze of her audience. Under their look, her body swells to tremendous proportions; the "small blot" of blood seeping from her crotch magnifies before the eyes of passersby. Where once her absent body bore no mark of its exchange, Tralala's body is so marked by the wounds of labor that, like the body of Marx's worker, it grows "larger and more vivid" until, in Scarry's words, "all attention to personhood or personality or spirit [is] made impossible." The reader who acknowledges not only the presence of Tralala's body but the absence of her subjectivity is suspended uneasily between subject and object, caught in a rupture that looking perpetuates rather than repairs.

Even as the conclusion of the narrative reminds the reader that he or she—like Tralala's cohorts—has a way out of the broken lot that Tralala does not have, it undermines the reader's apparent freedom. The very gaze that empowers Tralala's cohorts disempowers the reader, granting him or her not the assurance of a good deal but the vision of violation as its focus shifts from "plenty of money" to a plenitude of wounds. In "Rereading as a Woman," Nancy K. Miller observes, "To reread as a woman is . . . to imagine while reading the place of a woman's body; to read reminded that her identity is also re-membered in stories of the body" (355). The process of rereading in "Tralala" is a process not only of re-membering the body but of acknowledging its dismemberment; by the end of the story the reader can ignore neither Tralala's physical presence nor the subjective absence to which her broken, wounded body attests.

V

AMERICAN PSYCHO AND THE AMERICAN PSYCHE
READING THE FORBIDDEN TEXT

The appearance of the body in "Tralala" suggests a motion away from silencing and generalizing patriarchal forms and toward the acknowledgment of individual subjectivity. This is accompanied by the reader's realization that Tralala is not a disembodied capitalist but an embodied laborer whose body suffers the painful and dehumanizing consequences of violence. Bret Easton Ellis's controversial novel *American Psycho* investigates the impact of a capitalist mentality on conceptions of violence and the body much more openly than does "Tralala," yet Ellis's novel moves the reader through an almost precisely opposite narrative process. The horrific representations of violence in *American Psycho* image the victim's body with tremendous specificity, yet render the subjective presence of the victim less immediate to the reader.

In using money to make money, Marx's capitalist profits without labor; he trades in the abstract and the invisible at the expense of those whose bodies are visibly used up by his exploitation of them. Marx's descriptions of the capitalist's dealings stress their apparent magical quality, the ease with which the capitalist is able to make something out of nothing. In doing so, of course, the capitalist also turns something *into* nothing; he transforms human beings into material: "Production does not simply produce man as a commodity, the human commodity, man in the role of commodity; it produces him in keeping with this role as a mentally and physically dehumanized being" (*Economic and Philosophic Manuscripts*, 121).[1] The "increasing value" of the capitalist's world not only results in but depends upon what Marx describes as "the devaluation of the world of men" (107). Whereas Marx's work on economy traces capitalism back to its origin in the gritty sacrifice of the worker's mind and body, *American Psycho* pushes the capitalist mentality to an extreme that renders visible the machinery at work beneath its apparent magic. Patrick Bateman, the protagonist of Ellis's novel, manipulates not only money and stocks but the bodies that he transforms through violence.

As a successful capitalist, Bateman is able to buy whatever he wants, whether it be clothes, food, or human bodies. He quite literally purchases the opportunity to commit violence when a prostitute he injures during their first encounter balks at being rehired:

> Though she was still scared, a few shots of vodka in the back of the limo along with the money I'd given her so far, over sixteen hundred dollars, relaxed her like a tranquilizer. Her moodiness turned me on and she acted like a total sex kitten when I first handed her the cash amount—six bills attached to a Hughlans silver money clip—but after I urged her into the limo she told me that she might need surgery after what happened last time, or a lawyer, so I wrote out a check to cash in the amount of one thousand dollars. . . . (284)

Christie's fear for her welfare, a fear made legitimate by the violence involved in her previous encounter with Bateman, is transformed into a sign of sexuality through the mysterious power of capital. Reading her reluctance as a tantalizing "moodiness," Bateman is able to remake the prostitute into a "total sex kitten" by presenting her with money. As in "Tralala," the prostitute's economy involves erasing the presence of the wounded body; here, however, we see the transaction from the perspective of the john who can erase the body's wounds by waving a check. In his own example of the transformative power of money, Marx describes an individual who is lame but uses his capital to hire two dozen feet, thus overcoming his bodily disability (167). The *Psycho* incident literalizes Marx's metaphor for capitalism by pointing to the way in which Bateman's money allows him the opportunity not only to remake a body that his own violence has damaged but to repurchase that body, claiming it as the object of further violation.

I.

The power of the john, who is able to repair and repurchase even a damaged body by producing money, anticipates the explicitly violent force of the psychotic killer who is able to transform the individual subjective body into typical, physiological matter by producing a weapon. As a critique of the dangers of '80s capitalism, *American Psycho* suggests that not only the john but any powerful capitalist manipulates and violates bodies in the process of buying and selling. The psycho, then, merely extends logically the assumptions of capitalism as he translates human bodies into commodities subject to both physical and economic manipulation. Norman Mailer has encapsulated this thesis as follows:

> *American Psycho* is saying that the eighties were spiritually disgusting and the author's presentation is the crystallization of such horror. When an entire new class thrives on the ability to make money out of the manipulation of money, and becomes altogether obsessed with the surface of things—that is, with luxury commodities, food, and appearance, then, in effect, says Ellis, we have

entered a period of the absolute manipulation of humans by humans: the
objective correlative of total manipulation is coldcock murder. (159)

The excessive distancing of the capitalist from the physical operation of labor
may cause him to conceive of the body as so entirely alienated that he no
longer need recognize it as human, subjective, capable of pain. In *American
Psycho*, Ellis attempts to unveil the machinery that creates the magical
illusions of a psycho-capitalist world in which the wealthy and beautiful have
the power to transform anything into anything.

Even as the content of Ellis's novel seems to push toward a critique of the
capitalist's magic, however, the narrative itself participates in the creation
of its own dangerous illusions. If money is, as Marx describes it, an "al-
mighty being" (169), a "divinity" (167) capable of transforming anything
into its opposite, Bateman is the god of this novel. As a character, the
psycho's actions are repellant, his intentions visible even as they are violent.
As a narrator, however, he partakes of a kind of magic less visible and
ultimately more dangerous.

As Bateman's acts of violence reduce human will and subjectivity to material that he is free to manipulate, the narrative representation of his victims
authorizes the very manipulation that it would appear to criticize. The ability
of the body to speak to the reader, to express subjectivity (as Tralala's body
increasingly does throughout her story), is gradually decreased in *American
Psycho* by the continual rendering of body parts in purely conventional terms.
Ellis's narrator perceives the women around him as physical conventions: "a
. . . hard body with a perfect ass and great full tits" (97). His victims are
nameless, and the chapter titles most often refer to them only by gender:
"Girl," "Tries to Cook and Eat Girl," "Girls," "Girls," "Girls." Even when
distinguishing physical characteristics are presented the narrator manipulates them into a typical image:

> She's blond and slim and young, trashy but not an escort bimbo, and most
> important, she's white, which is a rarity in these parts. . . . [Y]ou could easily
> mistake her for one of the NYU girls walking home from Mars, a girl who has
> been drinking Seabreezes all night while moving across a dance floor to the
> new Madonna songs, a girl who perhaps afterwards had a fight with her
> boyfriend, someone named Angus or Nick or . . . Pokey, a girl on her way to
> Florent to gossip with friends, to order another Seabreeze perhaps or maybe
> a cappuccino or a glass of Evian water— (168–69)

Here, as elsewhere throughout the novel, the subjective expressivity of the
physical body is diverted onto a set of nonsubjective material objects loosely
associated with that body: Seabreezes, songs, Evian water. All of Bateman's
friends look the same because his narration replaces characterization with
the description of material commodities; when we meet a new character we
are told not who he is but what he is wearing:

> Scott Montgomery walks over to our booth wearing a double-breasted navy blue blazer with mock-tortoiseshell buttons, a prewashed wrinkled-cotton striped dress shirt with red accent stitching, a red, white and blue fireworks-print silk tie by Hugo Boss and plum washed-wool trousers with a quadru-ple-pleated front and slashed pockets by Lazo. He's holding a glass of champagne and hands it to the girl he's with . . . she's wearing a wool-crepe skirt and a wool and cashmere velour jacket and draped over her arm is a wool and cashmere velour coat, all by Louis Dell'Olio. High-heeled shoes by Susan Bennis Warren Edwards. Sunglasses by Alain Mikli. Pressed-leather bag from Hermes. (42)

Each individual is named not by a series of bodily features and personality characteristics but by the combination of objects with which they adorn themselves. These objects are described in intimate detail and marked by the names of their designers. The characters who wear the clothes, on the other hand, are often indistinguishable not only to the reader but to one another, as the novel's frequent episodes of mistaken identity reveal.

When the material covering the body is stripped away through violence, Bateman also reduces the body revealed beneath to matter that bears little trace of individual subjectivity. Attention to the body's individual character-istics is diverted by focus on the common physiological characteristics of all bodies, particularly their internal structure. With all his victims, Bateman uses his torture instruments to open up what is inside and bring it out, cutting out tongues, widening the opening of the mouth with nail scissors, reaching inside apertures to yank out the tubes and organs that sustain life. Because we very rarely see these characters before Bateman begins the process of torturing and murdering them, and because their distinguishing external features are rarely described, the reader comes to conceive of them as typical physiological specimens whose bodies will react to violence in typical ways. Throughout *Psycho*, traces of sentience are overwhelmed by representations that present the human body as a set of veins, internal organs, or bones that respond to pressure, heat, or electricity in various ways:

> He starts nodding helplessly and I pull out a long, thin knife with a serrated edge and, being very careful not to kill him, push maybe half an inch of the blade into his right eye, flicking the handle up, instantly popping the retina. . . . His eye, burst open, hangs out of its socket and runs down his face and he keeps blinking which causes what's left of it inside the wound to pour out like red, veiny egg yolk. I grab his head with one hand and push it back and then with my thumb and fore finger hold the other eye open and bring the knife up and push the tip of it into the socket, first breaking its protective film so the socket fills with blood, then slitting the eyeball open sideways, and he finally starts screaming once I slit his nose in two. . . . (131)

The victim's subjectivity is diminished here, not because the reader is made to concentrate on his surroundings or clothes, but because the reader is encouraged to focus on the structure of the eye being taken apart in various complicated ways. As Bateman opens the eyes of his victim to uncover what is hidden beneath, he unveils not a subject but an object, not an individual but a retina, a socket, an eyeball. The internal structure of the bodily organ, normally unnoticed and certainly not expressive of any subjectivity, is so foregrounded that the eye described seems unconnected to any specific person. Both the reader's recognition of the victim's presence as an individual subject and the victim's scream of pain are suspended until the end of the representation. The dehumanizing power of the psycho's violence is reinforced rather than exposed by a representation that concentrates on the anatomy of bodily violation rather than the immediacy of the victim's pain.

Narrative emphasis on the typicality of internal bodily structure is exaggerated by the didactic discourse that often accompanies representations of Bateman's acts of torture. The narratives of violence Bateman addresses to the reader provide detailed explications of the physiological source of the sights and sounds the body presents when opened and exposed:

> The ax hits him midsentence, straight in the face . . . splitting it open, his arms flailing at nothing, blood sprays out in twin brownish geysers, staining my raincoat. This is accompanied by a horrible momentary hissing noise actually coming from the wounds in Paul's skull, places where bone and flesh no longer connect, and this is followed by a rude farting noise caused by a section of his brain, which due to pressure forces itself out, pink and glistening, through the wounds in his face. He falls to the floor in agony, his face just gray and bloody, except for one of his eyes, which is blinking uncontrollably. . . . (217)

This representation places the reader in the position of a student being instructed on the physics and anatomy of a body governed not by will but by the mechanics of pressure and force. The reader sees geysers and pink, glistening matter, hears hissing and farting noises; rather than a head, the reader perceives bone and flesh that "no longer connect." Although Paul's eyes move and his body collapses, his actions emerge only as physiological responses. When the victim "falls to the floor in agony," even his pain appears as little more than a reflex reported by the psycho in the same offhand manner as the blinking of an eye.

As the psycho reduces human will and subjectivity to matter subject to his manipulation, female sexuality presents a particular threat; to Bateman, women's bodies suggest a notion of interiority that he must deny in order to continue existing in a world of pure commodities. The psycho's attack on female victims concentrates on defusing the Otherness of female sexuality by transforming female genitalia into undifferentiated matter. He kills one woman—a prostitute named Christie—by hooking up jumper cables to a battery and clipping them to her breasts. When the breasts explode, killing the woman, the narrator's representation focuses on the scattered fragments: "I have to open the venetian blinds, which are spattered with burnt fat from when Christie's breasts burst apart, electrocuting her, and then the windows, to air out the room" (290). Instead of glossing over the implications of his act, the narrator flaunts them. He temporarily reattaches the mutilated body parts to their human context, acknowledging them as "Christie's breasts," only to emphasize the way in which violence has severed the connection between object and subject, female body and embodied female. Under the force of the psycho's control, these body parts cease to retain any sign of female sexuality or personal identity as they are reduced to "burnt fat" and a bad smell.

The psycho's uneasy reflections on female Otherness often involve attributing absence to presence and presence to absence. His demand that the female body conform to a standard, male contour is made imaginatively possible as he speculates about the pleasure of "deflating" a woman's breasts as if they were no more than empty receptacles holding air. When confronted with the paradox of the vagina, whose presence is manifested in an interiority that appears as absence, Bateman finds the lack of substance even more difficult to confront. His description of a dead woman's body claims that "there's a black pit where her vagina should be" (290), seeming to assert his destruction of an organ that is largely an aperture or, in Bateman's own words, a "cavity." The psycho not only prides himself on his ability to "carve out" vaginas but talks about filling his health club locker with them: "In my locker in the locker room at Xclusive lie three vaginas I recently sliced out of various women I've attacked in the past week" (370). It is hard to imagine exactly what Bateman has "sliced out" or, indeed, what form such "vaginas," without the structures surrounding them, would assume. Clearly, however, the American psycho is invested in the idea of reducing the absence that is female genitalia to the presence of undifferentiated matter that he can manipulate. The psycho's demand reflects what Peter Brooks describes as "the male view of the female genitals as nothing, yet at the same time the object of an anxiety resolved in pejoratives . . . and nervous laughter . . . an antiphallus more powerful than the male member. Her sex is all the more powerful in that its mechanism remains hidden" ("Storied Bodies," 27). In fact, in being hidden, female sexuality ceases to appear mechanical at all; as such, it posits a magical order of its own that the psycho cannot destroy unless he is able to transform absence into presence. By bringing the interior to the surface, moving interior organs and female genitalia outside of the body within which they are housed, Bateman transforms subjectivity and interiority into typical and unexpressive matter; only then does female Otherness become a commodity that Bateman can control and discard.

Bateman's violence, then, enacts a literal process of commodification in which his female subjects are often reduced to undifferentiated matter that ceases to be recognizable as human. Body parts are reduced to malleable substance—"I start kneading her breasts with a pair of pliers, then I'm mashing them up" (290)—while solids become liquids—"her melted eyes [run] down her face with the tears and Mace" (305)—and the shapes of organs are transformed: "A few of her intestines . . . are mashed up into balls that lie strewn across the glass-top coffee table" (344). Bodies are broken into parts and lent a narrative equivalence to objects as one victim's arm becomes "a pipe," another's brain becomes "hunks of pink, fleshy meat" (328), and a stomach is compared to "the eggplant and goat cheese lasagna at Il Marliboro" (344). In the chapter entitled "Tries to Cook and Eat Girl" this resolution of the body into pure matter becomes explicit:

> In the kitchen I try to make meat loaf out of the girl but it becomes too frustrating a task and instead I spend the afternoon smearing her meat all over the walls. . . . I decide to use whatever is left of her for a sausage of some kind. . . . I grind bone and fat and flesh into patties, and though it does sporadically penetrate how unacceptable some of what I'm doing actually is, I just remind myself that this thing, this girl, this meat, is nothing, is shit. . . . (345)

Not only the psycho's actions but his narrative representations reflect how deeply invested he is in reducing the human form to matter that he owns and manipulates. The magic of his own capitalist enterprise depends upon his denial of the magical element of the human body; his violence extinguishes the spark of human subjectivity so that the bodies he violates both create and substantiate his view of the world: "Surface, surface, surface was all that anyone found meaning in . . . this was civilization as I saw it, colossal and jagged . . ." (375). Because Bateman's world is all surface, his torture and mutilation of victims consists of opening up their bodies to deny the mystery of interiority. Through violence, the psycho forces his victims not only to provide the matter out of which he constructs his universe but to participate in a world of commodities the emptiness of which any sign of their humanity would threaten to expose.

II.

Readers of *American Psycho* respond to the text not only with a sense of disgust at its protagonist but with a guilty acknowledgment of their own seeming complicity in his acts of violence. The public outcry that greeted the book even before it emerged on bookstore shelves led not only to one publisher's decision to cancel publication but to a series of personal outcries that testify to the novel's extraordinary power. George Corsillo, the artist who designed the jackets for Ellis's previous books, rejected the assignment for *American Psycho*. "I had to draw the line," he said publicly. "I felt disgusted with myself for reading it" (in Sheppard, 100). Jonathan Yardley of the *Washington Post* finishes his review of *American Psycho* with a vehement plea to the reader: "Of course, Ellis has every right to write [*American Psycho*] and Vintage, every right to publish it. But the rest of us have every right not to read it: as one who did so out of duty, and who feels thoroughly soiled by the experience, I can only urge—no, pray—that everyone else refuses to do so by choice" (75). Despite the fact that he read the book out of duty, Yardley feels "thoroughly soiled" by the experience, and prays that others will avoid reading the novel, while Corsillo, who presumably read *Psycho* for professional reasons, feels "disgusted" not at the contents of the book but "with [himself] for reading it." Norman Mailer observes that "One would like to throw the book away" but instead "reads on addicted to a vice that offers no pleasure whatsoever" (158). The self-directed criticism of these readers points to a source of discomfort that goes beyond the horrific contents of the novel. The message that these readers send implies a sense of powerlessness and complicity in the reading experience, a sense of being at once subjected to and guilty of violence. The vehemence with which Yardley communicates his plea to the reader not to pick up *American Psycho* creates a sense of the book's horror as communicable; although the contents of this novel are graphic and disturbing, even more disturbing is the sense conveyed by these readers that the book itself holds sway over any reader—no matter how critical—who chooses to open its cover.

What is missing in such responses is a sense of a particular reader's right to resist the message of the text, to read critically and actively rather than naively and passively. As Paul Smith discusses in *Discerning the Subject*, readers of a literary text—unlike the victims of the American psycho—are never passive victims of that text:

> . . . there is a distinction to be made between the subject-position prescribed by a text and the actual human agent who engages with that text and thus with the subject-position it offers. Clearly, any given text is not empowered to *force* the reader to adhere to the discursive position it offers. . . . [W]hat always stands between the text's potential or preferred effect and an actualized effect is a reader who has a history of his/her own. (34)

What Smith points to is the possibility of resistance, the ability of the reader to reject the subject-position offered by a text and to resituate him- or herself in that literary space. Why, given the validity of Smith's argument, does reading *American Psycho* not lead its readers to come away from the novel with a sense of their personal distinction from its protagonist/narrator? Given the character with whom the text asks us to identify, isn't reader rebellion the only logical response?

American Psycho succeeds in implicating the reader as well as Patrick Bateman in its universe of violence. It does so, not merely because it offers us identification with only one subject (which we, as individuals, could surely refuse), but because it offers us no definition of the subject we wish to resist. Patrick Bateman is at once the only character of the novel and no character at all. Although the subject of the book's actions, the first-person narrator of its events, he never assumes an identifiable subject-position that we can define and react against. The narrative carefully denies the reader a clear sense of both the literal and the psychological space that Patrick Bateman occupies. Although the psycho's attempts to deny the subjectivity of his victims—both through violence and through the representation of violence—constitute a form of terrorism, his own position in the narrative is marked not by an empowered subjectivity but by his refusal to be contained in a single subject-position. For the reader attempting to define and resist a character and narrator capable of immense brutality, the inability to locate the very subject against which the reader would react is one mark of the text's ultimate violation.

As a character, Bateman's actions are unpredictable, his motivations impossible to define. While almost all popular culture representations of serial killers are constructed around a narrative that makes sense of violence either through an explanation of the killer's psychosis or a revelation of some emergent pattern of violence, *American Psycho* frustrates the reader's desire to translate Bateman's unintelligible behavior into any kind of coherent form. The reader forced to read on as the psycho murders again and again comes no closer to understanding his motivations; acts of violence are framed neither by an exploration of the psycho's thoughts or emotions nor by flashbacks to his childhood or adult frustrations. Even the psycho's self-analysis, which announces itself as revelation, offers only empty insight:

> The smell of meat and blood clouds up the condo. . . . I'm weeping for myself, unable to find solace in any of this . . . sobbing, "I just want to be loved," cursing the earth and everything I have been taught: principles, distinctions, choices, morals, compromises, knowledge, unity, prayer—all of it was wrong, without any final purpose. All it came down to was: die or adapt. (345)

In this rare moment of introspection, the psycho explains himself to the reader; his explanation, however, is a mere amalgamation of stereotypes appropriated from bad movies and melodramatic novels. In Bateman's self-portrait, the merciless killer is really at heart only a child who wants to be loved or a human struggling to adapt to the harsh demands of a cruel world. These pictures of the psycho jibe neither with one another nor with anything we know of Bateman from the novel. The novel's refusal to answer our demand for psychological narrative not only frustrates but disturbs us. The American psycho has no psyche; in refusing to lend him one, Ellis also refuses to lend his readers a category through which to differentiate themselves from this killer.

Indeed, Bateman's psyche exists only as a compilation of materials, images, and acts borrowed from a culture all too familiar to Ellis's readers:

> I . . . [am] lost in my own private maze, thinking about other things: warrants, stock offerings, ESOPs, . . . GNPs, the IMF, hot executive gadgets, billionaires, Kenchichi Nakajima, infinity, Infinity, how fast a luxury car should go, bailouts, junk bonds, whether to cancel my subscription to *The Economist*, the

> Christmas Eve when I was fourteen and had raped one of our maids, Inclusivity, envying someone's life, whether someone could survive a fractured skull, waiting in airports, stifling a scream . . . a Rolls is a Rolls is a Rolls. (342)

Bateman's "personality" exists only as an assemblage of the properties of the world around him, a world stretched by the demands of capitalism to accommodate the objectification of subjects and the abstraction of objects. The exchange of concrete material is replaced not only by the invisible magic of money but by an economic language abstracted into numbers and abbreviations; meanwhile, abstractions of thought such as "infinity" are reduced to concrete objects, luxury cars marketed by advertisers. The psycho, like Marx's capitalist, thus emerges as a human aggregate of properties purchased rather than an individual bearing the mark of defining human characteristics. Marx observes:

> That which is for me through the medium of money—that for which I can pay (i.e., which money can buy)—that am I, the possessor of the money. The extent of the power of money is the extent of my power. Money's properties are my properties and essential powers—the properties and powers of its possessor. Thus, what I am and am capable of is by no means determined by my individuality. (167)

The only properties that belong to Bateman are those which he has purchased; the concept of individuality as defining and determining is undercut by the existence of the capitalist whose indeterminate potential to be anything or anyone is limited only by his supply of money.

Bateman's lack of subjectivity, which might appear to be a sign of weakness, thus emerges in Ellis's text as a mark of the psycho's empowerment. As Marx suggests, the capitalist's lack of personality does not suggest an inability to move toward desired self-definition; rather, it suggests the idea of a self unrestrained by individuality, invested with the capacity to manipulate the universe and unhindered by a sense of the boundaries that separate one subject or object from another:

> I am ugly, but I can buy for myself the most beautiful of women. Therefore I am not ugly, for the effect of ugliness—its deterrent power—is nullified by money. . . . I am stupid, but money is the real mind of all things and how then should its possessor be stupid? Besides, he can buy talented people for himself, and is he who has power over the talented not more talented than the talented? Do not I, who thanks to money am capable of all that the human heart longs for, possess all human capacities? (167)

As a character, the psycho purchases his good looks, not only by buying himself designer clothes, accessories, and a tan, but by lavishing money and attention on the beautiful women who accompany him to the trendiest restaurants, providing him not with sex but with the appearance of desirability;

Bateman refers to these women alternately as his girlfriends and as his "restaurant whores." The psycho constructs his image out of commodities that he attaches to his body and characteristics with which he surrounds himself; money is the glue that holds the properties he purchases together and allows the psycho to claim them as part of himself.

As a narrator, the psycho extends the capitalist's ability to appropriate any and all human capacities into forms of marked and unmarked narrative omniscience that leave the reader struggling to place him in the text. Bateman claims for himself the directed focus of the first-person narrator along with the omniscience of the third person. Indeed, the novel begins with page after page of description in which no mediation of vision or limitation of perspective is acknowledged: "The man passes under the fluorescent glare of a streetlamp with a troubled look on his face that momentarily curls his lips into a slight smile and he glances at Price almost as if they were acquainted but just as quickly realizes that he doesn't know Price and just as quickly Price realizes it's not Victor Powell and the man moves on" (7–8). It is only on page 8 of the text, with the sudden, jarring intrusion of the pronoun "I" into the narrative, that the reader is pushed to reevaluate as limited what had seemed to be the voice of an omniscient narrator; narrative rendering of the thoughts of the two characters described in this passage must now be read as Bateman's interpretation—rather than a mere transcription—of their thoughts.

As he appropriates the powers of the omniscient narrator only to intrude in first person, the psycho also appropriates his victims' suffering as an extension of his own subjective experience. There is no sense in this novel, as there is in the early part of "Tralala," that violence does not lead to suffering, that human bodies do not register pain. What appears to be an acknowledgment of the subjectivity of the victim, however, is actually an opportunity for the psycho to appropriate his victims—especially the female ones—in consciousness as well as body. The narrative of Ellis's novel seems to allow the victim to speak her subjectivity through the articulation of pain. In fact, however, that narrative appropriates the victim's voice as clearly as Bateman appropriates her body. Moments in the text that appear to offer a voice to resistance are moments in which the woman's subjectivity is most obscured, for in these moments the narrator not only strips the victim of the ability to voice her outrage but offers to the reader a resisting voice designated hers but really belonging to the violator.

In describing the details of torture, Bateman often ignores his own emotions and passions to focus instead on the experience of his victim. As he pauses in the midst of torture to smoke a cigar, he describes the response of one victim to his violation: "I light it with steady, bloodstained fingers, and her face, pale to the point of blueness, keeps contracting, twitching with pain, her eyes, dull with horror, close, then open halfway, her life reduced to nightmare" (247). The shift in narrative focus from violator to victim that seems to grant a momentary acknowledgment of female subjectivity in the midst of male empowerment is actually just the opposite; the psycho's imaginative rendering of his victim's pain forcibly asserts not her subjectivity but his power. Even as his representation seems to acknowledge the subjective presence of the victim, it renders her "pale" and "dull" in narrative as well as physical terms. The victim's life is indeed "reduced to nightmare," if not by violence then by a representation that acknowledges her presence only as an object in a fantasy of the psycho's creation.

In reading the moans, the twitches, and the tears of his victims, the narrator appropriates the women's agony as testimony of his omniscience: "I laugh when she dies, before she does she starts crying, then her eyes roll back in some kind of horrible dream state" (290). Such a representation reveals nothing about the victim and everything about the violator who wrestles away the woman's perspective to define himself as the creator of her nightmare, the maker of her horrible dream. In figuring his victims' pain, the psycho inverts normal conventions of representation whereby the spoken language or the body language of an individual expresses subjectivity: "Tiffany is tied up with six pairs of Paul's suspenders on the other side of the bed, moaning with fear, totally immobilized by the monster of reality" (304). Tiffany's consciousness is immobilized as effectively as her body by a representation that reads her moans as a sign of her weakness in the shadow of the psycho's strength. The narrator, in passing off his imaginative fantasies as truth, becomes the "monster of reality"; this oxymoronic phrase demonstrates the magical nature of this representational coaptation of the victim's body and points to Marx's statements about the ability of money to make the fantastical into truth: "money transforms the real essential powers of man and nature into what are merely abstract conceits and therefore imperfections—into tormenting chimeras—just as it transforms real imperfections and chimeras—essential powers which are really impotent, which exist only in the imagination of the individual—into real powers and faculties" (169). Through the magic of narrative, the subjectivity of the psycho's victim is transformed into a further manifestation of the psycho's own subjective experience.[2]

In the novel's representations, even the victim's pain ceases to belong to the victim and becomes part of the violator's text; value is established by a narrator who owns the means of representation in much the same way that the capitalist owns the means of production. In describing the power of the capitalist's tool, Marx claims that money "is the general confounding and compounding of all things—the world upside-down—the confounding and compounding of all natural and human qualities" (169). Like the capitalist who uses money to "confound" all things, to turn "the world upside-down," the narrator uses his power to resignify the victim's pain so that it expresses not subjectivity but its absence:

> Finally, in agony, after I've taken the coat off her face, she starts pleading, or at least trying to, the adrenaline momentarily overpowering the pain. "Patrick

oh god stop it please oh god stop hurting me. . . ." But, typically, the pain
returns—it's too intense not to—and she passes out again. . . . (246)

Even this brief moment in which one of Bateman's victims is allowed a voice
is framed by his mechanical depiction of her resistance as the battle between
adrenaline and pain, his denial of her subjectivity in the designation of her
pain as "typical."

A rare moment in which the psycho's veil of omniscience slips reveals the
way in which his subjectivity overwhelms the victim's in all the novel's
representations of pain: "She's barely gained consciousness and when she
sees me, standing over her, naked, I can imagine that my virtual absence of
humanity fills her with mind-bending horror" (327). The presence of the
psycho as visible subject in this sentence—"I can imagine"—exposes what is
a hidden presence in the representations above. Narrative becomes yet another tool in the psycho's economy of violence; like the capitalist's money,
the psycho's narration effects "the transformation of all human and natural
properties into their contraries" (167) as it denies the victim's subjectivity in
the very act of acknowledging it.

Narrative strategies for the manipulation of female subjectivity both echo
and exaggerate the psycho's physical manipulation of female form. The
connection between stifling the voice of female resistance and violating the
female body is clearly articulated in an incident that dramatizes in plot terms
Ellis's narrative technique:

> I lean in above her and shout, over her screams, "Try to scream, scream, keep
> screaming. . . ." I've opened all the windows and the door to my terrace and
> when I stand over her, the mouth opens and not even screams come out
> anymore, just horrible, guttural, animal-like noises, sometimes interrupted by
> retching sounds. "Scream, honey," I urge, "keep screaming." I lean down, even
> closer, brushing her hair back. "No one cares. No one will help you. . . ." She
> tries to cry out again but she's losing consciousness and she's capable of only
> a weak moan. I take advantage of her helpless state and, removing my gloves,
> force her mouth open and with the scissors cut out her tongue, which I pull
> easily from her mouth and hold in the palm of my hand, warm and still
> bleeding, seeming so much smaller than in her mouth, and I throw it against
> the wall, where it sticks for a moment, leaving a stain, before falling to the
> floor with a tiny wet slap. (246)

As Bateman tortures Bethany, he does not physically stifle her screams; in
fact, he orders her to express them. In doing so, he appropriates her pain as
further evidence of his own empowerment, "confounding and overturning"
the very sign of her resistance. In articulating her own pain, the victim now
expresses not her resistance to his violence but the impossibility of disobeying
his command. As in the instances of narrative manipulation above, the
psycho's invitation to his female victim to voice her pain is actually part of
a plot to control that pain and rewrite it in his own terms. As he does so, her

cries become weaker and weaker, mere moans that testify to the ease with which he has not only forced her under his command but cleverly appropriated her power to resist. Her tongue becomes an object that he, the subject, owns; as he cuts it out and holds it in his hands, her voice is reduced to material that the psycho—not only as character but as narrator—manipulates for pleasure.

Bateman's portrayal of himself as a spectator of his own actions reveals the ease with which he moves from the role of character to narrator to reader of his own text. He frequently describes his actions in the passive voice, or expresses his inability to remember his role in dismembering and distributing the various body parts littered around his apartment: " A head has been nailed to the wall. . . . One of the bodies . . . has been defecated on" (306). Often, the narrator articulates the reader's position as his own so that the violence he enacts assumes a cinematic quality. What is entertainment or art or fiction to us is also entertainment or art or fiction to the psycho, who watches his victim turn "in slow motion, like in a movie," and observes not "my gloved hands" but "the gloved hands" that close around the victim's neck (245). By claiming our position as his own, the psycho closes the distance between reader and violator, exposing the act of watching as an integral part of the act of violation.

At points the narrator uses this self-consciousness for what seems intended to be a kind of ghastly comic effect: "with a pair of scissors I start to cut off her dress and when I get up to her chest I occasionally stab at her breasts, accidentally (not really) slicing off one of her nipples through the bra" (246). Similarly, he joins us as a member of the audience to watch his own reactions to his violent acts:

> I can already tell that it's going to be a characteristically useless, senseless death, but then I'm used to the horror. . . . I'm not mourning, and to prove it to myself, . . . I use a chain saw and in a matter of seconds cut the girl in two with it. (329)

Bateman's need to "prove" his emotions to himself points to the split he establishes between viewing narrator and violating character, even in the midst of the first-person present-tense narration. This distanced portrayal of his own emotional experience is identical in kind to portrayals of the victims' emotional experience, suggesting an equivalence between the two that the narrator frequently elaborates upon. After a horrific procedure that leaves the victim's innards hanging out of her mouth and her whole body twitching, the narrator shifts to a new paragraph that begins: "The aftermath. No fear, no confusion. Unable to linger since there are things to be done today . . ." (305). By deliberately eliding the subject in these sentences, the narrator leaves the reader to supply the missing referent and to discover, after a few sentences, that "the aftermath" of violence refers not to its consequences for the victim but for the violator, not to her fear and confusion, but to his.

The ease with which the narrator slides from one subject-position to another—from violator to spectator and even to victim—blurs the lines between these positions and enlists the reader in a violent and confusing plot. The result of such narrative manipulation is the absence of Patrick Bateman as a coherent subject and the blurring of agency that leaves us, as readers, often uncertain about who acts and who is acted upon in the novel. The narrator thus manipulates the reader into a situation in which the possibility of resistance is undercut by the reader's inability both to define the subject of the narrative and to locate his or her relationship to that subject.

Even as Bateman seeks to control and coopt any threatening signs of opposing value systems, then, the reader desperately attempts to assert distinction and difference in value from the novel's narrator. Although the search for plot and character is frequently frustrated in postmodern literature, this novel's refusal to answer our demand for psychological narrative not only frustrates but disturbs us. Ultimately, the relentless force of a text that promises but never delivers, that posits as verity what we have no way of verifying or rejecting, pushes the reader into a narrative world with very few stable points of reference. Having claimed for himself every possible stereotyped identity, Bateman ultimately releases his hold on all subject-positions to fall into what seems an admission of his purely artificial subjectivity:

> . . . there is an idea of a Patrick Bateman, some kind of abstraction, but there is no real me, only an entity, something illusory, and though I can hide my cold gaze and you can shake my hand and feel flesh gripping yours and maybe you can even sense our lifestyles are comparable: *I simply am not there.* It is hard for me to make sense on any given level. Myself is fabricated, an aberration. I am a noncontingent human being. My personality is sketchy and unformed, my heartlessness goes deep and is persistent. (377)

For the reader pushing toward the conclusion of *American Psycho*, this passage emerges as a moment of revelation that finally reveals nothing. Bateman fails to make sense on any given level because the context in which he announces himself—both as a series of somethings and as nothing—offers the reader no verifiable point of reference by which to assess truth or falsehood. Even Bateman's confirmation of the reader's resistance to the illusory subject-positions he has adopted authorizes not the reader's right to resist but the reader's powerlessness to interpret knowledgeably. Bateman wants to claim that he is everything and that he is nothing, and he is not beyond claiming both at once. Even as he reveals that he has no self, that he is fabricated, the psycho's revelation is itself a fabrication; such manipulation ultimately redirects the frustrated reader's attention back to the psycho's narrative power to revel in his own protean variability and the reader's apparent powerlessness to resist that reveling.

The disgust that readers of *American Psycho* direct toward themselves as well as the text and its protagonist/narrator may be seen as a response to such manipulation. Shock and horror at being subjected continuously to the psycho's brutality and offered no apparent means of resistance may push the reader to grasp the one avenue of escape that seems to remain. That avenue is to accept the psycho's conclusion that the bodies we see are already dead, that the stripping of life, vitality, subjectivity, is so inevitable that in order to confront the psycho's violence we would do best to deny the victim's presence from the beginning. In the pattern established by the narrative, the cringing, whining bodies of the psycho's victims testify to their universal powerlessness, as their resistance becomes formulaic and—even before it begins—failed. Like Tralala, who desperately stomps on the body of the sailor because it reminds her of his vulnerability, we as readers do our best to escape from this psychotic text through the denial of the humanity of the psycho's victims.

The psycho's torture scenarios often enact a form of violation that exaggerates the abject status of reader and victim alike:

> . . . I hold her head up, blood dribbling from her mouth, and make her watch the rest of the tape and while she's looking at the girl on the screen bleed from almost every possible orifice, I'm hoping she realizes that this would have happened to her no matter what. That she would have ended up lying here, on the floor in my apartment, hands nailed to posts, cheese and broken glass pushed up into her cunt, her head cracked and bleeding purple, no matter what other choice she might have made; that if she had gone to Nell's or Indochine or Mars or Au Bar instead of M.K., if she had simply not taken the cab with me to the Upper West Side, that all this would have happened anyway. *I would have found her.* This is the way the earth works. (328)

Given what we have seen of Bateman's ability to control his victims' bodies and subjectivity, we must admit that in *American Psycho* he does control how the earth works. The psycho not only violates this nameless woman's body but here makes clear the agenda behind his violation: to deny her will, to obliterate her subjectivity. His goal is not only to torture and murder her but to make her see that torture and murder as inevitable, necessary, conclusion. Insofar as the novel terrorizes the reader, it is because it denies the reader's subjectivity in just such a way. The nameless girl being forced to watch a video—a representation—of torture serves as an embodiment of the reader who is forced to observe violation after violation. The very pattern of the narrative, its obsessive repetition, its refusal of variation, its relentless monotony of violence, denies not only the end of violence but the possibility that such violence could end. The reader finds him- or herself forced to negotiate a text that asserts narrative omnipotence and seems to deny the reader even the power of resistance. Ellis's narrator wields his power unchecked so that he acts on the reader in much the same way that the psycho acts on his victims; we as readers are produced by the very text that alienates us, seemingly denied the right not only to define but to resist the subject-position that the novel offers us.

American Psycho, then, is a forbidden book not because it invites us into forbidden territories but because, once there, it coopts our essential properties as readers, conspiring to appropriate even our right to resist. Like the psycho's victims, the reader must offer up his or her subjectivity to a monster who dons it as a mask that perpetuates his power as violator. The novel's lack of closure, characterization, and plot make it archetypally postmodern; its subject matter, however, strips away our theoretical interest in play even as it entraps us in a game not of our own making.

Deprived of the power to negotiate this work textually, angry readers have applied their resistance outside the novel's parameters in the attempt to block its publication and sale. Critics' exhortations not to buy the book, one publisher's decision not to market it, the attempts by various organizations to prevent the novel from being sold, all target resistance to the text in its status as commodity. The book is figured as something inherently infectious. Once picked up, it cannot be thrown away; once touched, it soils the reader, regardless of his or her individual characteristics. Underlying these attacks is the assumption that the reader, like Marx's capitalist or the American psycho, will be remade by the commodities he or she purchases. Having bought a way into Ellis's fictional world, the reader is caught up in a process of consumption both painful and slow; in taking in the novel, the reader appears less consumer than consumed.

Such a view of the text, even as it attends to the important issue of commodification, ignores the particular status of the literary text as commodity. As Raymond Williams points out in "Base and Superstructure in Marxist Cultural Theory," treating a work of art as an "object" ignores the way in which it is different from—and not only similar to—other commodities. In literature, Williams observes,

> what we permanently have are not objects but *notations*. These notations have then to be interpreted in an active way. . . . The relationship between the making of a work of art and its reception is always active, and subject to conventions. . . . [T]his is radically different from the production and consumption of an object. (421–22)

Ellis's ability to obscure the distinction between "object" and "notation" in his text is perhaps the most important aspect of the work's power. Readers' efforts to attempt to control the text of *American Psycho* through the book's commodity status point to the sense of powerlessness that the novel manages to instill in its readers; resistance is forced outside the text because the reader, like the reader/viewer that Black describes in *The Aesthetics of Murder*, is seemingly relegated to the status of passive observer. Ellis's narrative not only fails, in Chambers's terms, to "designate itself . . . as a site of discursive oppositionality," but actually seems to appropriate the reader's resistance as part of its textual power (43).

In interviews and public statements, Ellis attempts to authorize the work by simultaneously invoking and denying its literary status. He claims, on the one hand, that the work is a cultural analysis of '80s capitalism that uses violence *only as a metaphor*; the novel, therefore, is not *about* violence but about the dangers of the materialistic ethic which that violence signifies. When asked about the horrific descriptions of torture, rape, and mutilation contained within his literary work, however, Ellis is quick to respond that such representations are taken directly from the testimony of serial killers and from public records of their actions.[3] Within the context he offers for the work, then, its representations of violence are both purely literary and absolutely factual, both mere metaphor and bare fact. In Ellis's text, the psycho's identity exists simultaneously as pure material—as a combination of the objects and persons with which he surrounds himself—and as pure abstraction: "I simply am not there," the psycho says. "Myself is fabricated" (377). Ellis's contextualization of his work implicitly claims that it, too, is both a mere combination of cultural materials and an utter fabrication. Like the psycho, who claims that he is everything and that he is nothing, Ellis, too, is not beyond claiming opposing identities for his text.

The novel's critics, however, most often bring to the text a set of interpretive conventions situated in only one of the two frameworks between which Ellis negotiates. Those who place the text within the framework of capitalist greed read Ellis's representations of torture as purely sensationalistic; many imply that, having run out of ideas as a writer, Ellis uses the materials of violence to sell a text devoid of any literary status. Within such a context, the issue of *representation* is often underplayed and violence emerges as a stock ingredient added to a market commodity to increase its value. Others focus not on Ellis's materials but on his failure to transform them into the stuff of literature. Such a critical perspective underlies Norman Mailer's literary assessment of the novel. Given the assumption, Mailer claims, that works of fiction may legitimately address any human concern, we must approach Ellis's text not with horror at its choice of contents but with a critical eye to the way in which he transforms his novelistic materials into human insight. "Since we are going to have a monstrous book with a monstrous thesis," Mailer claims, "the author must rise to the occasion by having a murderer with enough inner life for us to comprehend him. . . . We cannot go out on such a trip unless we believe we will end up knowing more about . . . the real inner life of the murderer" (220). Ultimately, Mailer concludes that Ellis does not translate his materials into art; his failure of vision makes him less than successful as a literary fabricator.

Perhaps because it focuses either on Ellis's materials or on his transcendence of them, much of the criticism of *American Psycho* leaves important questions about the novel unanswered. Why, if Ellis taps into the materials of violence merely to sell his book, has his book created such an uproar when others that use similar sources pass unnoticed into the hands of the American public? Why, if Ellis's artistry is so limited, does one, in Mailer's own words, "read on addicted to a vice that offers no pleasure whatsoever"? Because they do not attribute literary complexity to the text, critics like Mailer bear the consequences of reading *Psycho* without recognizing the way in which it constructs its own terms of readership. The novel's inability to transcend its own materials, its seemingly endless repetition of details, its exhaustive description of commodities, seem to lend it, like the commodities it describes, "object" status; unlike an object, however, the novel depends for its very existence upon the imagination of its readers. The confusion, disgust, and felt complicity of many readers of *American Psycho* testify to the space between object and notation even as the novel blurs that distinction; our control over the act of interpretation seems to disappear beneath the force of a text that naturalizes itself as object even as it appropriates the participation of its readerly subjects.

Although the contents of *American Psycho* are extremely disturbing, even more disturbing is the narrative's ability to draw attention away from the representational process it enacts. In announcing itself both as material and as fiction, the narrative manages to obscure the space that lies between the two, a crucial space that we might designate *representation*. Ellis's narrative, despite his claims to the contrary, is neither pure violence nor pure art; by responding to it as one or the other, we ignore the process and the consequences of his translation of cultural material into artistic form. As readers, then, we need to recognize what is at stake in the process of representing and the act of reading violence. As we do so, we need not abdicate our access to particular texts; instead, we should reclaim our powers as readers from them.

The force of narrative is not material; it is incapable of knocking us down and stifling our resistance. Because reading is such an intimate experience, however, its form of violation is perhaps almost as frightening. Unless we assert our right to read representations of violation critically, skeptically, oppositionally, we become the victims of a narrative force that our own participation as readers helps to create. Oppositional reading, then, implies not just opposition to the actions occuring in a novel, to the characters that perpetrate them, or even to the narrator that describes them, but opposition to the very terms of readership implicit in the text. Only in locating and defining those terms can we become oppositional readers as well as readers of oppositional texts.

VI

"KNOWN IN THE BRAIN AND KNOWN IN THE FLESH"
GENDER, RACE, AND THE
VULNERABLE BODY IN *TRACKS*

Rape begins, like many other forms of violence, with the painful confrontation of two bodies; more importantly, however, its dynamics originate out of two opposing experiences of embodiment. For the male violator, embodiment emerges as a source of strength rather than vulnerability. Often imaged as solid, fixed, powerful, the body of the rapist is capable not only of asserting his presence but of appropriating, reshaping, and violating the female body so that it conforms to the dictates of his pleasures. The male body, then, functions as a tool that extends the power of subjectivity out into a larger universe that the violator can remake within the configurations of his own desire.

For the rape victim, on the other hand, embodiment is a source of vulnerability rather than power. Fixed within her body, the woman is unable to shield herself from the force of the violator as he pins her within the confines of a form over which he assumes control. Beneath the violator's hand, the rape victim's body becomes a text on which *his* will is inscribed, a form that bears the mark of his subjectivity even as she cannot divorce it from her own. Within such a scenario, the entanglement of subject and body allows the violator to assume control of both and the victim to assert power over neither. The image of bodily penetration is thus bound up with an assault on subjectivity in which the victim is annihilated from both inside and outside; the woman's body continues to allow the violator access to her subjectivity even as the power of agency is stripped away from her, imprisoning her in a material form over which she as subject has no control.

The dynamics of rape are further complicated when the victim of sexual violence is a woman of color for whom the experience of embodiment cannot be separated from the experience of oppression. In such a case, the rapist's physical appropriation of the female body as the object of his desire may exaggerate a sense of powerlessness that the victim experiences daily within a hegemonic culture that defines her body as the source of her Otherness.

The increased statistical vulnerability of women of color to the violence of rape is a daily and constant threat to personal autonomy that intensifies an already difficult struggle to claim the power of subjectivity. In the literature of African American, Hispanic, and Native American women, then, the dynamics of rape often become intertwined with the dynamics of oppression.

In *I Know Why the Caged Bird Sings*, Maya Angelou describes her own childhood experience of rape by observing, "The act of rape on an eight-year old body is a matter of the needle giving because the camel can't. The child gives, because the body can, and the mind of the violator cannot" (65). In such a case, the victim's body becomes the imprint on which the rapist's identity is forcibly inscribed, her own being the mark of his desperate claim to power. In raping, the violator not only assaults his victim but turns her presence into an absence that she may be unable to reclaim. The destructive power of such an assault is heightened when its victim already experiences her claim to her own body and subjectivity as tenuous. The twelve-year-old rape victim in Cherrie Moraga's *Giving Up the Ghost* describes the rapist's attempt to penetrate her young body as a literal and figurative process of transforming her into a hole: "there was no hole / he had to make it / 'n' I see myself down there like a face / with no opening / a face with no features. . . . HE MADE ME A HOLE!" (42–43). In Moraga's representation, the subjectivity of the young victim is effaced by a rapist who not only violates her physically but makes her *see herself* as a featureless absence, a hole. The apparent intimacy of physical closeness and the absolute denial of the victim's subjectivity converge to lend the rapist an awful power that the torturer/protagonist of Maria Irene Fornes's *The Conduct of Life* describes by saying, "It is a desire to destroy and to see things destroyed and to see the inside of them" (*Plays*, 82).

That assault from the inside defines not only the anatomy of the rape experience but the invisible operation of a hegemonic culture that constructs the woman of color, like the rape victim, as a featureless absence. In "Poem about My Rights," June Jordan links the experience of rape with the self-destructive act of internalizing the values of a dominant culture: "I am the wrong / sex the wrong age the wrong skin. . . . / I am the history of rape / I am the history of the rejection of who I am / I am the history of the terrorized incarceration of / my self . . ." (*Passion*, 86, 88). As an act in which physical and emotional violation converge, in which the external force of the violator is necessarily contained within the most intimate space of the victim, rape is an assault often imaged as self-destruction, an experience defined by the literal violation of the boundaries of anatomy *and* autonomy. Such an experience of fragmentation, as Jordan observes here, is also the fundamental experience of a woman attempting to claim an identity in a culture that defines her as the weakness against which to measure its own strength or the absence that serves only to mark its presence.

The attempt to unveil the oppressive mechanisms of a dominant culture that governs through sign and metaphor leads many women writers of color not merely to metaphorize rape but to trace the way in which its material dynamics are experienced, interpreted, or appropriated by both victim and violator. In this chapter, I will explore the vulnerable body as it emerges within the dynamics of rape and oppression in Louise Erdrich's *Tracks*. *Tracks* not only investigates the psychological effects of rape as an act that can "terrorize and incarcerate" women within their own bodies; it also explores the way in which that experience of vulnerable embodiment is exaggerated by the victim's internalization of essentialist assumptions about race and gender.

Although the rape that takes place early in Louise Erdrich's *Tracks* is perpetrated against Fleur Pillager, the "strong and daring" Native American heroine of the novel, the reader's access to that rape is mediated through the perspective of Pauline, the young mixed-blood Native American woman who both witnesses and narrates the crime.[1] The psychological consequences of Fleur's rape—either for the victim or the violators—are never fully addressed in the novel; Fleur's rapists die shortly after they attack her, while Fleur herself never articulates her pain or acknowledges that the rape took place. It is, then, only in Pauline's imagination that the act of violation remains present in the novel.[2] Its impact on *her* character surfaces not only in her recounting (or, according to other characters in the novel, fabrication) of the incident but in the images of sexual violation that permeate the psychological landscapes through which Pauline moves both as character and as narrator. Although critics of Erdrich's novel have largely ignored the rape, it is impossible to disentangle Pauline's understanding of race, gender, and power from her response to Fleur's violation.

The intersection of issues of race and gender complicates any discussion of the sexual violence represented within Erdrich's novel. In exploring the ideological function of criticism that takes gender as its starting point, recent feminist critics have pointed to the danger of using feminist theory to reinforce the values of a dominant race and class system.[3] Reading rape in the context of Erdrich's text makes visible dynamics that often operate invisibly in texts by white authors. The body, as *Tracks* reveals, is marked not only by sex but by race, and the dynamics of intimate violence may be written within narratives highlighting both. In the case of Erdrich's novel, however, critics have focused almost exclusively on the issue of race.[4] Because it is structured as a series of chapters narrated alternately by Nanapush and Pauline—the elder tribesman and the young mixed-blood woman aspiring to whiteness— Erdrich's novel is often read as a struggle between traditional Native American life and the dangerous lure of white acculturation. The tensions that emerge in *Tracks*, however, stem from differences of gender *and* race, as the prominent place of Fleur's rape early in the novel demonstrates. The challenge that Erdrich's novel poses to the critic is the challenge to avoid privileging one category of difference over another. In order to claim herself as subject, Pauline must negotiate her identities as both woman and mixed-blood Native American; the division of those identities can be effected only artificially, in intellectual rather than practical terms. My discussion of Erdrich's novel, insofar as it makes use of categories of race and gender, tends to separate in theory what cannot be divorced in practice, to isolate in the very act of articulating connection. My attempt, nonetheless, is to gesture toward the points of intersection that cannot properly be named by exploring in dialogic rather than dualistic terms the rape that constitutes one center of Erdrich's novel.

In the figure of Pauline, Erdrich offers us a character suffering from both racial and gender disempowerment. As a woman whose body is not marked by the conventions of femininity and a "half-breed" caught between her white and Native American backgrounds, Pauline is trapped in the margins of cultural definition. *Tracks* traces her attempt to reclaim a subjectivity that has been appropriated by others by turning against a body that she defines as the source of her Otherness. Pauline images her own vulnerability—as a woman and a Native American—with a vocabulary of violation that grows out of her experience of listening, against her will, as Fleur is raped. A discussion of the dynamics of rape in the novel begins to unveil the way in which Pauline's understanding of herself as subject is caught up in essentialist notions of the body that lead, ultimately, to her literal and figurative self-destruction.

The issue of how Pauline's body is read by others surfaces immediately in the novel as she travels to Argus to live with her aunt and work in the butcher shop there. Because the men who surround her in the shop fail to read the conventional signs of "femaleness" on her skinny teenaged form, Pauline's body seems to disappear before their gaze:

> I was fifteen, alone, and so poor-looking I was invisible to most customers and to the men in the shop. Until they needed me, I blended into the stained brown walls, a skinny big-nosed girl with staring eyes. . . . Because I could fade into a corner or squeeze beneath a shelf I knew everything: how much cash there was in the till, what the men joked about when no one was around, and what they did to Fleur. (15–16)

Gendered neither male nor female, Pauline's body ceases to exist in the men's world; unmarked by the signs of gender difference, it "blends" and "fades" into a landscape controlled and interpreted by men. Her subjectivity also remains unacknowledged as, caught in the space between the cultural labels of male and female, Pauline becomes "no one." In a patriarchal society, as Mary Ann Doane observes, "to desexualize the female body is ultimately to deny its very existence" (79). Seemingly bodiless, Pauline does not interact with the men around her but becomes instead the observer, the witness, the watcher.

In racial as well as gender terms, Pauline's subjectivity is consistently denied. She responds to the powerlessness of her position as a Native American in a white world not by questioning the values of the dominant culture but by internalizing those values to see herself through the mediation of the white gaze. "I wanted to be like my mother, who showed her half-white . . . ," she remarks early in the novel. "I saw through the eyes of the world outside us. I would not speak our language" (14). As the words of Pauline's disavowal reveal, her claim to white identity is effected only at the cost of self-alienation. The split implied in separating her white being from her Native American self is revealed as she simultaneously claims and disavows her native language: "I would not speak *our* language." Similarly, her decision to appropriate "the eyes of the world outside *us*" implies the internalization of a vision that necessarily redefines *us* as *Other*. In Pauline's case, to see herself through the eyes of the world, to define herself through the images of a dominant culture, is a form of self-violation that perpetuates the white culture's negation and destruction of the Native American Other. Her own assumptions of a fundamental Otherness bind her to a destructive vision of herself as not-white that parallels and exaggerates the powerlessness of her presence beneath a male gaze that defines her as "no one."

Fleur's rape unsettles the dominance of a patriarchal, white gaze in the text by challenging the notion of Pauline's bodily invisibility and exposing the dynamics of self-violation that underlie her disavowal of the racial self. Until the point at which Fleur is raped, Pauline's occupation of the space between female and male, Native American and white, seems to lend her a perverse kind of power; the looker but never the seen, her gaze does not seem to originate out of a body that circumscribes perspective. Unattached to any single form or subject position, Pauline seems to possess a kind of liberating fluidity emphasized by descriptions of her body. The novel's early representations emphasize the insubstantiality of Pauline's "skinny" form; as she describes herself as a "moving shadow" (22), only her "staring eyes" locate her in the novel's early scenes (16).

Not surprisingly, then, Pauline's response to Fleur's rape is to close her eyes to the act she witnesses, almost as if the loss of vision will bring about the complete erasure of a body already imaged as invisible. As the men whom Fleur has humiliated at cards corner her inside the smokehouse and rape her in punishment, Pauline is paralyzed by the recognition of a vulnerability she shares with Fleur, and responds by attempting to escape from her own body:

> The men saw, yelled, and chased [Fleur] at a dead run to the smokehouse. . . . That is when I should have gone to Fleur, saved her, thrown myself on Dutch the way Russell did. . . . He stuck to his stepfather's leg as if he'd been flung there. Dutch dragged him for a few steps, his leg a branch, then cuffed Russell off and left him shouting and bawling in the sticky weeds. I closed my eyes and put my hands on my ears, so there is nothing more to describe but what I couldn't block out: those yells from Russell, Fleur's hoarse breath, so loud it filled me, her cry in the old language and our names repeated over and over among the words. (26)

Despite Pauline's decision not to speak the language in which Fleur cries out, Fleur's articulation of pain remains intelligible to her; Pauline's disavowal of her Native American identity cannot undo her connection to the "old language." Similarly, Pauline's attempt to move outside the body that not only makes her vulnerable to rape but links her in sensory terms to Fleur's painful experience proves ineffectual as well. Pauline's futile efforts to block out awareness of Fleur's violation only call attention to her physical presence as witness; as Fleur's body disappears from this representation of rape, the image of Pauline closing her eyes and putting her hands over her ears directs the reader's focus toward the very body that Pauline would erase.

The reader's attempt to access the details of Fleur's rape, then, is frustrated not only by the mediating force of Pauline's narration but by its emphasis on *Pauline's* experience of her body during the rape rather than Fleur's. When the reader finally "witnesses" Fleur's violation many pages later, the materiality of violence is once again obscured as Pauline recalls not the rape itself but her dreams about it. Erdrich's interpolation of such dreams into the plot of her novel in part reflects her appropriation of Native American traditions based on a mythic or symbolic epistemology.[5] As a character caught between Native American and white religions, experiences, and conventions, Pauline authors a narrative that foregrounds questions of interpretation as it moves between "imaginary" and "real" events; that narrative, as Catherine Rainwater argues, "vexes the reader's effort to decide upon an unambiguous, epistemologically consistent interpretive framework" (407). Although Rainwater does not address Pauline's narrative of the rape, it most clearly exposes the implications of the reader's suspension between opposing interpretive frameworks:

> I relived the whole thing over and over, that moment so clear before the storm. Every night when my arms lowered the beam, it was my will that bore the weight, let it drop into place—not Russell's and not Fleur's. For that reason, at the Judgment, it would be my soul sacrificed, my poor body turned on the devil's wheel. And yet, despite that future, I was condemned to suffer in this life also. Every night I was witness when the men slapped Fleur's mouth, beat her, entered and rode her. I felt all. My shrieks poured from her mouth and my blood from her wounds. (66)

Despite Pauline's apparent revelation of the details of the rape—"the men slapped Fleur's mouth, beat her, entered and rode her"—the reader remains dislocated in a scene of violence that offers him or her few points of material reference. The origin of these images in Pauline's dreams exaggerates the already blurred line between the experiential and the imagined, just as Pauline's rendering effaces the boundaries between her body and Fleur's. The reader's attempt to assign cause and effect or to place the location of victim, violator, or observer is frustrated by Pauline's confusion of material and immaterial categories. Despite Pauline's physical distance from the rape, for example, she renders its impact on her in material terms as she describes her shrieks and her blood pouring from Fleur's body. Although Pauline covers her "staring eyes" during the rape, she cannot escape from the scene in either body or mind, and her obsessive reenactments of the crime force her into the position of a voyeur who witnesses the violation of a body that dissolves into her own form.

The reader's attempt to access the materiality of violence in this representation is thus frustrated by a narrative that moves the reader away from the empirical dynamics of violation into a semiotic universe in which it is impossible to disentangle mind from body, imagination from materiality. As these categories become blurred within the text, the narrative propels the reader away from the immediacy of the rape which it represents and discourages the reader from connecting Fleur's violation to the empirical dynamics of rape. As I have argued in my introduction, the act of reading a representation of violation is defined by the reader's suspension between the semiotic and the real, between a representation and the material dynamics of violence which it evokes, reflects, or transforms. "Semiotics," as Teresa de Lauretis observes, "specifies the mutual overdetermination of meaning, perception, and experience, a complex nexus of reciprocally constitutive effects between the subject and social reality, which, in the subject, entail a continual modification of consciousness; that consciousness in turn being the condition of social change" (*Alice Doesn't*, 184). Representations of violence locate the readerly subject at the "nexus of reciprocally constitutive effects" that may ultimately result in a transformation of attitudes about empirical as well as textual reality. Because the language of fiction is by definition never simply referential, however, fictional representations of violence that disorient the reader by manipulating experiential conventions may obscure any connection to empirical violence.

Such readerly disorientation may account for the glaring absence of a discussion of Fleur's rape in the criticism of Erdrich's novel. Even the most current analysis of *Tracks*, which focuses on gender issues as they affect the construction of Pauline's subjectivity, lacks a single reference to the incident of sexual violence with which Pauline's narrative begins.[6] Such an omission can be explained only by exploring the way in which both Pauline and the reader of *Tracks* interpret the presence of the vulnerable body. As Pauline conflates the materiality of her body with the hegemonic culture's semiotic construction of it, the reader engages with a series of representations that obscure the materiality of the body in favor of its semiotic construction. Both Pauline and the reader, then, negotiate between empirical and semiotic realities; as Pauline reduces the semiotic to its material counterpart, the reader is pushed toward enacting the opposite process.

As Pauline's narrative dissolves the representational boundaries between body and mind, it magnifies the immaterial dynamics of the reading process to heighten the reader's experience of the text and the violence represented within it as imaginative constructs. The reader, whose access to the materiality of violence is always problematized by the operation of representation, encounters an absence of referentiality even at the level of plot. Even as Pauline struggles to deal with an act of violence that remains urgently present in her mind, the events of the rape are continually displaced for the reader by Pauline's reflections about them. In her initial description of Russell's attempt to lock the rapists into the meat lockers, for example, Pauline states, "He strained and shoved. . . . Sometimes, thinking back, I see my arms lift, my hands grasp, see myself dropping the beam into the metal grip. At other times, that moment is erased" (27). Even this simple bodily act becomes an issue of interpretation as the reader comes to access Pauline's experience only through the mediating force of an imagination capable of creating and erasing realities.

Pauline's vexed relationship with her body thus intrudes upon the reader's experience of the text through the force of a narrative that represents without transition empirical and imaginary events. In Pauline's dream recollection of the rape quoted above, Russell is able to respond to the horror of the rape physically while Pauline "bears the weight" of the beam on the freezer door imaginatively; it is her "will" that drops the latch and not her body. The confusion of mind/body categories evident in Pauline's narrative thus operates not only to deny the reader material reference but to mark Pauline's double vulnerability; Pauline experiences not only the pain of a rape that she resists imaginatively but the guilt of complicity in a crime in which she appears not to intervene physically. As the boundary between body and imagination dissolves, Pauline suffers the consequences of a seeming disembodiment that implicates her as passive witness to Fleur's suffering but does not protect her from imaginative vulnerability to Fleur's pain.

After the rape, Pauline's reflections on the gaze reveal her attempt to renegotiate the position of powerlessness into which the rape forces her. If her own body enforces her reluctant perception of Fleur's violation yet offers no physical medium through which to resist the rape, Pauline envisions an alternative body that resists rather than invites vulnerability:

> Power travels in the bloodlines, handed out before birth. It comes down through the hands, which in the Pillagers are strong and knotted, big, spidery and rough, with sensitive fingertips good at dealing cards. It comes through the eyes, too, belligerent, darkest brown, the eyes of those in the bear clan, impolite as they gaze directly at a person.
>
> In my dreams, I look straight back at Fleur, at the men. I am no longer the watcher on the dark sill, the skinny girl. (31)

Pauline's focus on the physical texture of these powerful hands, which are "strong and knotted, big, spidery and rough, with sensitive fingertips," renders the body that she ascribes collectively to the Pillager family surprisingly tactile and immediate in contrast to the vague abstraction of Pauline's individual form. As the "watcher" whose skinny body blends into darkness and the mixed-blood Native American who sees herself only as not-white, Pauline lacks the substantiality of the Pillagers. Even her gaze is seemingly sourceless, its trajectory indirect; originating out of no concrete form, it is capable of "looking straight back" at the other only in Pauline's dreams. Unlike Pauline, who sees "through the eyes of the world outside us," the Pillagers possess a "direct" and unmediated gaze imaged in part by the physical presence of eyes that assert their owners' embodiment *and* subjectivity. Both "darkest brown" and "belligerent," these eyes provide an anchor for the penetrating gaze that issues from them; their claim to materiality is also a claim to subjectivity that Pauline implicitly contrasts with her own inability to affirm her presence in either category.

The interpenetration of body and subject in Pauline's imaging of the gaze reflects in part her own struggle with the notion of biological determinism and racial identity. The power implicit in the Pillager form travels, in Pauline's analysis, "in the bloodlines, handed out before birth"; the body, in such a view, carries the mark of identity and determines not only the physical configuration of an individual but the power and variety of subject positions available to him or her. If their pure "bloodlines" lend power and solidity to the Pillager gaze, Pauline's own family status as a mixed-blood Native American seems to deny her access to that power, as her description of the Puyats reveals:

> During the time I stayed with them, I hardly saw Dutch or Regina look each other in the eye or talk. Perhaps it was because . . . the Puyats were known as a quiet family with little to say. We were mixed-bloods, skinners in the clan for which the name was lost. (14)

Located biologically in the space between Native American and white, defined by the mixing of two racial bloodlines, the Puyats lack a stable base from which to affirm their presence. The quiet demeanor of Pauline's relatives and their inability to "look each other in the eye" contrasts sharply with the strong hands and belligerent gazes of the Pillagers. The fear of Pauline's father that she will change if sent to the white town—"'You'll fade out there,' he said, reminding me that I was lighter than my sisters. 'You won't be an Indian once you return.'" (14)—is imaged in bodily terms, as the white world's assault on an Indian identity marked so weakly on Pauline's body that she is in danger of dissolving into the whiteness that her father defines as nothingness.

In racial as well as gender terms, then, Pauline's body threatens to fade into invisibility. Because the novel constructs Pauline's marginality within a framework that is self-consciously racial, criticism has tended to focus exclusively on her role as a half-breed whose perspective has been coopted by the dominant white culture. As Trinh T. Minh-ha theorizes, however, any such isolationist reading can be said to reinscribe the very Euro-American dynamics that critics of *Tracks* attempt to unveil. Minh-ha states, "The idea of two illusorily separated identities, one ethnic, the other woman (or more precisely female), again, partakes in the Euro-American system of dualistic reasoning and its age-old divide-and-conquer tactics" (104). Only by restoring the link between Pauline's racial and gender identities is it possible to explore the full implications of the rape scene with which Pauline's narrative begins and to which it continually alludes.

Within the deterministic frame that Pauline posits, Fleur's status as a Pillager dictates that her hands be marked by strength and her gaze defined by its penetrating stare. As the rape makes clear, however, Fleur's body is not merely a racial text, the strength of her Native American name not the only signifier of her power or powerlessness. Fleur's cultural heritage is imaged throughout the novel as a source of a mystical strength; more than once, she survives her own drowning, manipulates the lives and deaths of others, and moves into and out of different physical forms. Fleur's inability to escape the female form that makes her vulnerable to rape is thus all the more shocking. Within the context of sexual violence, Fleur's strength is overwhelmed by males and her body transformed from the source of the penetrating gaze to the object of penetration. Although Pauline frames the rape with references to Fleur's mystical powers, culminating in the tornado that eventually results in the death of the rapists, the experience to which Pauline returns again and again is the moment of violation itself, a moment in which Fleur is defined not by racial empowerment but by gender powerlessness.

Both in imaging Fleur's rape and in reenacting it in different forms, Pauline attempts to come to terms with her own vulnerability to violation. Like her attempt to respond to racial otherness by denying her Native American identity, however, Pauline's effort to escape the vulnerability she experiences as a woman by destroying the body that is the most visible manifestation of that vulnerability only succeeds in reinscribing the dynamics of violation that she fears. Although the novel begins with Pauline's rejection of the Native American self that she defines as Other, the rape propels her to view the marks of her gender as signs of her powerlessness as well; after Fleur's violation, the gaze that she comes to adopt as she sees "through the eyes of the world outside us" is not only white but male. Pauline's attempt to appropriate the vision of the empowered only results in the continued reinscription of her identity as Other; her borrowed eyes are anchored in a body that intrudes again and again to reinforce her vision of her own insignificance: "Clarence was the one I should have tried for, I saw that, but I also saw what he saw—the pole-thin young woman others did, the hair pulled back and woven into a single braid, the small and staring eyes that did not blink . . ." (74). Pauline's representation of her body reinscribes its object status even as she attributes the process of objectification to the male gaze: "I also saw what he saw." Having internalized the gaze of the oppressor, Pauline images her own eyes as static; her wooden, motionless look defines her not as subject but as object. Even as she attempts to appropriate the power of the gaze, Pauline becomes overpowered by it; as long as she defines herself according to what she is not—white, Pillager, male— Pauline remains uncomfortable in her own body.

That discomfort is revealed again as Pauline images the power of men in the same way she imaged the power of the Pillagers: in the strength and solidity of their hands. Describing her failed encounter with a potential lover, Pauline claims, "I hadn't liked the weight of Napoleon's hands, their hardened palms. I hadn't liked seeing myself naked, plucked and skinned" (74). This passage renders the female form both transparent and malleable; assigning weight and solidity to the male body, Pauline contrasts Napoleon's "hardened palms" with her own vulnerable nakedness. Although Pauline consents to the sexual interchange that she describes here, she images the physical act that is not rape as a form of psychic violation. In "forcing" her to see herself "naked, plucked and skinned," Napoleon metaphorically strips away the layer of protection that would allow Pauline to claim autonomy as both body and subject. Ironically, of course, it is Pauline who is the subject of her own violation as she reduces herself to the object of a gaze that originates in her consciousness rather than in Napoleon's eyes.

Pauline's horror at being "skinned" beneath the force of Napoleon's gaze reflects her notion of the body as a kind of container which houses the subject within; the skin, then, becomes the boundary between body and subject, the protective layer that is the final physical barrier to a self vulnerable to intimate violence. "Naked, plucked and skinned," the female form becomes a permeable structure invaded by a masculine body that Pauline images as hard, substantial, anchored: "With my clothes gone, I saw all the bones pushing at my flesh. I tried to shut my eyes, but couldn't keep them closed, feeling that if I did not hold his gaze he could look at me any way he wanted" (73). Pauline's fear of violation is not merely a fear of physical assault; it is a fear that her body itself will dissolve, her skin melt away, to unveil to the masculine eye the very bones that support her frame. The male gaze, it seems, contains the power not only to see those bones but, in isolating them, to reconstruct them into a form of its own making. Lacking a sense of herself as stable subject, Pauline collapses into a body that serves not as the shield she desires but as a passageway into the self. The subject "contained" by those bones, it becomes clear, exists only incidentally as it is created by others. In looking at her "any way he wanted," Napoleon possesses the power to make her anything he wants, and although she seems determined to hold his gaze to keep him from doing so, Pauline's internalization of his perspective guarantees that she will continue to construct herself as an absence in the shadow of his presence.

Pauline's response to such vulnerability is to disavow the physical form through which others gain access to her as subject. "Plucked and skinned" beneath the male gaze, Pauline can assert her identity as desiring subject rather than victim only by abandoning her body. She succeeds in enacting her desire for her cousin Eli only by attaching herself to another body in the text, a body that she images as opaque and invulnerable:

> With the dim light cloaking us together, I could almost feel what it was like to be inside Sophie's form, not hunched in mine, not blending into the walls, but careless and fledgling, throwing the starved glances of men off like the surface of a pond, reflecting sky so you could never see the shallow bottom. (78)

"Hunched" in her own form, Pauline sees her body as a kind of prison; its boundaries constrict her even as they remain permeable to others. Pauline's extreme self-consciousness pushes her to attribute to the male gaze the power of penetrating her flesh to the bones. The "careless and fledgling" Sophie, on the other hand, deflects that gaze; Pauline images Sophie's body as a barrier that refuses penetration by "throwing off" the male look.

"Cloaked together" with Sophie, Pauline gains imaginative access to a form that she associates with strength rather than vulnerability. In the scenes that follow, Pauline appears to gain pleasure without exposure; she does so by thrusting Sophie's body between Eli's and her own so that her own form becomes invisible: "Eli stared after her [Sophie] and saw through me, still as the iron wedge I sat on, dark in a cool place. He could not see into the shadow" (81). Using Sophie's body to deflect attention away from her own, Pauline seems to achieve the kind of invisibility that she associates with invulnerability after Fleur's rape. In the scenes that follow, Sophie and Eli come together in a passionate encounter that Pauline claims to have orchestrated herself.

As the encounter proceeds, however, the dynamics of rape from which Pauline attempts to escape reassert themselves:

> And then, as I crouched in the cove of leaves, I turned my thoughts on the girl and entered her and made her do what she could never dream of herself. I stood her in the broken straws and she stepped over Eli, one leg on either side of his chest. Standing there, she slowly hiked her skirt. . . . She shivered and I dug my fingers through the tough claws of sumac, through the wood-sod, clutched bark, shrank backward into her pleasure. . . . He lifted her and brought her to the water. She stood rooted, dazed, not alert enough to strip off her dress. . . . She waited in shallow mud, then waded in, obedient. . . . He ran his mouth over her face, bit her shoulder through the cloth, held her head back by the pale brown strands and licked her throat. He pulled her hips against him, her skirt floating like a flower. Sophie shuddered, her eyes rolled to the whites. . . . (83–84)

Although Sophie participates in this encounter physically as she straddles Eli, hikes her skirt, and wades into the water, the absence of any sense of will or volition on her part exaggerates Eli's violent manipulations of her pliable body; as he bites her shoulder, holds her head back by the hair and pulls her hips against him, Sophie not only fails to "throw off" his glance but loses the power of her own vision; "her eyes rolled to the whites," Sophie's presence in the scene is reduced to that of a mechanical puppet or a frightened animal.

Although it is Eli who physically manipulates Sophie's body, Pauline casts herself as the orchestrator of this scene of violation. Physically distanced from the scene, Pauline emerges not only as its observer but as its author; in her representation of the event she, rather than Sophie, remains the subject of an encounter that Sophie "could never dream of herself." The powerlessness that Pauline experiences during Fleur's rape results in her attempt to sever the subject/body connection that makes her vulnerable to male manipulation. As her mind is "cloaked together" with Sophie's body in this scene, however, the result is not an escape from the dynamics of rape but a reinscription of them. Detached from her own body, Pauline uses her imagination to violate Sophie—"I turned my thoughts on the girl and entered her." Having "entered" Sophie, "stood" her on the straw, and made her behave in ways she cannot understand, Pauline strips Sophie of her presence and reduces the body that she appropriated for its strength to the form of a lifeless puppet: "They [Sophie and Eli] were not allowed to stop. . . . I was pitiless. They were mechanical things, toys, dolls wound past their limits" (84). By robbing Sophie of her subjectivity and making her assume the postures of another's will, Pauline serves as the orchestrator of yet another rape. As long as she is unable to imagine sexual intercourse without violation, Pauline can achieve pleasure only by placing someone else in the position of experiencing pain. By the conclusion of this scene, Sophie's "careless and fledgling" form becomes weakened and physically vulnerable, her body the object of Pauline's physical as well as imaginative manipulation: "she [Sophie] sank to her knees in the sour mud, hung her mouth open and went limp so I had to drag her" (84).

In the attempt to escape from the vulnerability of her own body, Pauline not only recreates the dynamics of rape and reduces Sophie to the role of powerless victim but offers herself no lasting access to invulnerability. As long as she remains attached imaginatively to Sophie's body, Pauline cannot sever her connection to Sophie's pain. After Sophie returns home, Pauline relates, "I heard [Bernadette] laying into Sophie with a strap, and I felt it, too, the way I'd absorbed the pleasure at the slough, the way I felt everything that happened to Fleur" (86). Ultimately, the kind of detachment that Pauline longs for escapes her; her attempt to liberate herself from her own body by attaching herself to another form fails. As Sophie and Eli come together before her eyes, the woman who envisioned herself as "hunched" in her body remains "crouched in the cove of leaves," the cramped posture of her body asserting its uncomfortable material presence even in the midst of a scene over which Pauline claims imaginative control.

For the reader, then, Pauline's body emerges as the one stable presence in a scene that propels the reader toward what Catherine Rainwater describes in another context as "an hermeneutical impasse" (410). Because the reader's access to the bodies of Eli and Sophie is only through the path of Pauline's mind, it is impossible to disentangle the material dynamics of their encounter from her imaginative rendering of it; the reader is suspended between a natural and supernatural interpretation of the scene. If, as Pauline claims, she has a mystical control over Sophie's mind, then an imaginative form of rape occurs: "I turned my thoughts on the girl and entered her." If Pauline simply projects her obsessions on two lovers, as the text sometimes seems to suggest, issues of violence and consent associated with any sexual encounter between an adult and a minor still haunt the scene and are unearthed by Pauline's portrayal. The reader of Fleur's rape cannot know if an act of violence occurred; the reader of Sophie and Eli's encounter cannot know whether the act that occurred was violence. As in the portrayal of Fleur's rape, interpretive issues so encircle this portrayal that the process of representation becomes foregrounded and the material dynamics of violation obscured.

Pauline's attempt to escape the dynamics of violation underlies not only her sexual manipulation of Sophie and Eli but her decision to reject her cultural heritage and embrace the tenets of Catholicism. In responding to a statue of the Virgin Mary, Pauline recontextualizes Christian myth by situating Mary's experience within the paradigms of sexual violation rather than religious epiphany:

> Perhaps, I thought, at first, the Virgin shed tears . . . because She herself had never . . . been touched, never known the shackling heat of flesh. Then later, after Napoleon and I met again and again, after I came to him in ignorance, after I could not resist more than a night without his body, which was hard, pitiless, but so warm slipping out of me that tears always formed in my eyes, I knew that the opposite was true.
>
> The sympathy of Her knowledge had caused Her response. In God's spiritual embrace She experienced a loss more ruthless than we can imagine. She wept, pinned full-weight to the earth, known in the brain and known in the flesh and planted like dirt. She did not want Him, or was thoughtless like Sophie, and young, frightened at the touch of His great hand upon Her mind. (95)

Pauline's appropriation of the vocabulary of sexual violation rather than religious symbolism highlights Mary's experience as "the Virgin" and rewrites "God's spiritual embrace" as a form of rape. Tracing the loss the Virgin experiences at the hand of God to the connection between body and subject, Pauline reveals the extent to which the physical violation of rape is inextricably tied to the violator's assault on female subjectivity. The blurring of material and psychological categories in Pauline's description of the Virgin's rape reveals the double empowerment of the male violator and the consequently heightened vulnerability of his female victim. Like Napoleon, God seems to possess a physical solidity that marks his body as an extension of his power; imaged here in material as well as spiritual terms, God enacts his wishes by touching his frightened victim with "His great hand."

The strength of materiality that the male violator displays here, however, is not attended by the consequent limitations of spatial and physical boundaries. "[F]rightened at the touch of His great hand upon Her mind," the young Virgin is the victim of an assault that seems to acknowledge no proper division of surface or category. The male God is capable of penetrating the Virgin Mary's mind as well as her body; it is the double-edged aspect of this rape that makes the loss she experiences "more ruthless" than can be imagined. In an inversion of the violator's position, the victim is bound by the limitations of a materiality which controls her but over which she has no control: "She wept, pinned full-weight to the earth, known in the brain and known in the flesh and planted like dirt." Never directly imaged, the Virgin's body exists only as a negative presence that restricts, defines, and fixes her. "Pinned" and "planted" to her physical form, she is attached to a body over which she is denied autonomy. Her "flesh" becomes an extended surface through which the violator can access her vulnerable subjectivity, but not a means of extending her own will into space.

Napoleon's ability to penetrate Pauline's skin with his gaze, to dissolve what she images as the boundary between body and subject, is reenacted here as the Virgin Mary is "known in the brain and known in the flesh." In playing on the biblical connotations of the verb "to know," this passage forges a connection between the rapist's assault on the body and the corresponding assault on subjectivity figured here as knowledge of the victim's brain. Both forms of intimacy involve a penetration of boundaries that the subject uses to define herself, a cooptation of being that dissolves the autonomous self as it erases the physical space between violator and victim. As the physiological penetration of the victim's body allows the violator literally to come inside her, rape is experienced as a form of self-destruction marked by the subject's seeming complicity in her own violation.

Pauline's response to her own body during and after Fleur's rape can best be understood as a response to the dynamics of rape revealed through her representation of the Virgin Mary. Pauline's attempt to make her body invisible during the rape results from her panicked recognition of its visibility and her resulting vulnerability. Describing herself as "hunched" in her form, Pauline reveals imagistically the tension she experiences between her body and the subject "contained" within it; the parameters of her body seem not only to constrain the presentation of herself as subject but to fix her in a hostile space and prevent her from dissolving into nonbeing. It is through her body that Pauline, like the Virgin, is "pinned full-weight to the earth," reduced to an object that can be seen and known not only in the flesh but in the brain. Her wariness of her own body, then, results in part from the fact that it exists as a text that she never authors but through which others are free to read into her subjectivity as well as her materiality.[7]

As the novel continues, Pauline devises other strategies to escape her vulnerability, each of which results in an equally destructive conclusion. In her desire to avoid being defined, fixed, either as woman or as Native American, Pauline attempts to disavow the body which bears traces that others can use to construct her identity. Rather than asserting authorship of a body that has been misread and manipulated, Pauline attempts to liberate herself by destroying the physical form that others view as text. Such a desperate claim to empowerment, however, perpetuates the very dynamics that it seeks to overturn; having internalized a hegemonic system of interpretation, Pauline engages in numerous acts of self-violation that merely reinforce the dominant culture's reading of a body over which she is unable to claim the power of signification.

Because it is not merely physical but emotional assault that she fears, not merely the violation of the body but a corresponding violation of the mind, Pauline attempts to preserve some semblance of autonomy by defining herself as the agent of her own assault. Unsuccessful in her attempt to sever the connection between herself as subject and her physical form, she attempts instead to define and control that connection. By willing the destruction of a body she is incapable of rendering invulnerable to violation, she attempts to use that body to reassert the power of a subjectivity equally threatened. In doing so, Pauline turns to the Christian ideology of self-sacrifice as rationale for embracing the role of self-violator:

> At the convent my hands cracked. The knuckles were tight and scabbed. . . . At night, I did not allow myself to toss or turn for comfort, but only to sleep on my back, arms crossed on my breasts in the same position as the Virgin received the attentions of our Lord. . . . I put burrs in the armpits of my dress and screwgrass in my stockings and nettles in my neckband. . . . I let my toenails grow until it ached to walk. . . . (151–52)

By willingly embracing her status as victim of physical pain, Pauline attempts to reduce violation to its material origin and preempt any corresponding assault on her subjectivity. Having figured the Virgin Mary's impregnation as a type of rape, Pauline casts herself in the Virgin's role not mentally but physically; her literalist attempt to recreate the physical configurations of the assault—she sleeps on her back with arms crossed on her breasts "in the same position as the Virgin"—functions as a means of deflecting the real horror of a violation the physical consequences of which are but one small component. Pauline's efforts to manipulate, mark, and assault her body represent a negative form of empowerment through which she attempts to preempt the force of a violation she sees as inevitable.

Whereas the Christian mode of sacrifice that Pauline appropriates as her model is aimed at destroying individual subjectivity to effect a greater union with God, Pauline's self-destructive actions function as an attempt to reclaim the power of her own subjectivity from the domination of others. In choosing to suffer at her own hand, Pauline removes her body from beneath the hands of the violator, be he man or God. Embracing a physical pain that she sees as in some sense inevitable, Pauline uses suffering to affirm her presence and reconstitute herself as subject:

> That night in the convent bed, I knew God had no foothold or sway in this land, or no mercy for the just, or that perhaps, for all my suffering and faith, I was still insignificant. Which seemed impossible.
> I knew there never was a martyr like me.
> I was hollow unless pain filled me, empty but for pain. . . . (192)

In the context of Pauline's earlier fear that the male gaze would strip away her skin to reveal the hollowness within, her body continually threatened to open up into a revelation of absence. Here, she reveals the strategy by which she has seemingly reclaimed that body as a tool to affirm her presence. Pauline invokes the self-abnegating vocabulary of Christianity only to undercut it; the pain that she has embraced functions not to erase her presence as subject but to reveal the impossibility that she is "still insignificant." If earlier in the novel she as subject was reduced to an object constructed by the male gaze, here her fundamental emptiness is filled only by the pain that she embraces.

Pauline's fear of being "skinned" beneath the male gaze results from a sense of her own insubstantiality as subject; even the bones that "push" at her flesh are defined by motion rather than constancy, contributing to the image of Pauline's form as malleable material unrestricted by a defining structure, be it the parameters of a subject position or the constraints of a skeleton (73). Instead of choosing to use such elasticity to construct herself as subject, however, Pauline burns away the physical flexibility that marks, in her mind, a malleability of self. Despite excruciating pain, she deliberately submerges her hands in boiling water, literally skinning herself so that others will be unable to skin her:

> Later, when the binding was excruciatingly changed, I shed a skin with the dirty wrapping. Every few days I shed another, yet another, and I drank or ate whatever my Sisters brought, I fattened in bed, took on subtle heft. . . .
> New flesh grew upon my hands, smooth and pink as a baby's, only tighter, with no give to it, a stiff and shrunken fabric, so that my fingers webbed and doubled over like a hatchling's claws. (195–96)

Unable to free herself of the skin that in her mind marks the margin between subject and body, Pauline attempts to limit others' ability to access her through it. The "new flesh" that results from her act of self-violation is no longer flexible skin that can be made or remade into many different configurations. This skin is defining, taut, a "stiff and shrunken fabric" that cripples the movement and autonomy of the subject who wears it, but resists the manipulation of others. Pauline has remade her own body in such a way that it cannot be taken from her; in doing so, however, she sacrifices its ability to enact her will or desire. The price of her invulnerability is the loss of the nerves that link the subject with the physical world. Her hands encased in scar tissue, Pauline locks herself within her body even as she locks others out.

Only by burning away her skin is Pauline able to create for herself a body that speaks the kind of invulnerability she associates with whiteness as well as maleness. Pauline describes the members of her family as "mixed-bloods, skinners in the clan for which the name was lost" (14). The slang term "skinners" suggests both Pauline's sense of entrapment within a skin that can be identified as half-white by Native Americans and half-Indian by whites, and her fear of being "plucked and skinned," having the self beneath the skin revealed to the world.

Just as the models through which Pauline attempts to liberate herself from the vulnerable female body are inexorably structured around the dynamics of rape, so the models she chooses to liberate herself from the racial body are structured around and lead toward racial oppression. Having chosen the Virgin Mary and Christian mysticism as her models, Pauline is forced to embrace a hegemonic logic that leads racially to genocide just as it leads physically to self-mutilation. Directed by Christ to "fetch more" Indian souls for his heaven, Pauline states that that "is what I intended by going out among them with the net of my knowledge. He gave me the mission to name and baptize, to gather souls. Only I must give myself away in return, I must dissolve. I did so eagerly" (141). With her "net of knowledge," Pauline intends to gather the spirits of dead Indians, pulling their souls away from their bodies to a foreign yet more powerful culture where they will be met by the figure of Christ "dressed in glowing white" (140). In gathering up the souls of her community and collecting them for a white God, Pauline "gives herself away" even as she snatches up the souls of others. Her eagerness to distance herself from the racial identity that in her own mind defines her is reflected in the verb that she chooses to describe the process of losing herself; Pauline literally wants to "dissolve," to break down her body so thoroughly that it can be reconstituted in a form of her own making.

Having mutilated and destroyed the body that marks her as Other, however, Pauline is still unable to distance herself sufficiently from her Native American identity. In the effort to eliminate every trace of her connection, she makes one last trip to a homeland that she now describes as "the kingdom of the damned":

> I had told Superior this would be my one last visit to Matchimanito before the day of my entrance as novice, after which I would repudiate my former life. I knew I would not see Pillagers, Kashpaws, or old Nanapush again after that. . . . They could starve and fornicate . . . worship the bones of animals. . . . I would have none of it. I would be chosen, His own, wiped clean of Fleur's cool even hand on my brow, purged of the slide of Napoleon's thighs. . . . (196)

In her eagerness to "repudiate [her] former life," Pauline translates the haunting attachments that she cannot escape psychologically into physical images that render them visible and manipulable. Pauline's desire to be "wiped clean" or "purged" of Fleur's hand and Napoleon's thigh is really a desire to escape the sense of vulnerability that the presence of each elicits in her; once again, the body emerges as the material surface on which Pauline projects conflicts of the mind. Having inflicted violence upon her own body, she uses that "purged" form to engage in a physical battle with the Indians, a battle that serves as the culmination of her war with her own racial and gendered self.

As she leaves the convent to pilot herself into the midst of the lake with her scarred hands, Pauline for the first time defines her body by its strength rather than vulnerability: "naked in my own flesh . . . I tumbled forward when the boat slammed on shore, scrambled upright on the balls of my feet, ready and strong as a young man" (201). No longer experiencing her body as an object created by the male gaze, Pauline likens herself to a young man and asserts her nakedness as a strength rather than a weakness. Her probing gaze now penetrates the bodies of others to unveil their fragility and randomness; looking to the shore, she describes the bodies of the people she sees: "They were such small foolish sticks strung together with cloth that in the heat of my sudden hilarity I nearly tumbled over the side . . ." (197). For the first time in the novel, other bodies seem contingent to Pauline while her own appears essential; beneath her gaze, individual subjects fragment into images of "small foolish sticks" connected not of necessity or reason but "strung together" haphazardly. Although Pauline's shrunken hands pin her within her body in much the same way that the "great hand" of God pins Mary to the earth, she experiences this self-inflicted limitation as liberation. Pauline's response to her physical mutilation cannot be understood outside the dynamics of rape revealed in her discussion of the Virgin Mary; the inviolability she associates with masculine power is an experience of mind as well as body. "This," she claims, "was how God felt: beyond hindrance or reach" (197–98).

Having boiled away the skin that would lend others access to the subject she sees "contained" within it, Pauline now experiences herself as invulnerable to the manipulation of others; she proclaims her own strength by asserting Fleur's weakness: "I was important, beyond their reach, even Fleur's though she must have been hiding in the cabin, weakened by my act, for I caught no glimpse of her" (198). Pauline's hostility toward Fleur may be traced to her identification with her; in order to assert her own strength, Pauline must obliterate her connection to Fleur. Her attempt to do so, however, is as unsuccessful as her attempt to render herself inviolable by destroying her own body. With the newfound strength of a body she images as masculine, Pauline turns against Fleur only to emerge as the victim of her own assault:

I screamed at her, but the wind flattened out my words.

Her figure swelled into relief, as if the force of my yell enlarged her. Her hair was covered by a scarf white and brilliant as the moon rising. . . . But the rest of her was planted tight. Her heavy black clothes, her shawl, the way she held herself so rigid, suggested a door into blackness.

I stood before it and then she turned, so slowly I heard the hinges creak. A moment and I was inside where I could not breathe and water filled me, cold and black water of the drowned, a currentless blanket. I thought I would be shut there, but she turned again and off she walked, a black slot into the air, a passage into herself. A crushing sadness. I was glad when night approached. (200)

In its allusions to a vocabulary of rape present throughout the text, this passage appears at first to reinforce Pauline's notion of her own empower-ment by defining her voice as the "force" that swells Fleur's figure. As Fleur's body appears to enlarge in response to Pauline's words, it loses its solidity to become a flexible form shaped by the violence of Pauline's will. Fleur's malleability is accompanied by an entrapment within the confines of the physical; like Sophie and the Virgin Mary, Fleur too emerges as "planted," pinned in one place by her physical form. Defined by the confines of a physicality that simultaneously restricts her motion but allows others to access her, Fleur's body becomes both a "black slot" defined by emptiness and a "passage into herself" through which others can manipulate her sub-jectivity, or the emptiness that emerges in its place.

In order to appropriate the violator's power to effect such manipulation, however, Pauline must detach herself from Fleur to claim a psychological as well as a physical distance from the victim's subjectivity. Although Fleur's figure seems to swell in response to the "force" of Pauline's yell, that force turns against Pauline. Unable to overcome her identification with the victim, Pauline herself is imaged as swollen, "filled" with the "cold and black water of the drowned" in the same way that she was "filled" with Fleur's cries of pain during the rape (26). Pauline's self-conscious repudiation of her female body, like her rejection of her racial self, barely masks a knowledge of her own vulnerability that turns her every act of violence into a form of self-violation. Because she continues to define herself as Other even as she projects that Otherness onto an external force that she attempts to destroy, it is not only Fleur but Pauline who is "weakened by [Pauline's] act." Although Pauline gratefully embraces the coming of the night, then, its darkness will fail to obscure distinctions that emerge not from the visible configurations of bodies but from the constructed notions of identity that Pauline cannot escape.

The futility of Pauline's attempt to render herself invulnerable by repo-sitioning herself within the dynamics of violation rather than rejecting them becomes most apparent in her attack on Napoleon. Pauline's murder of Napoleon enacts in visible terms the violence of her attempt to "repudiate" her Native American self; in her increasingly desperate effort to destroy her connection with her Native American background, she mutilates and murders the Indian "devil" who would defy her white God. The carefully mapped racial and religious symbolism of this scene may overwhelm the reader's understanding of its gender dynamics. Pauline's newfound confidence in her body not only leads her to image herself as male but to image her murder of Napoleon as a rape in which she is cast in the role of violator rather than victim:

> There was an odd pleasure to the tiny stinging blows and in the words, which tightened me from nape to heels. . . . I felt his breath, a thin stream that swept along my collarbone and my throat as we crushed close. And then I seized him and forced myself upon him, grew around him like the earth around a root, held him still.
>
> . . . He began to pound beneath me like a driving wind and I went dizzy with the effort of holding on, light and dry as a fistful of matches. He rose, shoved me against a scoured log, rubbed me up and down until I struck. I screamed once and then my tongue flapped loose, yelled profane curses. I stuffed the end of the blanket in his mouth, pushed him down into the sand and then fell upon him and devoured him, scattered myself in all directions, stupefied my own brain in the process so thoroughly that the only things left of intelligence were my doubled-over hands.
>
> What I told them to do, then, they accomplished. My fingers closed like hasps of iron, locked on the strong rosary chain, wrenched and twisted the beads close about his neck until his face darkened and he lunged away. I hung on while he bucked and gagged and finally fell, his long tongue dragging down my thighs.
>
> I kicked and kicked away the husk, drove it before me with the blows of my feet. (202)

This act, like Pauline's initial juxtaposition of her own strength with Fleur's weakness, seems to reflect Pauline's newfound empowerment. Pauline's representation evokes the vocabulary of sexual violence to image a scene in which two bodies, "crushed close," are described as "tightening," "pounding," and "driving" against one another. The rape that plagues Pauline throughout most of the novel is reenacted in this final scene. This time, however, Pauline emerges as the violator rather than the helpless observer; "I seized him," she proclaims, "and forced myself upon him." The assault on subjectivity that is part of rape is also recreated here; as Pauline the character forces herself upon Napoleon, Pauline the narrator delays even the acknowledgment of her victim's identity until after she has murdered him.

In recasting her role within the rape scenario rather than rejecting the dynamics of rape, however, Pauline moves once again into the domain of self-violation. When she attacks Napoleon, the imagery of Pauline's narrative suggests that the violation is double-edged. For most of the representation Pauline, while the aggressor, emerges not as the actor but as the individual being acted upon. Napoleon's motions are described with direct action verbs: he pounds, shoves, and rubs her. When Pauline "strikes," on the other hand, her action emerges only as a reaction to Napoleon's physical manipulation: "He rose, shoved me against a scoured log, rubbed me up and down until I struck." Pauline's actions seem only to reinforce the solidity and stability of Napoleon's body. When she says that she "forced [herself] upon him, grew around him like the earth around a root," her body is the one being transformed. The word "force" does not suggest one form imprinting itself upon another, but a form molding itself to another; even as Pauline "rapes" Napoleon, she is unable to escape the malleability that defines the victim's experience of violence. Although Pauline goes on to "devour" Napoleon, he does not dissolve; rather, Pauline herself fragments as her interior is bruised and broken outward: "I pushed him down into the sand and then fell upon him and devoured him, scattered myself in all directions, stupefied my own brain in the process." In this representation, "devouring" emerges as a form of self-violation, just as "force" emerges as a form of weakness; Pauline's categories of identity have become so self-destructive that her very means of expression has inverted.

Even as Pauline casts herself as rapist, then, her experience seems closer to that of the rape victim. The character who lamented Mary's pain as she was "known in the brain and known in the flesh" becomes the agent of a similarly double-edged assault against herself; as Pauline attacks Napoleon, she also attacks herself, not only damaging her body but "stupefying" her "own brain." Throughout the book Pauline has sought to break the intimate connection between body and subject, hoping to achieve the violator's status of physical power and emotional inviolability. Having envisioned the body as the physical locus of a subjectivity always vulnerable to assault, Pauline effects her liberation only by becoming the victim of a "rape" that she herself initiates. Whereas Fleur's body serves as "a passage into herself," Pauline's body now appears to bear no trace of her existence as subject. Having "scattered [her]self in all directions," Pauline can no longer be located in or through her body: "the only things left of intelligence," she claims, "were my doubled-over hands." Whereas before she violated her body to forestall the possibility of others' violation, here she assaults the very connection between mind and body, "stupefying" the synapses that register physical pain and psychological violation just as she burned the nerves from her hands. Pauline's hands—like the hands of men, of God, of the Pillagers—now appear to serve as an extension of her power rather than a sign of her vulnerability. "What I told them to do, then," she observes, "they accomplished. My fingers closed like hasps of iron . . . " (202). Her body, no longer a passageway to the self, is imaged here as a tool that she controls as if from a distance.

Pauline's newfound distance from her body allows her to finger her own wounds with a kind of detached bemusement. Having seemingly forestalled any assault on her subjectivity, she now views her body as a surface on which the marks of physical violation are inscribed in imagistic patterns: "I had committed no sin. . . . I could certainly prove that over doubt, for I was marked here and there, pocked as if we'd rolled through embers, stamped by his molten scales in odd reddened circles, in bruises of moons and stars" (203). Pauline's detachment from her body culminates in her aesthetic rendering of the marks of her own violation. Citing her wounded body as evidence of Napoleon's assault, Pauline claims the bruises and abrasions on her body as a register of the legitimacy of her violence but not a register of her own pain. Pauline's strategic assertion of her connection to this wounded body is a tactic for further empowerment; having severed the essential link between body and subject, she appears to reclaim that bond at will even as she continues to reject the vulnerability coincident with it. For perhaps the first time, Pauline reads her body as a text the signification of which she controls.

The motion away from materiality and into textuality also defines the reader's initial experience of Pauline's assault on Napoleon. The mythic tone and surrealistic imagery of Pauline's representation intensify the reader's confusion about agency and materiality in the text. While this assault is represented, unlike Fleur's rape, the representation invokes so many imaginative and literary conventions, so unsettles the line between mind and body and victim and violator, that the reader is distanced from its material dynamics. The physically exhausted and mentally unstable Pauline begins her assault on Misshepeshu by dropping a rock from the boat, and seeing it wake the monster "in [her] mind" (197). Encountering the monster on land she is blinded by the fire and sees "double, or not at all in the flickering glow" (202). In the representation that follows, the reader also seems to see double or not at all, never knowing quite how the bodies represented are making contact, and whether these bodies operate by material laws or by some supernatural dynamism.

Although at times the representation seems to push toward a revelation of material bodies, the reader cannot assume that physical effects will follow from physical causes. Physical wounds are not enumerated; the violence instead batters Pauline's "self" and "brain." Material forms are replaced by images of roots, wind, matches, and logs, and even words become "black lake pebbles." As the categories of mind and body that separate dream from reality and words from objects are lost, the reader experiences the representation as a dynamic but primarily semiotic experience in which the empirical dynamics of violence emerge only in a murky, confusing light. Catherine Rainwater discusses the way in which the reader's experience of Pauline's narrative is complicated by the intersection of conflicting Christian and Native American religious codes.[8] That experience, I would argue, is complicated here by the way in which the narrative unsettles epistemological and hermeneutic distinctions encoded in Western conventions of reading. As Pauline's narrative moves freely from material to immaterial categories, the reader searches for a single interpretive frame that will reconcile a representation that is neither realistic nor fantastical.

When, at the end of the portrayal, the fantastical Misshepeshu emerges as the very real and very dead Napoleon Morrissey, however, the reader is suddenly propelled toward recognition of the material consequences of Pauline's act:

> I kicked and kicked away the husk, drove it before me with the blows of my feet. A light began to open in the sky and the thing grew a human shape, one that I recognized in gradual stages. Eventually, it took on the physical form of Napoleon Morrissey.
> As the dawn broadened, as the fire shrank and smoldered, I examined each feature and confirmed it for the truth. . . .
> There was hard work to do, then. I dragged him by the suspenders down a crooked path, into the woods, and left him in high weeds. (202–203)

As the "husk" that Pauline kicks before her is transformed into the heavy materiality of Napoleon's "physical form," the reader is forced to revise his or her perception of Pauline's assault on Misshepeshu.[9] Pauline continues to insist that Napoleon's body may or may not be present: "How could I have known what body the devil would assume?" (203). For the reader, however, the revelation of the violated body also reveals how far toward a purely semiotic conception of violence the reader has been pushed by Pauline's confusion of material and immaterial categories. As Pauline recognizes the need to drag Napoleon's body into the woods, her description of that act as "hard work" exposes not only the material weightiness of Napoleon's body but the contrast between the difficult task of hauling that body away and the apparent ease with which she almost magically murdered her victim. As the reader is propelled toward an acknowledgment of the empirical dynamics of violation, what seemed a symbolic reenactment of a possibly imaginary rape emerges as a representation of murder.

The reader's awareness of the material, victimized body in the text thus undercuts Pauline's subsequent, and apparently victorious, attempts to efface her own materiality by literally reconstructing her physical form:

> . . . then I realized I was still naked, with no covering. I rolled in slough mud until my arms and breasts, every part of me was coated. . . . I was a poor and noble creature now, dressed in earth like Christ, in furs like Moses Pillager, draped in snow or simple air. . . . I rolled in dead leaves, in moss, in defecation of animals. I plastered myself with dry leaves and the feathers of a torn bird . . . so that by the time I came to the convent . . . I was nothing human, nothing victorious, nothing like myself. I was no more than a piece of the woods. (203–204)

Even as it displays Pauline's apparent liberation from the confines of her bodily form, this passage reveals her inability to escape completely from the assumptions of biological determinism. Although she seems to claim the power of resignification that allows her to make her body speak for her,

Pauline is able to do so only after she obliterates all trace of her actual physical form. As she undertakes to remake herself as subject, the lengths to which she goes to obscure her body reveal her fear of its betrayal. Only when "every part of [her]" is "coated" with mud—the breasts that define her as woman, the dark skin that marks her as Indian—is Pauline able to reclaim her body as the ground from which to assert herself as subject. After rolling in slough mud, Pauline images herself not as a woman covered with grime but as a being "draped in snow or simple air." Such rhetoric moves toward a myth of origin, a rhetoric of purity and simplicity through which Pauline recasts herself as a "poor and noble creature" freshly created. Pauline's every effort to create herself anew as subject, however, is hampered by her need to destroy a self that she sees inscribed on her body each time she looks in a mirror or into the eyes of another.

Here, as earlier in the novel, Pauline's claim to subjectivity is deeply entangled with her attitude toward a body that she must destroy or obscure before she can make it speak for her. Pauline's essentialist assumptions about the body dictate that even the most self-conscious manipulations of her physical form emerge in the shadow of a body that speaks the powerlessness of race and gender. Because the body that she images as "draped in snow" will continue to bear the traces of the dominant story that she has whited out, Pauline's every act of assertion must be accompanied by an act of erasure. As long as she continues to read the inscriptions of a hegemonic culture on her form, Pauline's claim to the power of signification remains a purely negative one; "I was," she asserts at the end of this scene, "nothing human, nothing victorious, nothing like myself" (204).

Pauline's long struggle to remove herself from the disempowered, easily violated position of an embodied Native American woman in a white patriarchal culture seems to her to have succeeded. The reader is aware, however, that the mechanisms Pauline chooses to avoid violation simply victimize her again. Pauline falls prey to the fact that her subjectivity can be constructed by others, but at the same time she has imbibed the notion that the body determines the self. Rather than trying to resignify the socially constructed self, Pauline accepts these social constructions; the only way she sees to live with her body is to sever body, which bears the marks of race and gender, from self. Pauline undertakes the severing process with the only models available to her: rape of physically vulnerable women by men, Christian mortification of the flesh, and the destruction of Native American spiritual culture through white cultural imperialism. The book records the crossing and recrossing of these modes of oppression and self-violation, and the transitional points in Pauline's life—Fleur's rape, her vision of the Virgin Mary, her murder of Napoleon, and her final induction into the convent—all involve such nexuses.

This is not to say that in the book rape serves as a metaphor for racism, or vice versa, or even that the two are mutually reflexive symbols. Erdrich offers us a character suffering from both racial and gender disempowerment who manages to combine them into a single set of symbols, and allows us to witness how racial and gender oppression can work together in a dynamic of psychological self-violation. Rather than simply despising Pauline for the absurd lengths to which her denial of identity takes her, Erdrich asks us to understand how the fear of rape, arising out of physical embodiment, can interact with the sense of disempowerment and bodily self-consciousness promulgated by racism.

Pauline's efforts to create a new subject, an "I," that is "nothing like [her]self" culminate in her return to the convent and her decision to take the veil.[10] Such a decision involves not only a denial of her culture and a rejection of her past but a literal veiling of her body and redefinition of her identity. For Pauline, whose deterministic assumptions about race, gender, and the body have consistently undercut her efforts to create herself anew, the Catholic church seems to offer a ready-made identity that extends even to the level of a new name. Having donned the "camphor-smelling robes" of the nun, Pauline goes forward to draw a name from the Mother Superior's hand:

> I prayed before I spread the scrap of paper in air. I asked for the grace to accept, to leave Pauline behind, to remember that my name, any name was no more than a crumbling skin.
> *Leopolda.* I tried out the unfamiliar syllables. They fit. They cracked in my ears like a fist through ice. (205)

In this passage, Pauline reveals her essentialist assumptions even as she attempts to deny them. While the insubstantiality of the scrap of paper and the arbitrary process of selection point to the social constructedness of identity, Pauline's description of the ritual points the reader back toward an essential link between name and subject or body and subject. She does not ask for the grace to "leave the name 'Pauline' behind" but simply to "leave Pauline behind"; the signifier of her name blends in the reader's mind with the person that it identifies, suggesting that she could not abandon the name without abandoning the person.

Even Pauline's assertion that a name is "no more than a crumbling skin" dissolves into its opposite as the terms of Pauline's metaphor jar uneasily with the reader's experience of the novel. Paralleling the name with the body, Pauline asserts that neither is capable of determining identity. Her description of the body's insubstantiality, however, is belied by the violence of her earlier efforts to destroy her physical form; the words "crumbling skin" strike a reader who has witnessed Pauline's brutal attempts to contain, cover, and burn away her own skin as eerily passive.

Racial and gender issues meet at the nexus of violence because, Erdrich shows us, essentialist assumptions about the relationship between body and self generate violence from within and from without. The violent oppression of the Native Americans justified by the essentialism of white culture is paralleled and exaggerated by Pauline's more subtle and intimate form of essentialist violence. Pauline's story emerges as a perverted *bildungsroman*, the tale of a young woman who overcomes the disadvantages of her birth to access a position of some power in the dominant culture; given Pauline's assumption of an essential link between body and subject as well as the pervasive racism and sexism of her society, however, such success can only come through violence perpetrated against the body to which inhere the disadvantages of birth. Pauline succeeds at overcoming her Native American identity and her female vulnerability only through a form of self-violation that ultimately reinscribes rather than reverses her powerlessness. To have done otherwise would have involved a level of self-consciousness about the social construction of identity and power not available to a young Native American woman who continues to see, in her own words, "through the eyes of the world outside us."

The body in *Tracks*, then, emerges as a material presence on which Pauline projects her essentialist notions of race and gender and a narrative absence seldom acknowledged in the reader's semiotic construction of the novel's violence. Pauline's narrative points to a definition of intimate violence that acknowledges its material and immaterial consequences; "known in the brain and known in the flesh," the victim of violence is assaulted not only as body but as subject. Pauline's attempt to preserve her subjectivity by manipulating the materiality of her body represents one response to these dynamics; because she fails to acknowledge the way in which that body's significance is constructed by the interpretation of a hegemonic culture, however, Pauline's material manipulations of her form fail to lend her the inviolability that she seeks. The reader ignores the materiality of the vulnerable body to focus on the way in which it is constructed in the act of representation; the reader's concentration on Fleur's rape as a literary or symbolic phenomenon may blind him or her to the dynamics of violation that the text naturalizes. As Pauline fails to recognize the textuality of the body, then, the reader may fail to acknowledge the materiality of the text. Critical analyses of the novel that ignore its representations of intimate violence in favor of a symbolic recasting of the material dynamics of violation accept the narrative's semiotic invitation without recognizing its potentially radical unsettling of the very process of semiosis. Caught between the materiality of violence and its semiotic construction, the reader who charts the dangers of Pauline's essentialist response to the violability of the body must also be wary of completely dematerializing a violence the dynamics of which return us, not only as victims but as readers, to the urgent presence of the vulnerable body.

NOTES

Preface

1. A historical analysis of the emergence of violence in twentieth-century literature remains to be written. Such studies have been undertaken about different historical periods; see, for example, Richard Slotkin's classic work, *Regeneration through Violence*, and David Brion Davis's *From Homicide to Slavery*.

2. A few forays into these complex issues have emerged in recent criticism. See, for example, the discussion of race and violence in Trudier Harris, *Exorcising Blackness*, and Ronald T. Takaki, *Violence in the Black Imagination*. Two collections of essays on gender and violence have been published since 1990; see Katherine Anne Ackley, *Women and Violence in Literature*, and Lynn A. Higgins and Brenda R. Silver, *Rape and Representation*.

Introduction

1. For an excellent discussion of current theories of the body, see Frances E. Mascia-Lees and Patricia Sharpe's introduction to *Tattoo, Torture, Mutilation, and Adornment*.

2. The most recent study of violence in American fiction, Michael Kowalewski's *Deadly Musings* (1993), argues otherwise. Unfortunately, because Kowalewski's study appeared after this book was already in press, the specifics of his argument cannot be addressed here. The theory of reading violence that follows argues against the central assumption of Kowalewski's book, the notion that "the only presence violence has in fiction is verbal" (4).

3. Earlier studies of violence in literature also tend to ignore the way in which the readerly subject constitutes and is constituted by the textual scene of violence. In *Violence in the Arts*, John Fraser warns that "certain presentations of art reinforce and in a sense confirm the psychopathological vision of the violators" (24). Frederick Hoffman distinguishes between representations which "do violence to their human subjects" (*The Mortal No*) and those which do not. Leslie Fiedler, in *Love and Death in the American Novel*, warns against what he describes as "horror pornography": "And now, even as a hundred years ago, such readers relish thinking that the sadist fantasies in which they find masturbatory pleasure are revelations of social disorder, first steps toward making a better world" (499–500). Such distinctions, even as they assess the effect of individual works, have little to say about the *process* of representing and the *experience* of reading violence; in concentrating on the consequences of meaning but not its production, they empower the text with an almost magical ability, in Hoffman's terms, not only to represent but to "do violence."

Although such works of criticism may offer the reader a kind of guidebook to representations of violence, they do not offer a theoretical inquiry into ways of reading that unveils the way in which the conclusions to which they respond are generated. The absence of the reader as anything but a passive receptacle for meaning in these critical scenarios may stem in part from the way in which representations of violence often appear to appropriate the reader's participation—or even resistance—as part of their force. In certain representations, the reader's participation may be usurped by a narrative that forcefully aligns the reader's gaze with the perspective of victim, observer or violator; portrayals of violence are often constructed so that the power of readership seems to disappear before the irresistible pull of representational effect.

4. Throughout this section of his book, Black elides the distinction between reader and viewer to use the term "reader-viewer." Although I adopt this term in my discussion of his study, I address the problematics of such a term when I discuss the distinctions between film and novel conventions in an earlier section of this introduction.

1. Reading Rape

1. Robert Dale Parker is the first critic to discuss the function of the narrative gaps in *Sanctuary*. Parker does not concentrate, as I do here, on the reader's evolving experience of the text or on Faulkner's manipulation of that experience through the exaggeration of literary convention. Instead, he situates the gaps in *Sanctuary* in the context of other gaps in Faulkner's writing and concludes by reading the novel's trial scene as a reversal of the narrative process of elision. Whereas I argue that the trial scene exaggerates the dynamics of reading already present in the novel, Parker argues that it represents a "sudden change to certainty" that results in "a frightening clarity absolutely antithetical to Faulkner's other novels" (84).

2. Terry Heller uses Iser's theories of reading to a different critical end in "Terror and Empathy in Faulkner's *Sanctuary*." For a psychoanalytical discussion of Temple's rape that also marks the reader's complicity in the crime, see Homer B. Pettey, "Reading and Raping in *Sanctuary*." Diane Roberts explores the thematics of rape in the novel, focusing on Temple's control over her own narrative of the crime, in "Ravished Belles."

3. In "The Elliptical Nature of *Sanctuary*," John T. Matthews explores the function of ellipses throughout the novel. Whereas my discussion of the rape focuses on the reader's response to the text's elliptical representations, Matthews concentrates on the role played by Horace Benbow within the novel. "The pressure that keeps out of the book the depiction of Temple's assault," Matthews claims, ". . . may be traced to Horace, as he eludes both his own and society's complicity in Temple's fate" (254).

4. See Elaine Scarry's discussion of pain and language in *The Body in Pain*.

5. Despite this radical pre-telling of the rape story, the camera's ultimate representation of the rape is, in fact, intricately bound to the rhythms of the male violators. At one point in the act of violation, for example, the camera shifts to a bottle that bounces with increasing fury on the video machine on which the victim is raped until, at the moment of the violator's climax, the bottle smashes to the floor.

6. The notion of pain and violence as "world-destroying" is taken from Scarry, pp. 4–29.

7. I use the term "uncritical reader" to account for the fact that not all readers—male or female—will be swept up by the novel's formal mechanisms of captivation.

2. Reading Torture

1. It is not always simple, of course, to separate our sensory, experiential knowledge of the body from the way in which it is culturally constructed. In *Bodies That Matter*, Judith Butler questions the very notion of what we accept as "materiality." Although I find her argument a useful challenge to contemporary thought, my own study assumes the body's material immediacy as well as its constructed presence. As Peter Brooks observes in *Body Work*, the body functions not only as psychosexual construction, cultural product or biologic entity, but "is all of these, often all at once, to writers and readers" (xii).

2. Orwell's description of the prisoners as they watch the chinless man being beaten is similar to Faulkner's description of the blind man who "watches" while Temple is raped in *Sanctuary*. While the prisoners sit "quiet, their hands crossed on their knees" (Orwell, 196), the old man sits "in his chair in the sunlight, his hands crossed on the top of the stick" (Faulkner, 99). Initially, the reader is aligned with the silent/blind

observer in both novels; in *1984*, however, Orwell goes on to undercut the reader's passive response to violence by forging a new connection between reader and victim.

3. In "Behind the Door of *1984*," Judith Wilt uses the novel's final torture scene to discuss how torture can destroy the victim's identity by conflating interior and exterior worlds. Torture reveals those aspects of the victim's subjectivity that he or she is unwilling to confront, Wilt argues, making the face an insubstantial barrier between two mirroring realities. To extend Wilt's argument, I would observe that the narrative is also a point of interface between character and reader, a tenuous barrier narrowly disguised by conventions of reading that Orwell's representation dissolves in this scene.

4. All remarks from Helen Garrett are taken from an interview which I conducted with her in June 1991 at the New York headquarters of Amnesty International.

5. See, for example, "The Vocabulary of Torture" in Amnesty International's publication on Myanmar (New York, 1990).

3. Sweet Pain and Charred Bodies

1. See Jean Laplanche, *Life and Death in Psychoanalysis*.

2. See Peter Brooks, *Reading for the Plot*, pp. 264–85.

3. In Stanley Fish, *Doing What Comes Naturally*.

4. For a discussion of the way in which *The White Hotel* subverts the positivistic and male-centered assumptions of Freudian theory, see David Cowart, "Being and Seeming," and Mary F. Robertson, "Hystery, Herstory, History."

5. K. J. Phillips, in "The Phalaris Syndrome," offers an exhaustive analysis of the way in which the patterns of imagery in *The White Hotel* undercut Freud's analysis of Lisa's experience.

6. For another discussion of this point, see Cowart, "Being and Seeming."

7. Of course, "vehicle" and "tenor" are conventional terms only; recent criticism of metaphor has revealed that the firm distinction between these two aspects is in itself problematic.

8. In "The Phalaris Syndrome," K. J. Phillips opposes Thomas's novel to a post-Enlightenment tradition that appropriates violent imagery to describe the writing process. The patterns of imagery in *The White Hotel*, Phillips argues, ultimately affirm the value of empathy and community. Phillips fails, however, to make clear how Thomas impresses the reader with the immediacy of Lisa's pain.

9. For a cogent discussion of the debate surrounding Thomas's borrowing from Anatoli Kuznetsov's *Babi Yar*, see James E. Young, *Writing and Rewriting the Holocaust*, pp. 53–58.

10. Of course, Thomas's appeal to an actual historical account of the Babi Yar experience does not allow him to escape completely from the problematics of "grounding" his representation. While a metaphorically governed concept of history (see Hayden White, *Tropics of Discourse*) questions the very notion of historical fact, that issue is further complicated in the case of Thomas's borrowing by the fact that his source is a secondhand account of the experience described. As James E. Young observes, the text from which Thomas borrows is *itself* not a victim's testimony but a novelistic rendering "based upon the verbatim transcription of yet another testimonial source" (55).

4. Envisioning Violence

1. See, for example, Laura Mulvey's groundbreaking article, "Visual Pleasure and Narrative Cinema."

2. References to Marx are to *The Economic & Philosophic Manuscripts of 1844* unless otherwise noted in the text.

3. The film version of *Last Exit to Brooklyn* (Columbia, 1989) presents a striking

contrast to Selby's careful and relentless unveiling of Tralala's body. Early in the film, as in the book, Tralala appears as a conventional filmic body; the body of actress Jennifer Jason Leigh appears so much like all other perfectly turned movie-star bodies, even down to the Marilyn Monroe ash-blonde wig and black beauty spot, that the viewer perceives it as a convention rather than an individual material form. Director Uli Edel could, then, have offered a cinematic version of Selby's bodily unveiling by pushing Leigh's body farther and farther from the movie-star ideal to reveal pores, pimples, and sagging skin; instead, he simply musses her hair. The viewer is never made uncomfortable by the grotesque physicality of the body that emerges in Selby's novel as Leigh's body remains smooth, trim, and surprisingly intact.

Furthermore, although Selby forces the reader to recognize complicity in Tralala's objectification, Edel allows the viewer an escape through cinematic techniques that offer distance and moral justification. Rather than one painfully relentless scene, the rape appears in several short clips, intercut with scenes of a family party. The camera avoids showing Tralala's body, but frequently delivers a close-up of her face, clearly meant to remind us of her humanity. These close-ups, particularly one in which, in voice-over, Tralala's soldier lover tells her he will miss her, allow the viewer to affect self-congratulatory compassion for Tralala and to disassociate him- or herself from the rapists; at the same time, these close-ups fail to interrupt or unveil the viewer's voyeuristic experience of the rape. The portrayal ends with a young man who has loved Tralala from afar (a character created for the movie) rescuing her and bursting into tears. A surrogate for the viewer, this character seems to be intended to present a "moral center" for the scene, and to diffuse any guilt that might turn back on the viewer. As a newly covered and apparently unharmed Tralala reassures the boy, embracing him and saying "Don't cry," she completely reverses the message delivered by the naked, brutalized body of Selby's story.

5. *American Psycho* and the American Psyche

1. References to Marx are to *The Economic and Philosophic Manuscripts of 1844* unless otherwise noted in the text.

2. A recent popular culture representation that does acknowledge the victim's subjectivity even in the midst of apparent powerlessness can be found in Jonathan Demme's film version of *Silence of the Lambs* (Orion, 1991). Demme manipulates the conventions of film to render the subjective presence of the psycho killer's victims visually and verbally immediate to the viewer. Instead of representing the act of murder, Demme concentrates on the prelude to and consequences of violation. The film reveals the mutilated bodies of the killer's victims only briefly, and effectively brackets the material text created by the killer's knife with various verbal and visual portraits of the young women that restore the subjective presence that violence has obliterated. After the killer lures Catherine Martin into his van and slices off her blouse from behind, for example, the close-up of her naked back momentarily captures the killer's perspective as it brackets out of the frame every part of the victim's body and subjectivity but the skin that is the object of the killer's quest. Even that momentary glimpse is disrupted, however, by a close-up shot that individualizes Martin's skin; as the camera focuses on her freckles and moles, it renders the material surface on which the viewer focuses as part of an individual human body rather than the smooth and consistent fabric that the killer desires that body to be.

By concentrating in detail on the experience of Catherine Martin as she is trapped and imprisoned in a stone pit by the killer for several days, the film also lends the victim a voice of resistance. Even as the visual text of the movie traces the killer's activities and empowers him as a filmic presence, the victim's invisibility does not relegate her to absence. During every visually complicated and brightly colored scene that takes place in the killer's home, the viewer is distracted from the visual text of rich fabrics, colorful makeup, and exotic clothing by the constant verbal demands of the victim just offscreen. As her hoarse voice permeates the smooth visual representations of the killer's activities, Catherine's words assert both her personality and her capacity for resistance. Her voice becomes a powerful means of asserting her subjectivity not only in response to the threat of the killer's violence but in reaction to the shallow reassurances of the FBI agent who acknowledges her presence only to desert her in pursuit of the criminal.

3. See, for example, Ellis's interview on "Fresh Air" (WYSP, Philadelphia) on March 26, 1991.

6. "Known in the Brain and Known in the Flesh"

1. Pauline's narration, of course, represents only one of two narrative perspectives in the novel; for a discussion of the way in which Nanapush's narrative "masters" Pauline, see Daniel Cornell, "Woman Looking."

2. Although Fleur is the actual victim of rape, its effects are registered only through Pauline's presence in the novel. Fleur remains seemingly intact and emerges as a kind of romance figure whose mysterious presence in the novel lends her an aura of invulnerability to the material dynamics of rape. Pauline can thus be seen as Fleur's surrogate, the character who exposes the consequences of a rape written out of the romance world associated with Fleur in the novel. In the argument that follows, I will focus on Pauline's function in the novel, addressing Fleur's presence only as it relates to Pauline's experience. (My thanks to Andy Von Hendy for his discussion of Fleur.)

3. As Lorraine Gamman and Margaret Marshment point out, for example, psychoanalytic criticism's emphasis on gender as "the category which structures perspective" ignores other forms of power relations which also underlie processes of identification and objectification in narrative fictions (7). See also Jane Gaines, "White Privilege and Looking Relations."

4. See Catherine Rainwater, "Reading between Worlds"; James Flavin, "The Novel as Performance"; Victoria Walker, "A Note on Perspective in *Tracks*." The most recent critical essay on *Tracks* is the first to focus extensively on gender as well as race; see Daniel Cornell, "Woman Looking."

5. For a useful discussion of the symbolic imagination in Native American culture, see Paula Gunn Allen, *The Sacred Hoop*. Allen argues that "Symbols in American Indian systems . . . articulate . . . that reality where thought and feeling are one, where objective and subjective are one, where speaker and listener are one . . ." (71).

6. See Daniel Cornell, "Woman Looking." This absence is particularly interesting given the title of Cornell's article; the rape is not only the one event that Pauline is unable to "look" at but, I would argue, the single most important event underlying her attempts to revise her subject position.

7. The comparison between Mary and Sophie with which this passage ends points to the way in which Pauline's efforts to escape her own body have implicated her in the dynamics of violation that she here attempts to unveil. Like the Virgin Mary, who is "planted like dirt," her mind as well as her body assaulted by a male God, Sophie is stripped of her will and planted in shallow mud through Pauline's machinations; once there, "She stood rooted, dazed, not alert enough to strip off her dress" (83). In her attempt to disavow her vulnerability as victim, Pauline lays claim to Sophie's brain as well as her flesh; if Sophie is "thoughtless," as Pauline describes her here, she is so because Pauline has stripped her of autonomy, "rooted" her in a body that Pauline—and not Sophie—controls.

8. See Rainwater, "Reading between Worlds," pp. 407–13.

9. The transformation of an insubstantial "husk" into Napoleon's body represents

a motion toward acknowledging the human consequences of violence, a motion that reverses the reader's experience of Fleur's rape. In the earlier scene, Lily's attack on Fleur is prefigured by his violent encounter with the sow:

> The sow screamed as his body smacked over hers. She rolled, striking out with her knife-sharp hooves and Lily gathered himself upon her, took her foot-long face by the ears, and scraped her snout and cheeks against the trestles of the pen. . . . She reared, shrieked, and then he squeezed her . . . his arms swung and flailed. She sank her black fangs into his shoulders, clasping him, dancing him forward and backward through the pen. (25)

Although this representation moves toward aestheticization by imaging the interaction between Lily and the sow as a dance, it acknowledges the painful force of the assault on the animal's body with an immediacy that is absent in the novel's representation of the rape that follows. The horror of Fleur's suffering is, in a sense, deflected onto the representation of the pig's struggle with Lily. By contrast, the assault on Fleur that occurs shortly thereafter in the novel renders the material consequences of violence almost invisible. The Napoleon scene reverses this motion by unveiling the supernatural creature or inhuman "husk" that Pauline manipulates as a human being whose body bears the consequences of her violence. (My thanks to Anne Fleche for our conversations on the function of the sow.)

10. Pauline, of course, emerges as the sadistic Leopolda of *Love Medicine*; her actions in that novel are rendered more intelligible in light of her experiences as Pauline in *Tracks*.

WORKS CITED

Ackley, Katherine Anne, ed. *Women and Violence in Literature: An Essay Collection*. New York: Garland, 1990.

Allen, Paula Gunn. *The Sacred Hoop*. Boston: Beacon, 1986.

Angelou, Maya. *I Know Why the Caged Bird Sings*. New York: Bantam, 1970.

Arendt, Hannah. *On Violence*. New York: Harcourt, 1970.

Armstrong, Nancy, and Leonard Tennenhouse, eds. *The Violence of Representation: Literature and the History of Violence*. New York: Routledge, 1989.

Bard, Morton, and Diane Sangrey. *The Crime Victim's Book*. New York: Basic, 1979.

Barthes, Roland. "Striptease." *Mythologies*. New York: Hill and Wang, 1972. 84–87.

Bernheimer, Charles. *Figures of Ill Repute: Representing Prostitution in Nineteenth-Century France*. Cambridge, MA: Harvard University Press, 1989.

Bersani, Leo, and Ulysse Dutoit. *The Forms of Violence*. New York: Shocken, 1985.

Bettelheim, Bruno. "Violence: A Neglected Mode of Behavior." In *Violence in the Streets*, ed. Shalom Endleman. Chicago: Quadrangle, 1968.

Black, Joel. *The Aesthetics of Murder*. Baltimore: Johns Hopkins University Press, 1991.

Brooks, Peter. "Fictions of the Wolf Man: Freud and Narrative Understanding." In *Reading for the Plot: Design and Intention in Narrative*. New York: Vintage, 1985.

———. *Body Work: Objects of Desire in Modern Narrative*. Cambridge, MA: Harvard University Press, 1993.

———. "Storied Bodies, or Nana at Last Unveil'd." *Critical Inquiry* 16 (August 1989): 1–32.

Brownmiller, Susan. *Against Our Will: Men, Women and Rape*. New York: Bantam, 1976.

Butler, Judith. *Bodies That Matter*. New York: Routledge, 1993.

Caws, Mary Ann. "Ladies Shot and Painted." In *The Female Body in Western Culture*, ed. Susan Rubin Suleiman. Cambridge, MA: Harvard University Press, 1986.

Chambers, Ross. *Room for Maneuver: Reading (the) Oppositional (in) Narrative*. Chicago: University of Chicago Press, 1991.

Cohen, Ted. "Metaphor and the Cultivation of Intimacy." *Critical Inquiry* 5.1 (1978): 1–12.

Cornell, Daniel. "Woman Looking: Revis(ion)ing Pauline's Subject Position in Louise Erdrich's *Tracks*." *Studies in American Indian Literatures* 4.1 (Spring 1992): 49–64.

Cowart, David. "Being and Seeming: *The White Hotel*." *Novel* 19.3 (Spring 1986): 216–31.

cummings, e. e. *The Enormous Room*. New York: Liveright, 1982.

Davis, David Brion. *From Homicide to Slavery: Studies in American Culture*. New York: Oxford University Press, 1986.

de Lauretis, Teresa. *Alice Doesn't: Feminism, Semiotics, Cinema* . Bloomington: Indiana University Press, 1984.

———. "The Violence of Rhetoric: Considerations on Representation and Gender." In *Technologies of Gender*. Bloomington: Indiana University Press, 1987.

de Man, Paul. "The Rhetoric of Temporality." In *Blindness and Insight: Essays in the Rhetoric of Contemporary Criticism*. Minneapolis: University of Minnesota Press, 1983.

Dimen, Muriel. "Power, Sexuality, and Intimacy." In *Gender/Body/Knowledge*, ed. Alison M. Jaguar and Susan R. Bordo. New Brunswick: Rutgers University Press, 1989.

Doane, Mary Ann. "The 'Woman's Film.'" In *Re-Vision: Essays in Feminist Film Criticism*. Frederick, MD: American Film Institute, University Pubs, 1984.

Ellis, Bret Easton. *American Psycho*. New York: Vintage, 1991.

Erdrich, Louise. *Tracks*. New York: Harper & Row, 1989.

———. *Love Medicine*. Boston: G. K. Hall, 1984.

Faulkner, William. *Sanctuary*. New York: Vintage, 1987.

Fiedler, Leslie A. *Love and Death in the American Novel*. New York: Stein and Day, 1966.

Fish, Stanley. "Withholding the Missing Portion: Psychoanalysis and Rhetoric." In *Doing What Comes Naturally: Change, Rhetoric, and the Practice of Theory in Literary and Legal Studies*. Durham, NC: Duke University Press, 1989.

Flavin, James. "The Novel as Performance: Communication in Louise Erdrich's *Tracks*." *Studies in American Indian Literatures* 3.4 (Winter 1991): 1–12.

Fornes, Maria Irene. *Plays*. New York: PAJ Publications, 1986.

Fraser, John. *Violence in the Arts*. New York: Cambridge University Press, 1974.

Gaines, Jane. "White Privilege and Looking Relations: Race and Gender in Feminist Film Theory." *Screen* 29.4 (1988): 12–27.

Gamman, Lorraine, and Margaret Marshment. Introduction to *The Female Gaze: Women as Viewers of Popular Culture*. Seattle: Red Comet Press, 1989.

Harris, Trudier. *Exorcising Blackness: Historical and Literary Lynching and Burning Rituals*. Bloomington: Indiana University Press, 1984.

Heller, Terry. "Terror and Empathy in Faulkner's *Sanctuary*." *Arizona Quarterly* 40 (1984): 344–64.

Higgins, Lynn A., and Brenda R. Silver, eds. *Rape and Representation*. New York: Columbia University Press, 1991.

Hoffman, Frederick. *The Mortal No: Death and the Modern Imagination*. Princeton: Princeton University Press, 1964.

Hunter, Lynette. *George Orwell: The Search for a Voice*. Milton Keynes, England: Open University Press, 1984.

Iser, Wolfgang. *The Act of Reading: A Theory of Aesthetic Response*. Baltimore: Johns Hopkins University Press, 1978.

Jordan, June. *Passion*. Boston: Beacon, 1980.

Kowalewski, Michael. *Deadly Musings: Violence and Verbal Form in American Fiction*. Princeton: Princeton University Press, 1993.

Kristeva, Julia. "Psychoanalysis and the Polis." In *The Politics of Interpretation*, ed. W. J. T. Mitchell. Chicago: University of Chicago Press, 1983.

Laplanche, Jean. *Life and Death in Psychoanalysis*. Baltimore: Johns Hopkins University Press, 1976.

Mailer, Norman. "Children of the Pied Piper." *Vanity Fair* 54.3 (March 1991): 154–59, 220–21.

Mailloux, Steven. *Interpretive Conventions: The Reader in the Study of American Fiction*. Ithaca: Cornell University Press, 1982.

Marx, Karl. *Capital*. Ed. Frederick Engels. Trans. Samuel Moore and Edward Aveling. New York: Modern Library, 1906.

———. *The Economic and Philosophic Manuscripts of 1844*. Ed. Dirk J. Struik. Trans. Martin Milligan. New York: International, 1984.

Mascia-Lees, Frances E., and Patricia Sharpe, eds. *Tattoo, Torture, Mutilation, and Adornment: The Denaturalization of the Body in Culture and Text*. Albany, NY: State University of New York Press, 1992.

Matthews, John T. "The Elliptical Nature of *Sanctuary*." *Novel* 17 (Spring 1984): 246–65.

Miller, Nancy K. "Rereading as a Woman: The Body in Practice." In *The Female Body in Western Culture*, ed. Susan Rubin Suleiman. Cambridge, MA: Harvard University Press, 1986.

Moraga, Cherrie. *Giving up the Ghost*. Albuquerque, NM: West End Press, 1986.

Mulvey, Laura. "Visual Pleasure and Narrative Cinema." *Screen* 16.3 (1975): 6–18.

Nagler, Michael M. *America without Violence*. Covelo, CA: Island, 1982.

Naylor, Gloria. *The Women of Brewster Place*. New York: Penguin, 1983.

Novitz, David. *Knowledge, Fiction and Imagination*. Philadelphia: Temple University Press, 1987.

Orwell, George. *1984*. New York: NAL, 1961.

Parker, Patricia. "The Metaphorical Plot." In *Metaphor: Problems and Perspectives*, ed. David S. Miall. Brighton, Eng.: Harvester, 1982.

Parker, Robert Dale. *Faulkner and the Novelistic Imagination*. Urbana: University of Illinois Press, 1985.

Pettey, Homer B. "Reading and Raping in *Sanctuary*." *The Faulkner Journal* 3.1 (Fall 1987): 71–85.

Phillips, K. J. "The Phalaris Syndrome: Alain Robbe-Grillet vs. D. M. Thomas." In *Women and Violence in Literature: An Essay Collection*, ed. Katherine Anne Ackley. New York: Garland, 1990.

Prince, Gerald. "Notes on the Text as Reader." In *The Reader in the Text: Essays on Audience and Interpretation*, ed. Susan R. Suleiman and Inge Crosman. Princeton: Princeton University Press, 1980.

Rainwater, Catherine. "Reading between Worlds: Narrativity in the Fiction of Louise Erdrich." *American Literature* 62.3 (September 1990): 405–22.

Ricoeur, Paul. *The Rule of Metaphor*. Trans. Robert Czerny. Toronto: University of Toronto Press, 1979.

Roberts, Diane. "Ravished Belles: Stories of Rape and Resistance in *Flags in the Dust* and *Sanctuary*." *The Faulkner Journal* 4.1–2 (Fall 1988/Spring 1989): 21–35.

Robertson, Mary F. "Hystery, Herstory, History: 'Imagining the Real' in Thomas's *The White Hotel*." *Contemporary Literature* 25.4 (1984): 452–77.

Russell, Diana E. H. *The Politics of Rape: The Victim's Perspective*. New York: Stein and Day, 1984.

Scarry, Elaine. *The Body in Pain: The Making and Unmaking of the World*. New York: Oxford University Press, 1985.

Scholes, Robert. *Protocols of Reading*. New Haven: Yale University Press, 1989.

Selby, Hubert Jr. *Last Exit to Brooklyn*. New York: Grove Weidenfeld, 1988.

Sheppard, R. Z. "A Revolting Development." *Time* 136.18 (October 29, 1990): 100.

Singer, Alan. *A Metaphorics of Fiction: Discontinuity and Discourse in the Modern Novel*. Tallahassee: University Presses of Florida, 1983.

Slotkin, Richard. *Regeneration through Violence: The Mythology of the American Frontier*. Middletown, CT: Wesleyan University Press, 1973.

Smith, Paul. *Discerning the Subject*. Minneapolis: University of Minnesota Press, 1988.

Sperber, Murray. "'Gazing into the Glass Paperweight': The Structure and Psychology of Orwell's *1984*." *Modern Fiction Studies* 26 (Summer 1980): 213–26.

Takaki, Ronald T. *Violence in the Black Imagination*. New York: Putnam, 1972.

Thomas, D. M. *The White Hotel*. New York: Pocket Books, 1982.

Trinh T. Minh-ha. *Woman, Native, Other: Writing Postcoloniality and Feminism*. Bloomington: Indiana University Press, 1989.

Walker, Victoria. "A Note on Perspective in *Tracks*." *Studies in American Indian Literatures* 3.4 (Winter 1991): 37–40.

White, Hayden. *Tropics of Discourse: Essays in Cultural Criticism*. Baltimore: Johns Hopkins University Press, 1978.

Williams, Raymond. "Base and Superstructure in Marxist Cultural Theory." In *Rethinking Popular Culture*, ed. Chandra Mukerji and Michael Schudson. Berkeley: University of California Press, 1991.

Wilt, Judith. "Behind the Door of *1984*: 'The Worst Thing in the World.'" In *Modernism Reconsidered*, ed. Robert Kiely and John Hildebidle. Cambridge, MA: Harvard University Press, 1983.

Yardley, Jonathan. "A Dirty Book by a Dirty Writer." *Boston Globe* (February 28, 1991): 75.

Young, James E. *Writing and Rewriting the Holocaust: Narrative and the Consequences of Interpretation*. Bloomington: Indiana University Press, 1988.

INDEX

LAURA E. TANNER is Assistant Professor in the Department of English at Boston College.